Ever since Colonial days Fairfield has been one of the most historic, romantic, and cultured sections of South Carolina.

The county is often referred to as "the Low-Country county in the Piedmont." Its culture has a distinct flavor all its own and its people have been known for their gentility and character for generations.

Mr. Bolick began making sketches for this book more than seven years ago and has done over one hundred intricate pen-and-ink drawings of the buildings that have passed their century mark. Each illustration has its own story, told in simple descriptive words.

A FAIRFIELD SKETCHBOOK is an absolute must for those who live in or are descended from Fairfield. It is a treasure for all who love the area, the rich cultural history of our state, or simply the beautiful and the romantic, anywhere.

Aside from the drawings with their historical and architectural appeal, the text will prove valuable for those interested in genealogy, history, and folklore.

Julian Stevenson Bolick was born and reared in Georgetown, South Carolina. His father, the late Leland L. Bolick, and his mother, nee Margaret Estelle Stevenson, were both natives of Fairfield.

Mr. Bolick is a gifted artist with pen and ink; as a hobby, he sketches old buildings and delves into their histories.

His earlier publications — GEORGE-TOWN HOUSELORE, 1944, WACCA-MAW PLANTATIONS, 1946, GEORGE-TOWN GHOSTS, 1956, and THE RETURN OF THE GRAY MAN, 1962 — are well-known to lovers of South Carolina history and folklore.

His mother, a daughter of Fairfield who is proud of her heritage and her Scotch-Irish background and is a lover of her native soil, at first hinted to him, later suggested, and finally demanded that he make a sketchbook of her native county and of the home of his father.

The task of making the illustrations and assembling the material was begun seven years ago. The book is dedicated to his mother, who was directly responsible for its being and who wrote the introduction to Lebanon, her girlhood home.

A FAIRFIELD SKETCHBOOK

A
FAIRFIELD
SKETCHBOOK

by

JULIAN STEVENSON BOLICK

with

INTRODUCTION
by
KATHLEEN LEWIS SLOAN

and

SECTIONAL CONTRIBUTIONS
by

JACOBS BROTHERS
Clinton, South Carolina

Copy Number_____

Limited Edition 750 Copies

To

My Beloved Mother

Who as

MARGARET ESTELLE STEVENSON

Was born, reared, and married in

OLD FAIRFIELD

the place that she has loved

and cherished

down through

the years.

CONTENTS

CONTENTS – Continued

SKETCHES

CONTENTS – Continued

SKETCHES

ACKNOWLEDGEMENTS

The author acknowledges his grateful appreciation to the kind people of Fairfield who have given of their time and helped so generously in assembling information for this book; also to the families who have cared for and preserved the grand old buildings and homes and who, even in our busy modern world, have retained the dignity, warmth, and genteel humility for which the natives of Fairfield have been famous for generations in dispensing their genuine hospitality. Tribute is also paid to the builders, known or forgotten, of the churches, public places, and residences, both elegant and modest, who have passed on but who have left us landmarks to love, honor, and point to with pride.

He is also grateful to Mrs. Eloise Stevenson Morris and the Fairfield Chamber of Commerce for allowing him the use of their files; to Mrs. Kathleen Lewis Sloan for the Introduction; to John N. LeMaster, Jr., Charles E. Thomas, Mr. Bryan Roberts, Mrs. Katherine Pearson Tomlin, Mrs. Estelle S. B. Dill, Mrs. Etta A. Rosson, Mrs. Maymie Weir Stevenson and each one helping with the sectional descriptions and individual histories; to John Holland Hunter, who gave generously of his time and talent; to Mrs. Alice Gaines Sloan, who edited the manuscript; and to the many natives of the county who helped and encouraged with their information and interest. Also to Mr. Harris McDonald, who did painstaking research into the records of the Winnsboro houses, Miss Zelma Brice, Mrs. Frank Vetoe, Mrs. Myrtle Henry Wilkes, Miss Kathleen Lemmon, Mrs. Albert McMeekin, Mr. Hamp Macfie, Mrs. Cleo Clowney Hall, Mrs. Sarah Hall Arnette, Mrs. Pattie Frick, Mrs. Nelle E. McMaster, Mr. and Mrs. Charles E. McDonald, Miss Julia Faucette, Mr. Thomas McDonald, and last but not least, Mr. G. M. Ketchin and "The News and Herald."

INTRODUCTION
by
KATHLEEN LEWIS SLOAN

A SHORT HISTORY OF FAIRFIELD COUNTY

*To the Turn of the 20th Century, with Brief Mentions of Latter-Day People
and Events and Places*

by

KATHLEEN LEWIS SLOAN

Fairfield County was in early times a part of Craven County when the Lords Proprietors ruled the Province of Carolina. It was also once a part of the Camden District of South Carolina.

Fairfield is located in the "median" between the upcountry of this state and the lowcountry. That it is neither upcountry nor lowcountry goes without saying; and part of the answer that it is "different" may lie in the original blending of the two elements which formed the background of its people.

These two elements were:

(1) The Scotch-Irish, who followed the trails down through Pennsylvania, Virginia, and North Carolina — some families settling along the way, either permanently or for brief periods — with a few subsequently creating a new frontier in the hills and valleys and along the rivers of what would eventually become Fairfield. Here they constructed their small log cabins in the midst of the most picturesque scenery possible to find.

(2) Those from Charleston and the coastal regions, the English and French Huguenots, whose families had already been in Carolina for several generations, highly cultured, well-educated, genteel.

Added to these was a sprinkling of German, Swiss, and Welsh.

The combination was rare — bravery, energy, religious fervor, stubbornness, elegance, refinement, industry, thrift, ingenuity, education, all leading up to a birthright of aristocracy.

Which of the original, sizeable elements arrived first, following the close of the Cherokee War in 1760, is a matter of conjecture. But, according to the historian Ramsay, the end product was better than the original — gold tempered to unusual worth and brilliance.

Logan, the historian, relates that the very first settler was a man named Thomas Nightingale, a Yorkshireman by birth, who had emigrated to America.

Nightingale, a true sportsman and lover of horseflesh, built the New Market race course near Charleston, where races were held for the first time on February 19, 1760.

That was twenty years after his arrival in Fairfield in 1740 when he established a cow pen on Little Cedar Creek, located six miles from where the county seat, Winnsboro, would eventually rise. This was the same spot later owned by General Strother, whose name lives on in the railroad station off the highway near Broad River and in the community.

Nightingale, therefore, may have been either directly or indirectly responsible for the migration to Fairfield of Charlestonians and others from the lowcountry

— especially so since he had such success raising horses and livestock on the lush grasses and tracts of canes that abounded in the wild, beautiful fields.

Many, however, from the lowcountry, came in later years for other reasons: to escape the scourge of malaria, and for schooling under private tutors.

Following Nightingale, as the first settler, was Howell, a man from the Congaree, who a little afterwards built a similar cow pen at Winn's Bridge (Bell's Bridge) on Little River.

Close together came Purmont Carey and John Hughes, former soldiers together, who took up lands in the forks of the Broad and Little Rivers. About the same time arrived Daniel Rees, a blacksmith from Pennsylvania, who obtained a warrant for three hundred acres, settling farther up, on the same stream.

In the fifties came Solomon McGraw, Richard Spencer, James Leslie (who had originally settled on Raiford's Creek), and James Andrews, who had been in the Province of Carolina for some time.

Warrants were issued in 1749 and tracts surveyed later for Thomas Conoway of Virginia, who had been in the area for about four years, and Conrad Adler, who brought with him two slaves. Adler had been a resident of Carolina for some time. Three Pennsylvanians, Thomas Owen — who established a mill — Lawrence Free, and Jacob Conomore, in 1752 petitioned for land along Wilkinson's Creek.

Mills' STATISTICS refers to early settlers (about 1745) being Colonel John Lyles and his brother, Ephriam, who located at the mouth of Beaver Creek on Broad River. The Lyleses were natives of Brunswick, Virginia, but had removed to Fairfield following a stay in old Butte County, North Carolina.

Richard Kirkland, also an early comer, settled near Wateree Creek about 1753. His lands, it is noted, were bounded by property owners Richard Greggrie (Gregory) and Joseph Cates.

Also included among the "firsts" were William Hart, John Mitchell, John Stubb, Moses Kirkland, Frederick Pines, Ann Lyther, Thomas Woodward, Job Meadows, William Phillips, William Harth, Albert Beam, John Marpole, James Rutland, Samuel Mobberly (Mobley), and Williams All.

Six grants were made between May 1764 and December 1774, totaling eight hundred acres, to John Waggoner. Waggoner was the same as Hans Wagner, who came to Fairfield and eventually adopted the English "John" for his Dutch name, Johan, of which Hans is an abbreviation.

Waggoner is remembered today by a small marker on Highway 215 as the man who built Fort Waggoner. Other similar forts stretching out in a chain from Beaver Creek to McCord's Ferry were those established by Phillip Raiford, John Hicks, P. Pearson, and James Andrews.

The purpose of the forts, which were built before the close of the Cherokee War in 1760, was for protection of the inhabitants who confined themselves within their walls in fear of the Indians. The occupants had only two kinds of food, fresh meat, provided by the men who made forays into the nearby forests, and bread brought by pack horses from Congaree.

Robert Mills tells in his STATISTICS an incident in connection with Fort Waggoner, which showed the sincere admiration and veneration the Indians held for the rattlesnake.

[2]

The first settlers were awed by the tremendous size and the apparent great age of the rattlers and eventually learned that they were never killed by the Indians because of the snake's custom of refraining from striking without first giving notice.

One day James Phillips, an occupant of Fort Waggoner, went out on a hunting party and on his return encountered a large rattler near the Fort. He shot it immediately, and, because of its immense size, decided to examine it. Upon cutting the snake open, he was horrified to discover a fawn in the stomach of the reptile! This story told by Mills was attested to by witnesses who were then living (1826).

INDIANS

Historians disagree on the fact that Fairfield was once a part of the Cherokee territory. One says that the Cherokees ceded it along with other lands in the nearby counties of Newberry, Laurens, etc. Another says that Fairfield served only as the "hunting grounds" of the Cherokees.

Fairfield was at one time or another traversed by parties of the Shawnee, Tuscarora and Chicasaw Indians and by the Mohawk, Seneca, and other tribes of the Six Nations.

Occupation in Fairfield was by Siouan tribes of the east, headed by the Catawbas, always friendly to the white man. Artifacts of the Catawbas were found in abundance around the Wateree, as well as in other parts of Fairfield; and to a lesser degree arrowheads, pottery, and other Indian remains have been unearthed throughout the county.

In recent years Hampton Island in the Broad River — inhabited only by goats — was opened up due to the new Pinner Bridge spanning it to join Fairfield and Newberry Counties. The island has proved a source of numerous arrowheads, pot shards, and other mementoes of the Indians.

Only two Indian place-names are left in the county, those of the Wateree and Catawba Rivers. The Eswaw Huppeedaw (Huppiday) — or Line River, which is said to have divided the empire of the Cherokees and Catawbas — is simply called the Broad River.

REGULATORS

The inhabitants of Fairfield — in those long ago days — seemed never to be without trouble of some sort. Following the end of the French and Indian Wars, the settlers faced a new threat in bands of terrorizers and robbers who invaded their homes and drove away their livestock. Seats of the courts were too far away, and the people had but little recourse to handle the situation as best they could.

This gave rise to the organization or associations which were known as "REGULATION", with those operating them known as "REGULATORS". The thieves were ferreted out, whipped, and their carefully set-up headquarters destroyed. Two or more noteworthy Regulators in Fairfield County were Moses Kirkland, an extensive landowner in Fairfield and across the River, and Thomas Woodward.

Woodward was described as a patron of orderly, good, honest men but suffered persecution later for his well-intentioned actions as Regulator. He was killed by a bandit.

At the dawn of the Revolution, Woodward was one of those who urged his countrymen to action, and he lived long enough to see his advice carried out. An oil painting of Woodward hangs in the Senate at the Capitol.

REVOLUTIONARY WAR

In Fairfield, supposedly, there were only two active Loyalists (Tories), the Phillipses. Colonel John Phillips, a friend of Lord Cornwallis, whose forces were encamped in Winnsboro, was instrumental in obtaining pardons for the seventy or more Whigs who had been condemned to death at the "Drum-head Court" held in that town.

When Cornwallis moved on, Phillips was left in charge of the Tories but — as in the fortunes of war — himself eventually became a prisoner of war in Camden.

The people of Fairfield "without exception" joined a petition that his life be "spared"; and when a pardon was granted he left America and returned to Britain.

The other Tory, his brother, James, returned to Winnsboro following the war. From his wife, relatives, and the townspeople, he received a cool reception. As time passed, however, he was restored in favor.

He became a staunch friend of General Richard Winn, the Virginian who gave his name to the small borough that had sprung up in the midst of the district.

Captain Winn had won glory at the Battle of Fort Moultrie and had taken part with valor in several others, the most noteworthy of which were those at York and Hanging Rock. In the latter, in what is now Lancaster County, he commanded a regiment of refugee militia, and was wounded during the fighting.

Winn, after the war, became a South Carolina leader. He was elected a brigadier general by the state legislature — in which he served for a considerable time — and rose to the rank of major general in the militia.

Winn was a cotton buyer, merchant, and land surveyor. In the Fairfield County Clerk's office are records of his work as a surveyor in some of the early land grants.

He was appointed superintendent of Indian Affairs for the Creek Nation in 1788, elected as a Democrat to the Third and Fourth Congresses (1793-1797), and served out Thomas Sumter's appointment to the Seventh Congress when Sumter resigned. Winn was re-elected to the Eighth and to the four succeeding Congresses, from 1803 to 1813. He was twice lieutenant governor of South Carolina.

In 1813 he removed to Tennessee where he became an outstanding citizen as a planter and a merchant. His home was on the Duck River, Maury County. He died December 19, 1818, and is buried in Winnsboro, according to best official sources in Washington. Though supposition has long been that he was buried in Tennessee, some years ago when plans were made to erect a marker to him, citizens of the area were unable to locate his grave.

During the years of his public service, Winn was one of those instrumental in establishing the state capital at Columbia and in laying out that city. At one time a street in Columbia bore his name.

THE COUNTY'S NAME

Legend gives Cornwallis the honor of having named Fairfield. Certainly he had ample time and opportunity to view the broad vistas during his stay in Winnsboro from October 1780 until early January 1781 when the fair fields could have come under his close scrutiny.

However, the late A. S. Salley, state historian, places the remark "fanciful" by the derivation of Fairfield. Robert Mills in his STATISTICS, describing the area as lying in a region temperate and salubrious, with fine views and in some places mountainous elevations, states:

"By the county court act (the work of the late Judge Pendleton), the upper county was divided into two counties. At that division the name Fairfield was first given to THIS section of the country, and *in all probability it owes its name to the mere good pleasure of the author of the act.*"

By an act ratified in 1769 the Province was divided into seven judicial districts, one of which was Camden District, which was named for the principal town within its border. In 1798 from the Camden District were formed Chester, Lancaster, Fairfield, Kershaw, and Sumter districts. In 1799 Richland was carved from Kershaw.

In 1868 its Constitution changed the entitlement to "County." A part of Fairfield in later years was annexed to Richland, that part nearest to and including the town of Blythewood.

Early records in the office of the Register of Mesne Conveyance of Fairfield go back into the 1730's. These fascinating records of Fairfield's early days — in their fancy Spencerian handwriting and with carefully drawn illustrations in colored inks — are perused frequently by genealogists and historians, who learn much about the people and the little-known facts of their existence, their customs, their adherence to the old English laws.

THE WARS AND THE COLORS

Fairfield's men have always served with honor when the call to the colors came; and often they have been there "fustest with the mostest."

Among the first uprisings against the Crown was one in Fairfield, the affray at Moberley's Meeting House, May 26, 1780; and another, larger one in March 1781 on Dutchman's Creek. In the latter a detachment of New York Volunteers under a Captain Gray attacked a body of militia, with serious losses to the Volunteers.

The Continental or regular army from Fairfield was commanded by Captain John Buchanan. Captain Thomas Woodward, Richard Winn, and Captain Robert Ellison were in command of several companies of state troops.

Among the Whigs of Fairfield who fought as brave patriots for the independence of this country were John Pearson (later a general in the militia), Colonel Aromanus Lyles, John Gray, Benjamin May, William Strothers, John Strothers, William and Joseph Kirkland, Robert Hancock, William McMorris, John Cook, Captain Balar, Captain Watson, Edward Martin, and John Winn, the brother of Richard.

In the War of 1812 there was Captain William McCreight's company of Light Infantry Volunteers; in the Seminole War were the Fairfield Volunteers, which included one of the county's most distinguished citizens, Nick Peay, one-time State Senator; the Mexican War, among whose heroes was Colonel A. H. Gladden, born in Fairfield, who later was a brigadier general in the Civil War; then, there were the two thousand or more — all heroes — who fought for the Confederacy, including Colonel James Henry Rion and General John Bratton. (Probably the last two well-remembered Confederate veterans in Winnsboro were Captain John Lyles, long-time Clerk of Court, and W. Harvey Flenniken.)

One of the local heroes of the Confederate War was Nick Myers of the Longtown section, who killed so many Yankees, and is a legendary figure in Fairfield today.

The later wars have also claimed Fairfield men, some paying the supreme sacrifice: World Wars I and II, and the Korean conflict. One of World War II's outstanding heroes is Winnsboro's General William Oscar Brice "who made the air safe over the Solomons" General Brice, a loyal "Confederate," raised the stars and bars over his post.

RELIGION

From its beginning, no part of the state is said to have had more religious communicants than Fairfield; and the first order of the day, after becoming settled in their crudely constructed huts, was for the people to congregate for worship of the Almighty.

In 1762 Jacob Gibson, a Baptist minister and teacher, came from North Carolina to sow seeds of refinement not only to his own flock but also to others. He lived in Fairfield for about forty years, and it is thought that he began the first school and was instrumental in helping to establish others.

Just prior to the Reverend Mr. Gibson's arrival, there was begun what is believed to have been the first *organized* religious congregation in Fairfield: Two Seventh Day Adventist groups of the period between 1740-1750. John Pearson served both groups as exhorter and lay preacher.

Another distinguished theologian, John Nicholas Martin, who was a Lutheran from Germany, built Bethesda Auf der Moven in southwestern Fairfield. The church was eventually located at the site of the present Crooked Run, a Baptist church, not far from the boundary of Richland County.

The Moberly Meeting House, an early house of worship, was begun by Episcopalians but was used by all denominations. E. G. Palmer began an early mission at Cedar Creek, also for Episcopalians, and was a principal in establishing St. Stephens at Ridgeway.

An early covenanter, the Reverend William Martin, one of whose churches was Mt. Olivet, is mentioned at length in Howe's HISTORY OF THE PRESBYTERIAN CHURCH.

Fairfield has today one of the few churches in South Carolina attended by Universalists, colloquially called the "No Hell Church." This historic church is located in what is called the "Dark Corner" of Fairfield.

In 1803 the Associate Reformed Synod of the Carolinas was organized May 9 at BRICK CHURCH, Fairfield. This, with the Synods of Pennsylvania, New York, and Scioto, Ohio, organized the General Synod in 1804 with headquarters in Philadelphia. The General Synod organization continued until it was agreed that each Synod become independent, and in 1822 the Synod of the Carolinas became the A. R. P. Synod of the South. In the Courthouse is a deed by Henry H. Crumpton to the members of the associate congregation of the Brick Meeting House on Little River, called EBENEZER. The deed, which covers the church building and includes a drawing of a plat or sketch, is dated June 2, 1793, and is recorded in Book "H" at page 171.

The Methodist Church movement in Fairfield County began about 1808. The Reverend James Jenkins was urged by Captain Buchanan's wife (who had leanings towards the Methodist Episcopal Church) to send an appointment to Winnsboro. The Reverend Mr. Jenkins preached first at the Courthouse. The Buchanans, Captain Harris and his wife, and Major Moore became the first five members of the local Methodist Church. In 1810 a church was dedicated, and the congregation was "greatly blessed" by visits from Bishop Francis Asbury at intervals between 1809 and 1814.

EDUCATION

Fairfield was an early educational seat, and in addition to reasons of health, many came to the location for school advantages for themselves and their children. In those days school was mainly for the rich, and not many could afford to send their children (sons) abroad for formal education.

Thus Mount Zion drew students from other states, as well as natives of South Carolina.

The Mount Zion Society was incorporated in 1777, shortly after the Declaration of Independence. The declaration of the Society was aimed toward ignorance, and the school that it established was mainly for orphans.

Later its charter was amended, and it became a college in 1785. In the succeeding years the illustrious seat of learning became only a high school, Mount Zion Institute; now it retains only the status of an elementary school, all the white high schools of Fairfield having been consolidated into Winnsboro High School at the beginning of the 1961-62 term. (Elementary schools are being retained in most communities at present.) Negro schools are Fairfield High, Gordon Elementary, and McCrorey-Liston.

The first principal of Mount Zion was the Reverend T. H. McCaule, a Presbyterian minister; the first five graduates became ministers of the gospel.

The Mount Zion Society is still in existence and still concerns itself with the education of youth. In contrast to its early days when the membership was made up principally of people from other sections, especially Charleston, the Society's membership is now drawn from Fairfield. In recent years the Society received as a gift from the United States Rubber Company the Fairfield Inn property. The Society in turn leased the Inn and the surrounding acreage to the new Fairfield Country Club, which operates a golf course, tennis courts, swimming pool, club house, etc. Money derived from this source is used by the Society to provide scholarships for higher education for deserving Fairfield youth.

Religion and education have always been closely tied together in Fairfield; and in any history of Fairfield it is difficult to separate one from the other.

Among Fairfield's original schools were the Jefferson-Monticello Academy (1800), to which, Robert Mills states, Thomas Jefferson was a "heavy contributor" because the institution bore his name; the Broad River Academy

(1824); the Manual Training School and Theological Seminary, later Furman University (1835).

The Feasterville Academy was begun in 1842; its first teacher was Mrs. Catherine Ladd, a patroness of the arts, who lived at the Boarding House with the students. Mrs. Ladd left the Feasterville Academy and moved to Winnsboro and is credited with having interceded successfully with Sherman's troops to save some of the town from torches. Mrs. Ladd's art works have been shown at the Fairfield Art Shows in recent years.

The Blythewood Female Institute, originally "Belle Haven" and located in Columbia, was relocated near the railroad station "Doko," and Dr. S. W. Bookhart was owner and principal.

Another thriving academy was in the heart of a wealthy settlement of Fairfield, a few miles from the Wateree River, in Longtown. The Longtown Academy afforded education for the children of such rich men as Nicholas Peay, who built his famous plantation house on a high ridge overlooking the river.

Little remains of Peay's empire today except the granite gate posts which guard the cemetery of the Longtown Presbyterian Church.

The house, never completed, was called "Peay's Folly." It grew out of the rivalry between Peay, the richest man in the upcountry, and Governor Manning to see whom could build the finest mansion. (Manning's home, "Millford," was in Sumter County. It is occupied by out-of-state owners today.)

Peay's house, "Melrose," built of bricks and Italian marble, with running water, and an observatory on its roof, bespeaks Fairfield's golden era, when plantation life was at its prime — perhaps the only opulent era that the small county has ever enjoyed.

Both Peay and his wife died before the Civil War, and the house was burned by Sherman's soldiers, despite the servants' pleas that it housed the couple's orphaned children. The story goes that a Yankee soldier lost his life as he greedily drank from the wine cellar as the flames licked about him.

Peay's slaves have been variously estimated between "two hundred" and "two thousand" and his holdings as nine thousand acres of land on which cotton was "King" because of the invention of the cotton gin.

Following the widow's death, the estate, managed for several years by the two executors of Peay's will, was plunged into litigation. The latter's heirs asked that a receiver be appointed to take the reins of "mismanagement" away from the executors. The Peay family was never able to regain some of the lands disputed in the litigation.

THE COTTON GIN

Almost every resident of Fairfield will tell you without hesitation that the cotton gin was invented by James Kincaid, native of Ireland, hero of Eutaw Springs. Though Whitney received accolades as the inventor, in Fairfield it is stated that the inventor stole the idea after visiting in Kincaid's home and watching the machine, which was originally intended to remove the burrs from sheep's wool. In Mr. Kincaid's absence, his wife allowed the Northerner to see the machine; he promptly made off for Savannah, Georgia, sketched the intricacies, and applied for a patent. Kincaid was a large cotton grower and served Fairfield for many years in the legislature.

RAILROAD

With slaves to produce cotton, and gins to make it ready for market, coming of the railroad was almost a necessity. With hundreds of bales, it was well nigh impossible to haul cotton by wagons during the late fall and winter months when rains made travel extremely difficult.

To one of Peay's neighbors goes the credit for the building of the railroad which today, as the Southern, follows closely the original roadbed of the Charlotte and South Carolina Railroad.

Edward Gendron Palmer of VALENCIA was also a large planter and is listed as one of the seventy-two men in South Carolina who owned between three hundred and five hundred slaves. (Record books of his transactions are carefully preserved today in the drawing room of VALENCIA, where his descendants live.)

Palmer grew so much cotton that he became "obsessed" with the idea that a railroad must be constructed for the convenience of Fairfield planters and others along the route into North Carolina, beginning at Columbia.

Many people pointed out that he was a "fool," but Palmer was a far-seeing man. Joining together with Mr. Peay, other extensive Fairfield planters, and the group from Charleston that had just launched the South Carolina railroad from Charleston to Hamburg, he began to raise funds.

In December 1846 an act was passed by the South Carolina Legislature, and in January a similar one by the North Carolina Assembly, authorizing the construction of the road. The Ridge Route was chosen — that favored by Palmer — which would pass through New Lands (as Ridgeway was then called).

On November 17, 1852, at a stockholders' meeting in Mecklenburg, North Carolina, County Courthouse, those present heard Palmer, the first president, declare, "Gentlemen, we have brought the road to completion." The railroad subsequently became known as "Palmer's Gin House Route" because it passed close enough for the president and his fellow Ridgeway-planters to load their cotton for marketing.

RIDGEWAY

The Palmers and the Thomases were among the early inhabitants of NEW LANDS. In the 1850's the little settlement had only four houses which could be seen from the depot: those of Arthur Craig, the railroad agent; Mrs. Catherine Ross Davis; Colonel Henry C. Davis; and James B. Coleman.

The Coleman home, built in 1854 of bricks made by his slaves, was known in rather recent years as the "Old Hotel." It is now the focal point of Ridgeway, having been restored as a community center and rechristened the CENTURY HOUSE.

St. Stephen's Episcopal Church of Ridgeway was built in 1854 and Aimwell Presbyterian in 1859. David H. Ruff came to Ridgeway after the Civil War, and, an ardent Methodist, founded Ruff's Chapel.

ROCKY MOUNT

Robert Mills in his STATISTICS predicted that Rocky Mount or Grimkiville (named in honor of Judge Grimki) would be a place of considerable influence. He spoke of the houses that commanded "a fine view of the Catawba

River, its numerous rapids, islands, and mountainous elevations along its banks for many miles." Mills had a particular interest in this river, as it was here that he engineered and built locks for the control of navigation.

The Great Falls of the Catawba River, however, were curbed many years ago by the Duke Power Company's Dearborn Plant and their waters lassoed for the use of electricity, an event Mills could not foretell.

The name "Dearborn" reaches back into the yellowed pages of history to the time of George Washington, when Dearborn, as Secretary of War in Washington's cabinet, visited the area.

Dearborn — on that visit — laid the cornerstone of a large building, and an European engineer arrived to direct the building of a large public works because of the government's interest in the fine water power of the area.

Here, too, according to Fairfield tradition, but not of official record, it was once planned to establish a military college for the United States, but it was subsequently located at West Point on the Hudson, in New York. However, a military academy called Mount Dearborn once existed in the vicinity. Bishop Francis Asbury who made several visits to Methodists in Fairfield between 1809 and 1814, notes in his Journal: "1809 — I met a congregation on Tuesday in a log cabin, ———— To my surprise a number of United States officers came up; I invited them in; these gentlemen are attached to an establishment at Rocky Mount ——"

WINNSBORO

Winnsboro was chartered in 1785 on the petition of Richard Winn, John Winn, and John Vanderhorst (correctly pronounced "Van Drost").

The original plat of the town may be viewed in the office of the Secretary of State of South Carolina.

In December 1832 the town was incorporated to be governed by an Intendant and Wardens. Today it operates with the Council-Manager system and a Mayor.

In those days the majority of the houses stood on one side of the street, with other streets laid out and "considerably improved." The town had its Courthouse and across the street a jail. Hangings on the public square were not out of the ordinary, and Fairfield is listed in history as one of the places in which Witchcraft abounded.*

The handsome Town Clock Building came later, some time around 1833, and the landmark is noted for its continuously running Roman Numeral clock with four faces. Missing now is the Town Clock's guardian, the Monument of the Confederate soldier, which had stood in the midst of Congress Street since its erection. In Winnsboro's renovation program in 1962, when the street was improved, the monument — over many protests — was moved and found a resting place just inside the gates of the hallowed Mount Zion Campus — still looking North.

Early Winnsboro consisted of a number of business houses and inns. There were two gin factories, a Masonic Hall, Market House, two houses of entertainment, a blacksmith and carriage shop, and eight or ten stores. About 1820 there were "approximately fifty private houses." Among special entertainments were quadrilles, fayres (fairs), and jousting tournaments.

---

*A Winnsboro attorney, Thomas K. McDonald, is an authority on this subject.

CIVIL WAR

Fairfield, like some other parts of South Carolina, fared badly during the Civil War. Homes and livestock were plundered and destroyed, and pillaging was conducted on a system both by the bummers, who arrived first, and the soldiers. This resulted in many goods leaving Fairfield forever, including jewelry, silver, art works, and fine books from those libraries which were not burned.

When Sherman's troops arrived, * the male population of Winnsboro had dwindled to two, a clergyman and a doctor.

About thirty buildings in the small town were destroyed — homes, stores, and other edifices, including the Episcopal Church — and a whole square at one time. In the two days the Yankees were in the town, much destruction took place. When the soldiers had gone, Pardee's Brigade remained on duty "for protection" and to wait for the troops of the Seventeenth, Twentieth, and Fourteenth Corps to catch up with the main body.

Then the mounted troopers were left, by the request of the citizens, because stragglers were terrorizing the women and children.

The Yankees marched east from Winnsboro on the road to Cheraw, the right wing crossing the Wateree at Peay's Ferry and the left wing at Rocky Mount. The cavalry, which detoured by Monticello and Feasterville, destroying as they went, was ordered to pillage Chester, where Beauregard had set up temporary headquarters, and then cross the Wateree with the left wing.

Beauregard's troops, retreating before Sherman as Columbia was being given over to the enemy, made camp at Blythewood.

On the nineteenth of February, 1865, Beauregard stopped for a midday meal in the Town of Winnsboro, moving on to White Oak for the night.

Following the war, the "Gay Nineties" were dull and lacked lustre in Fairfield. She lay stricken with poverty, the landed gentry without animals or tools to help them till the soil.

THE TEXTILE INDUSTRY

This period was the forerunner of the coming of the Textile Industry. In 1898 the sagging economy of the county was boosted somewhat by the establishment of the Fairfield Cotton Mills, begun with local capital. Its first president was Thomas Lauderdale, and J. M. Beaty was secretary and treasurer. The original plans, later doubled, called for five thousand spindles. In 1928 active management of the two mills — considerably enlarged and having changed ownership in the interim — was taken over by the United States Rubber Company.

It is now, of course, Fairfield's major industry, along with the next-in-line granite mining, pulpwood, and brickmaking. A few lesser manufacturing companies have been established in Fairfield in the past few years.

Fairfield, alluded to in the United States Government Survey in 1928 as tragically eroded with wasted lands, has made a fine comeback.

It is now known as the land of pines, ponds, and pastures and claims even a measure of prosperity. Agricultural pursuits are at an all-time low, large acreages being either owned outright by paper companies for producing pulpwood or in the government's soil bank.

---

*Fairfield has been "invaded" by several armies, Sherman's, Greene's and Cornwallis', etc.

The days of the tenant farmer are over. This is an era of mechanization, technical assistance, rural electrification, and an enlightened age.

The red clay hills sparkle green against the lush pine growth where dollars grow from their branches, and livestock meander 'cross the meadows, drinking from the numerous farm ponds — all of it adding up to jingling coins in the gentleman farmers' pockets.

POPULATION

Fairfield's population is now about double that of 1800 when there were ten thousand inhabitants, of whom two thousand were slaves. The ratio of Negroes to whites, sixty-forty in 1920, is changing in this modern age.

Continually Fairfield has exported its best asset, its children. Reared in gentility, educated to the utmost of their capacities, young people find greener fields and better economic advantages elsewhere. In Fairfield there is room for only a limited number of doctors, lawyers, scientists, teachers, ministers, and other professionals.

Those who leave, however, still retain the flavor of Fairfield, a characteristic which outsiders never understand but often admire.

The county has produced many outstanding people, including one governor, John H. Means, 1850-1852; many outstanding educators, including Professor R. Means Davis, who helped to revise the school laws in this state; several Negro educators; the theologian, Wm. Porcher DuBose, author D. E. Camak and the poet, his brother, M. B. Camak, and hundreds of others in various professions.

While exporting its own, Fairfield has very often received in return outstanding citizens from other areas, who have contributed much to the county's welfare.

Excerpt from History of
GREENBRIER AND RION

May 31, 1903, Benjamin Huger Heyward visited Fairfield County to look over the magnificent "Ten-Acre Rock." He had come at the request of his cousin, R. Goodwin Rhett of Charleston, owner, as "trouble-shooter" and was to stay one year to take over the active management of operations at Anderson Quarry.

Mr. Heyward spent the remainder of his life in Fairfield County, dying July 18, 1930, in a tragic accident on the site of the beautiful blue granite quarry. Operations since then have still remained in the hands of the Heyward family.

Benjamin Heyward, who settled at Rion with his family, became concerned about the lack of educational opportunities for children of the community. In his usual forceful way, he attacked the problem. He begged the parents to re-enroll their children at the Greenbrier School, which lacked accreditation, giving his word that upon their graduation they would be eligible for college. (Some of the community's students were attending Mount Zion Institute, and other schools.) He was backed in this proposal by Thomas W. Lewis, A. M. Blair (proprietor of the large company store at Rion), and other stalwarts of the community.

He procured a highly trained educator, Charles R. Spencer, a specialist in languages, math and the sciences, and placed him in charge. Many of the principles Mr. Spencer had learned at the University of Heidelberg in Germany and at the University of South Carolina, where he taught, were applied to the small school; and of its first graduates, two entered the University of South Carolina, achieving outstanding scholastic records.

As a reward for "good work", Mr. Heyward and his family entertained the pupils, both during the year and at the end of school. His daughters, chiefly Miss Mary Heyward, gave Virginia Reel dances for the students in the small parish house of the Episcopal Church which was established at Rion.

The annual picnic in May was a highlight for the community as well as the students. Riding the Rockton-Rion Railway — in which seats had been fashioned in open cars — the whole community went aboard at Green-brier School for the picturesque ride through the deep cut where the machinery of the 1920's had scraped through the clay for the little train's new bed.

The group passed through Rion (named for Colonel James Henry Rion, one of Fairfield's former first citizens). Anderson Quarry was at the end of the line, and here the students marveled at the views, scrambled over granite ledges, and listened for the call to dinner. Former students can recall the sight of the tremendous churns of ice cream, stacked against the granite walls, the finest treat of all the memorable day.

The little train is still a part of the Fairfield scene and during the week may be seen lugging tons of stone and crushed granite to the Southern terminal at Rockton. It is one of the last, if not the only, coal-burning trains in South Carolina.

MISCELLANEOUS ITEMS

The Greenbrier Methodist Church has been called Fairfield's most beautiful house of worship. It is constructed of native blue granite and is located across the road from where the other white frame church stood. The church-yard is enclosed with a blue granite wall of exquisite, delicate workmanship, which also encompasses the original church site. Here a marker to the early Church has been placed in a formal setting. To the rear of the marker is a monument to Hobbs, Fairfield's early granite quarrier.

Another of Fairfield's successful mining operations is the Blair Quarry at Blair.

For a little over twenty years Fairfield's rural areas have been lit by electricity, with the coming of Rural Electrification. The State Rural Electric Authority, which was established in the late 1930's, built Fairfield's first lines, which ran to White Oak, Blackstock, Lebanon and Salem Cross Roads. These lines preceded by about three or four years the establishment of the Fairfield Co-op in 1939. Rural telephones are now numerous in Fairfield.

Not far from Anderson Quarry, is the Parr Shoals Hydroelectric plant, begun by Henry Parr in 1915. Parr is the site of the first Nuclear Reactor plant in South Carolina and in the Southeast and will serve in many experimental and research capacities for large-scale commercial nuclear power stations. In September 1962 it was sealed off to make it vapor-tight. As a precautionary measure all of the inhabitants of Parr were moved out months before, as the construction began. The plant was activated in early 1963.

Fairfield in past days has seen the operation of three full scale "mineral springs," Shivar, at Shelton, Castles Springs, below Winnsboro on the road to Columbia and Harrison's in Longtown. Shivar grew into an extensive operation, eventually bottling soft drinks, but never resumed production following a fire in which the plant was destroyed. Castles Springs — the site of old-time community picnics — sold bottled water for health, as did Harrison's Spring in Longtown.

The owner of Castles Springs — long before electricity came to the rural areas — operated at Greenbrier a mercantile establishment lit by his own power plant and in which a telephone switchboard hooked up community telephones. The roadway between his home and store was brightly lighted, and this power also supplied ice for his early commercially operated ice house. Just up the road was Lewis' Store, an operation begun by James Carroll Lewis in 1912 and which is operated today by a third generation son of the family.

RAILROADS

In addition to the previously mentioned lines, one other branch of the Southern Railroad crosses Fairfield County. Its cargo in a large measure consists of pulpwood and brick from the manufacturing center at Richtex. The railroad has stations at Alston, Strother and Shelton, along the Broad River.

Fairfield's older homes, many of which are included in the ensuing sketches of Julian Bolick, reflect a great deal of the history of Fairfield and its peoples. Due to time, fires, and the ravages of wars, much is lost forever; and not a photograph or even a drawing or sketch of some of the early edifices can be located.

In Winnsboro, however, is to be found the county's oldest frame house, the present home of Mrs. Jean Smith Quattlebaum. Known locally as the *McCreight* house, located on Vanderhorst Street, the building is put together with wooden pegs; it is said that not a single nail was used in its erection.

People in Fairfield are fortunate in receiving news coverage. * Its own newspaper, THE NEWS AND HERALD, established in 1844 and whose motto is "Still Going Strong," has perhaps one of the finest editorial pages — written by its owner G. M. Ketchin — of the county newspapers in the state. It is interesting to read the files of this old paper, which are now in the Caroliniana Library at the University of South Carolina. How modern communication has changed can be especially noted when the newspaper in February 1865 was not aware on the date of publication that Columbia was being burned, and speaks hopefully that its little city (Winnsboro) will be spared.

RECREATION

Due in past years to the impounded rivers and streams, water recreation has become an important part of the life of Fairfield people. Cottages have sprung up along the Wateree, where the Fairfield Colony enjoy boating, fishing, bathing and water-skiing. Private ponds, stocked in plenty with various kinds of fish, provide pleasant diversion in recreation.

---

*Fairfield has one radio station, located on Hudson St. Extension, Winnsboro.

CONCLUSION

Who could deny that Fairfield has had a long and glorious history? Who can predict what her future will become?

As an industrial era, now in its cradle, sweeps over South Carolina, what part will Fairfield play?

Naturally, there will be many changes!

But its people will not change. Social life will follow some of its same patterns. And in years to come, some of the niceties of life will remain in Fairfield, one of the few places in the nation where visitors will still leave their calling cards at four o'clock!

REFERENCES

Howe	*History of the Presbyterian Church*
Mills	*Statistics*
Pearson	*Manuscript*
McMaster	*History of Fairfield County*
Obear	*Through the Years in Old Winnsboro*
Meriwether	*The Early Expansion of S. C.*
Lewis-Sloan	*Collection*
Wallace, Logan, Ramsay, Snowden	*Histories of South Carolina*
Files of	*The News and Herald*
Barrett	*Sherman's March Through the Carolinas*
Jacobs	*The Silk of the Trade*

READERS

Thomas K. McDonald, Sr., Moultrie D. Douglas, Norwood Obear, G. McMaster Ketchin, E. V. Lewis, and the Clerk of Court of Fairfield County who assisted with records, Walter W. Lewis.

PIONEER CABIN

This little abode is typical of the first homes that were built in Fairfield County by the early settlers. There are still a few of these to be found but they are fast disappearing.

The pioneers were rugged people. They literally chopped their way through the canebrakes and into the forests to establish their crude homes. Their first cabins were small, rough, and simple, but much labor and time were spent in constructing them.

To begin with, trees had to be selected and felled. The logs had to be hewn and sized by hand for the walls and roof timbers. Rocks were gathered, piled upon each other, and bonded together with mud mortar for a chimney. (Sometimes only sticks and mud were used for this necessary part of the building that supplied not only heat but the only cooking facilities.) If shingles were used for the roof, they had to be split and put on by hand. In many instances only brush thatch was used for a covering. The logs for the walls were mortised together, and the cracks between were chinked with mud. Usually there was only a dirt floor. Planks for flooring consumed so much time in the making that wood floors were added later and considered somewhat of a luxury.

While all this was going on, the pioneer and his family found their only shelter from the wind and weather in a "lean-to" made of treetops and brush.

As time passed and families and fortunes increased, these little dwellings were added to or used for other purposes when their owners built larger and more comfortable homes. Very often the cabin was handed down to the first child in the family when he or she married, and was used by them until they could do better. In other instances the cabins were used as barns, storehouses, or slave quarters.

Some time during its existence that particular house was covered with rough boards that have now weathered into a silvery gray. The grains in the wood stand out prominently due to their long years of exposure, and some of the planks are twisted and warped from the blistering sun and icy rains of many seasons.

This humble little house has no historical significance except for the fact that it has stood for almost two centuries in spite of the ravages of time, fire, storms, and constant use. It remains a silent survivor of a time, era, and way of life that we have almost forgotten in our fast, lush living of the twentieth century.

I

PIONEER CABIN

PART I

RIDGEWAY
AND
LONGTOWN

RIDGEWAY

RIDGEWAY'S FIRST SETTLERS
by
CHARLES E. THOMAS

The earliest settlers of the Ridgeway area of lower Fairfield District appear to have been Scotch-Irish Presbyterians. In Doctor George Howe's HISTORY OF THE PRESBYTERIAN CHURCH IN SOUTH CAROLINA (Columbia, 1870), he states, "In October 1799, a society on Cedar Creek petitions supplies, and prays it may be known on the minutes of Presbytery by the name of AIMWELL." However, in the old Session Book of the Aimwell Presbyterian Church in Ridgeway is the statement, "On the first Saturday in January, 1840, the semicentenary was observed and 63 dollars was subscribed for the board of publication." This places the origin of Aimwell Church as 1790.

When John Rosborough and his wife, Ann Cubit, moved to Ridgeway from Lebanon section of Fairfield in 1790, they "brought with them a fervent desire to organize a church," wrote Mrs. E. D. Goodson for the 150th anniversary of Aimwell in 1940. The first services were held in the Rosboroughs' home on the site of the present Century House in the town of Ridgeway. The first church building appears to have been erected about 1799 on land on Cedar Creek, given the previous year by Francis Robinson. The Reverend George Reed or Reid was the first pastor, and served for seven years. Mr. John Rosborough was ordained as the first elder. Following the Reverend Mr. Reed, Aimwell was served by the Reverend William G. Rosborough, who, Howe tells us, was prepared at Mount Zion College, and received under the care of Presbytery in April 1793.

The first church was burned. A second log church was built on a site near the present Bethlehem Colored Church across the street from the Crumpton House in Ridgeway, and this church was used until 1833. This marked the erection of Aimwell on the site of the present cemetery on land given the Presbyterians by Edward Gendron Palmer of Valencia. This building was erected in 1833; the fourth building was dedicated November 18, 1859. This building was described in later years by the late Eloise Davis Ruff as "white, foursquare, with a recessed porch and columns. There were two doors opening on the porch, and in the enclosed ends were concealed the steps leading up into the gallery where the colored servants sat. In the body of the church were three rows of pews. A melodian, given by Miss Sallie Means, stood near the pulpit. The choir was composed of Mrs. Henry Davis, Miss Ann Thomas, and Miss Mattie Rosborough, with Miss Sallie Means at the melodian. Behind the church, built of sturdy logs, was the session house, with a huge log fireplace," concluded "Miss Eloise" as she remembered Aimwell about the time of the Confederate War.

Early members of Aimwell and residents of lower Fairfield District were the Rosboroughs, Robinsons, Craigs, Kennedys, Hoods, Walkers, Gozas, Hunters, Campbells, Clevelands, Boulwares, and Colemans. Some of the first settlers had come from Scotland and Ireland by way of Virginia and North Carolina, whereas others, like John Rosborough, had come directly to South Carolina by way of Charleston from Ireland during the potato famines of the late 18th century. He had married Ann Cubit in Carolina after she came to Beaufort with her English sea captain father.

In the late 1800's about 1885 Aimwell built a frame church in the town of Ridgeway, and it was used primarily for prayer meetings for the greater convenience of the members. The church in the cemetery was eventually taken down, and given to the colored Presbyterians, and rebuilt on the Smallwood Road just south of the town limits. Like its parent white church in the town both have been brick veneered in recent years and continue to serve their respective congregations, the fourth Aimwell serving the colored people, and the fifth Aimwell serving the white congregation. In the days of the first and second churches, and the early days of Aimwell in the cemetery, the colored members were listed in the same congregation and attended the same services. Church segregation in the South is an outgrowth of the Civil War. Virtually all Southern churches had white and colored members before the War, and the Episcopal Church in South Carolina had more colored than white members.

ENGLISH AND FRENCH HUGUENOTS FROM THE LOWCOUNTRY

Edward Gendron Palmer of Saint James' Parish, Santee, Charleston District, came to Fairfield in 1824, the first of the lowcountrymen to move into this area and to exert an influence in the county out of all proportion to their numbers. Mr. Palmer had married Caroline, the daughter of Doctor James Davis, "eminent physician of his day," who lived at QUININE HILL near Columbia and who persuaded his son-in-law to migrate to the more healthful upcountry. Mr. Palmer purchased a plantation, BLOOMINGDALE, on Dutchman's Creek, several miles northwest of NEW LANDS as Ridgeway was then called. Not finding BLOOMINGDALE as healthful as he had hoped, Mr. Palmer temporarily moved into a house he owned on what is now Palmer Street in Ridgeway, while building VALENCIA.

One of the first to follow Mr. Palmer to the upcountry was Samuel Peyre Thomas of St. Stephen's Parish, Charleston District, who built VALLEY GROVE, the lands of which adjoined BLOOMINGDALE. Having received his Bachelor of Arts degree at Harvard College in 1825, S. Peyre Thomas returned to his birthplace BETAW on the Santee in St. Stephen's Parish. Here he awaited his twenty-first birthday, December 7, 1825, for the settlement of his late parents' estate. Writing his Harvard classmates from VALLEY GROVE in 1850 on the occasion of his twenty-fifth class reunion, Mr. Thomas states, "Upon becoming of age a few months after my returning home from college, I found myself in possession of ten negroes and about Two thousand Dollars. With this small property, I removed to Fairfield District and purchased a small farm and have ever since been engaged in the production of cotton." In 1834 Mr. Thomas married Jane Fears Rosborough, daughter of John Rosborough, whom he describes in another letter, now also in the Harvard Library Archives as "one of the most estimable men, and most correct in principle, that I ever knew." VALLEY GROVE was built in 1835, burned in 1841, and was described by Mr. Thomas as "very costly." The family lived in the former VALLEY GROVE kitchen for some years thereafter.

[21]

In the meantime, Mr. Thomas' plantation had been greatly enlarged by his wife's inheritance through her late father's death of lands adjoining VALLEY GROVE. Mr. Thomas then determined to build on this former Rosborough land, nearer Ridgeway, on the Longtown-Camden Road. Here he had commenced the building of MAGNOLIA less than a mile east of the village of Ridgeway when he died on June 28, 1854. MAGNOLIA was completed by his widow and sons and remained the family home until it was sold to settle the estate of his daughter, Anne (Mrs. Charles E. Thomas). Another house now occupies the site below St. Stephen's Church.

Through the influence of Messrs. Palmer and Thomas in lower Fairfield District, David Gaillard, Samuel DuBose, and Theodore DuBose of St. John's Parish also moved to Fairfield in this period, all of these settling near Winnsboro. With the opportunity of entering their sons at Mount Zion Institute, several lowcountry widows — Mrs. Isabella Peyre Porcher, Mrs. Sarah Palmer Couturier, and Mrs. Mary Gaillard, among others — also moved to Fairfield at this time. Through marriage and family connections General John Bratton and Mr. Isaac Dwight were also attracted to the county.

In the summer of 1835 John Peyre Thomas, M.D., elder brother of Samuel Peyre Thomas, travelled through Fairfield, visiting most of these lowcountry settlers of the upper country. Continuing to Greenville District, where he spent the summer with his wife, the former Harriet Jane Couturier, Dr. Thomas suffered the cruel blow of her death soon after the birth of their sixth child in Greenville. Dr. Thomas returned to Fairfield and determined to settle here, purchasing several tracts of land to make up MOUNT HOPE PLANTATION, most of which had been owned by the Kennedys and Rosboroughs.

The next year Dr. Thomas married his late wife's sister, Charlotte Henrietta Couturier, and brought her to MOUNT HOPE where their country plantation home was under construction.

RAILROAD AND TELEGRAPH THROUGH RIDGEWAY IN 1850's

Confederate Headquarters, February 17-19, 1865

Ridgeway takes its name from the ridge which bisects this lower area of Fairfield County between the Broad and Wateree Rivers. When the Charlotte and South Carolina Railroad, of which Mr. Edward G. Palmer of Ridgeway was the first president, was completed in 1850, the new railroad followed the ridge north of Columbia toward Winnsboro. Ridgeway drains east of the railroad into the Wateree River, and west of the railroad into the waters of the Broad River. Ridgeway, at an elevation of six hundred and twenty-five feet above sea level, is the highest point on the Southern Railway between Augusta, Georgia, and Charlotte, North Carolina.

The semaphore and telegraph lines marked the next great development through the county. The first telegraph line was run in 1854 and 1855, the wires being stretched from tree to tree. However, Ridgeway did not become a telegraph office until the latter part of the War, when the Confederate gov ernment established better provision for rapid communication. And the fact that Ridgeway had a telegraph office accounts for its "greatest and darkest days in history."

General Pierre Gustave Toutant Beauregard, commanding general of the Military Division of the West, Confederate States of America, established his headquarters at Ridgeway Friday, February 17, 1865, in the Coleman house, just across the street from the telegraph office. General Beauregard had evacuated Columbia that morning in advance of General Sherman's Union Army approaching the capital city across Broad River. General Beauregard maintained his headquarters at Ridgeway until Sunday, February 19, when it was ascertained that Sherman would advance north rather than toward Charleston or Wilmington through Camden.

General Beauregard with his staff travelled from Columbia to Ridgeway by way of the "Common Road," which roughly paralleled the Charlotte and South Carolina Railroad. After General Beauregard set up his headquarters in the BRICK HOUSE (now known as the CENTURY HOUSE), the first telegram that he sent from Ridgeway was to General Robert E. Lee in Richmond as follows: "Ridgeway, S. C., February 17, 1865, 9:30 P. M.

"Enemy having forced crossing of Saluda and Broad Rivers above Columbia, city had to be evacuated this morning. My forces are retiring to this place (Ridgeway). Everything possible shall be done to retard enemy's advance, but I cannot separate cavalry and infantry without fear of disaster, owing to the small number of latter, only 3,000 effectives. Moreover, having no supply trains, troops must move along railroads." Signed "G. T. Beauregard."

The next day, Saturday, Colonel Otey ordered 15,000 rations to be transported from Chesterville (now Chester) to Ridgeway. Lieutenant General Wade Hampton, chief of cavalry, remained near Columbia in an effort to delay Sherman's march north, and to offer such rear guard action for General Beauregard as might be feasible and possible. The popular South Carolina cavalryman, Wade Hampton, had been promoted only a few days before this to the rank of Lieutenant General by special order of President Jefferson Davis. General Hampton sent to General Beauregard at Ridgeway on February 18 a most important message, which, if put into action, might have altered the fast close of the War. This was General Hampton's famous plan of attack to bottle up Sherman's army between the swamps of the Wateree River and the banks of the Broad River, and with reinforcements from General Lee in Virginia to destroy the Union Army in Fairfield County. Beauregard did not consider his army strong enough to attempt such action, and did not execute Hampton's plans. There were only minor skirmishes between the armies after Sherman entered South Carolina, and his scorched earth policy was carried through with little hindrance.

SAINT STEPHEN'S EPISCOPAL CHURCH
by
CHARLES E. THOMAS

The second Ridgeway church after Aimwell, Presbyterian, was Cedar Creek Mission, organized by the Episcopalians in 1839, when the Reverend Cranmore Wallace held the first Episcopal services in the AIMWELL MEETING HOUSE and baptized several Davis, Palmer, and Thomas children. In 1825 and 1826 the Reverend Edward Thomas, a missionary of the Advancement Society, had visited Fairfield and preached at the Courthouse at Winnsboro. However, it was not until Mr. Edward Gendron Palmer fitted up a house on what is now Palmer Street in Ridgeway, in 1841, that the Ridgeway Episcopalians had a place to worship. This is the homesite of the late Robert Charlton Thomas, now the home of Mr. John Jones.

The widow of Doctor James Davis, Mrs. Catherine Ross Davis, who had moved to Ridgeway and built IVEY HILL (the site of the Ridgeway Public School) after the death of her husband in Columbia in order to be near her daughter, Mrs. Edward G. Palmer, gave in the early 1850's ten acres of land on which Saint Stephen's Chapel was built. Bishop Davis consecrated Saint Stephen's on August 4, 1854, as a chapel of Saint John's Parish, Winnsboro. The two Fairfield Episcopal churches had taken the names of the lowcountry parishes whence so many of their earliest members had migrated to Fairfield.

The earliest members of Saint Stephen's, in addition to the Davis, Palmer, and Thomas families, were the Peays and Meyers of Longtown and the Machettes of Dutchman's Creek. This marked the first of the German Lutherans in the area, some who became Episcopalians, as had the French Huguenots, such as the Gaillards and Couturiers, in the lowcountry.

One of the really great figures in the Episcopal Church of America, the Reverend William Porcher DuBose, a native of Fairfield County, served Saint Stephen's, Ridgeway, and Saint John's, Winnsboro, as rector immediately after the War, upon his return to his native state, from 1865 to 1868. Later, at the University of the South, Sewanee, as dean, chaplain, and professor for the remaining years of his long and fruitful life, Dr. DuBose through many writings became a world figure in the realm of philosophy and religion. He was called by English scholars "the wisest man on both sides of the Atlantic."

In more than forty years on the faculty of Sewanee, Dr. DuBose came to represent the Spirit of Sewanee, and to generations of students he became the Sage of Sewanee, revered by all who came under his quiet but powerful influence.

It is no singular coincidence that Fairfield County, with its rich religious and educational background of Scotch-Irish Presbyterians and Mount Zion College, its lowcountry English and French Huguenots in Saint John's and Saint Stephen's Episcopal Churches, its historic Methodism, and as the birthplace of the Associate Reformed Presbyterian Church, has given so many leaders to religion and education in the state, the South, and the nation. In its early years Mount Zion supplied the vast bulk of educated men to the Presbyterian ministry; and both Wofford College and South Carolina Methodism's great James Henry Carlisle, and Sewanee and the Episcopal Church's

SAINT STEPHEN'S EPISCOPAL CHURCH

II

scholarly William Porcher DuBose studied and later taught at Mount Zion, were both natives of Fairfield County.

The little church St. Stephen's that was built in 1854 is the oldest and one of the most beautiful landmarks at Ridgeway. It is a picturesque building, characterized by a steep gabled roof, giving it the appearance of an ancient Gothic chapel. Handsome stained-glass windows, deepset in narrow Gothic arches, further dramatize the architecture. The church was originally a frame structure, painted red. In the 1920's it was brick veneered, and in the 1940's a wing containing the parish house and Church School was added, enhancing, rather than detracting from, the original design.

The grounds consist of a well-kept cemetery, dotted with tombstones and graves bearing the names of the builders and early families. The churchyard is enclosed with a handsome wrought-iron fence and sturdy gateways.

THE CENTURY HOUSE
COLEMAN — RIDGEWAY GARDEN CLUB

The CENTURY HOUSE is one of the most imposing buildings in the town of Ridgeway. It is a massive, well-proportioned, two-story, solid brick house located almost in the center of the town. The large and ancient trees on the grounds give it a distinctive beauty and dignity.

The house was built in 1853 by James Buchanan Coleman, an extensive landowner. His properties were scattered from Blythewood, in the lower section of the county, to the DEVIL'S RACE TRACK community in the upper section. On locating in Ridgeway, he purchased the Rosborough home and a large tract of land from his friend, James Thomas Rosborough, M.D., some time before 1842 when Dr. Rosborough moved to Texas. Coleman family records indicate that this "two-story (Rosborough homestead) wooden house was near the BRICK HOUSE on the same level . . . with beautiful pink climbing roses on the piazza . . . large rooms on both floors and silver door-knobs and walnut stair-rails . . . built before 1800 by Dr. Rosborough's father, Mr. John Rosborough." The older Coleman children were born in the Rosborough house before Mr. Coleman built the BRICK HOUSE. The Colemans were hospitable and fond of company and entertaining; this is evidenced by the large and gracious home that they erected.

Before the construction of the house began, Mr. Coleman began making brick for it. For two seasons, after his crops were laid by, he used his plantation labor to make and burn the bricks. The kilns were located near the site of the present cemetery. With this task complete he began the actual construction. Plantation labor was also used for this operation, under the careful supervision of the owner and his capable wife. The lumber and materials used came mostly from the plantation. In a little more than a year the building was completed, in 1854.

From its beginning the house was a social center of the community. Entertainments of all kinds were held here, sponsored by this unselfish couple, for more than two generations.

THE CENTURY HOUSE

III

When Mr. Coleman died, the property was left to his widow for her life. At her passing, the portion including the home became the property of their son, L. H. Coleman, who with his family occupied it for several years. Later it was rented and used as a hotel until it was bought by Mr. R. B. Sessions. The Sessions resided here a number of years and then sold to a Mr. Branham.

Several years ago the ladies of the Ridgeway Garden Club became interested in the old building, which was beginning to show its age and become rather run-down. Mrs. Iola Kennedy Bolick, a grandaughter of the builders, and who was born and spent most of her girlhood in the old house, was most enthusiastic over the proposed project by the Garden Club.

The house was put into good repair, renovated, and redecorated. The grounds were relandscaped and the old place has been restored. It is now one of Ridgeway's most cherished landmarks and serves as a community center where both young and old still enjoy the hospitality of the spacious old rooms that have afforded so much pleasure and enjoyment to the people of the town for over a century.

Situated on the new Charlotte and South Carolina Railroad, which hauled freight and passengers in 1856, the Colemans' commanding brick house became the center of social and business life in the newly developing community of Ridgeway.

With the coming of the War Between the States, the BRICK HOUSE entertained many visitors and travellers passing through Ridgeway, who came by train, stagecoach, wagon train, on horseback, and afoot. Refugees from the lowcountry of South Carolina and Georgia, as well as others from Virginia and North Carolina, became almost daily visitors in the Colemans' hospitable and well-provisioned home. Among those who are mentioned in family letters as guests in the BRICK HOUSE were Mr. Gibbons, "who was getting up funds to supply the Confederate Army . . . as well as the famous maker of 'Pin Money Pickles,' Mr. Kid, from Virginia . . ."

When General P. G. T. Beauregard, commanding general of the Confederate forces of the deep South, evacuated Columbia with the approach of General Sherman's Federal Army, Ridgeway was chosen as Confederate headquarters, both because of its railroad and telegraph office, and its strategic location in relationship to Columbia, to Alston on the Broad River and railroad, and to Camden on the Wateree and railroads to Charleston and Wilmington. No doubt the possible use of the Colemans' BRICK HOUSE for General Beauregard and his Staff's accommodation contributed to the selection of Ridgeway for temporary headquarters, as well.

While General Wade Hampton remained in the rear for delaying action and to keep General Beauregard informed of the enemy's movements, Ridgeway was the most important Confederate post from February 17 to February 19, with telegrams constantly being sent to Confederate leaders throughout the South, and trains bringing rations and supplies into Ridgeway to feed more than three thousand Confederate troops converging on the small town.

These three days and the three following remain the busiest and most exciting week in the history of Ridgeway and Fairfield and perhaps South Carolina. Hundreds of railway coaches passed through with refugees fleeing the burning and sacking of Columbia, baggage and freight cars loaded with household goods and luggage, bank notes, State and Confederate records,

IV

VALENCIA

foodstuffs, and cotton. Roads were a solid stream of wagons, carriages, carts, and animals, with many colored and white people on foot, as well, many carrying all their worldly goods on their backs with small children trudging along.

Refugees were followed by State Militia and Confederate troops, travelling by railroad train, wagon train, horseback, and afoot. The South Carolina Militia under Governor McGrath included the young cadets from the Arsenal Academy under their superintendent, Colonel John Peyre Thomas, who had grown up in Ridgeway. Colonel Thomas left the cadets along the common road long enough to visit in passing, his home, MOUNT HOPE, to see his mother and sisters and younger brothers. Governor Isham Harris of Tennessee was among the refugees travelling through Fairfield during that eventful week.

Hardly had the Confederate troops passed through Ridgeway before the advance scouts and bummers of Sherman's Federal forces began arriving. A Diary kept at MOUNT HOPE during that dreadful week records that on "Monday (February 20), as we were hearing explosions and cannonading from Columbia, and we would listen in the yard and garden. Some of our soldiers had said, 'The next campfires you see will be the Yankees'" . . . The MOUNT HOPE Diary continues, "Tuesday, all the neighborhood was on fire; the stable smoking in the yard, the Railroad burning in the distance; Ridgeway Depot, three miles off, burning! Nothing but flames and smoke was to be seen all around . . ."

Many of the Ridgeway townspeople had stored their furniture in the Masonic Temple at the crossroads, thinking it might not be harmed, but it was burned after its contents had been scattered everywhere, according to one local resident. Mrs. Coleman, whose husband lay seriously ill, bravely met one of the Union officers and asked for his protection. The officer gallantly responded, taking personal charge of guarding the BRICK HOUSE and its builder in his last illness. Some have attributed this to the fact that the Union officer was shown Mr. Coleman's Masonic ring. So the BRICK HOUSE and its contents remained unharmed.

One of the Colemans described the BRICK HOUSE as it appeared soon after the war. She wrote, "Beautiful elm trees bordered the sidewalk just in front of the railroad station. Further back were cotton fields, and the vegetable and flower gardens with the beehives. Then the hill sloped sharply down to the spring near which the brick for the house had been baked by Grandfather's slaves. Mother says she remembers when the kilns were burning at night and what a beautiful sight the fires were from the upstairs bedroom windows of the old Rosborough House."

The new house was entirely of red brick, with bright green window blinds. Wide halls commenced at the double front doors off the first and second story piazzas. On the first floor the hall extended to the center of the house, where it entered the unusually large, long dining room which crossed the width of the house. Over the dining room was a similar large room upstairs for the dances and balls. Downstairs the front room on the right was the parlor, and on the left the gentlemen's parlor. Behind the parlors were downstairs bedrooms. One stairway commenced a short distance back of the parlor door on the left. There was another, smaller, narrower enclosed stairway from the dining room to the ballroom over it. This was for taking refreshments up-

VALENCIA

V

stairs for parties and receptions. Upstairs were four bedrooms, each with four-poster teester beds with steps leading up to the deep goose-feather mattresses.

The upstairs ballroom became a work room when a "Spinning Jenny and two large looms were installed during the War." Thread was spun, and woolen coverlets, thick white bedspreads, and other cloth were woven by a Mrs. Huffstetler, who came from the Dutch Fork section near the Broad River to do the spinning and weaving for Mrs. Coleman.

The builder of the BRICK HOUSE, J. B. Coleman, was born February 3, 1800, in Fairfield County near Ridgeway. He was the son of Charles Coleman, who had come to Fairfield from Virginia. State archives records show that Charles Coleman was an armorer to General Richard Winn (for whom Winnsboro was named) in the Revolutionary War. Pension records in the National Archives show that his father was Kadar Coleman. Charles Coleman owned large tracts of land and slaves between Ridgeway and Simpson's Turnout, according to the Coleman papers, and had sixteen children, "some very beautiful girls among them." Among the children of the Colemans born in the BRICK HOUSE was Thomas Hines Coleman, who became the founder of the Florida State School for the Deaf and Blind in 1885.

VALENCIA

PALMER

VALENCIA is an outstanding example of an old Southern plantation home. It rests upon a high hill overlooking lush, green woodlands as far as the eye can reach. It was built in 1834 by Edward Gendron Palmer.

Mr. Palmer was the first of the lowcountry planters to settle in Fairfield. He came from Saint James Parish, Santee. In 1824 he married Caroline Davis of Columbia. Her father, Dr. James Davis, was a prominent physician, who preferred the healthful climate of the upcountry to the malaria-infested lowcountry. It was he who influenced the young Palmers to settle in Fairfield. Edward Gendron Palmer acquired six thousand acres and built a fine new home for his new country seat. He called the plantation BLOOMINGDALE at New Lands.

This name, however, was short-lived. Not long after the Palmers moved into the house, Mrs. Palmer's brother, James Davis II, visited them. He had just returned from a grand tour of Europe, on which he had spent much time in Spain. The view from his sister's home reminded him so much of the landscape seen from his hotel room in Valencia, Spain, that he suggested that they call the new manor house VALENCIA.

This house is reminiscent of the plantation homes found in the lowcountry, where the Palmer family lived before coming to Fairfield. It is a large two-story frame house with a broad, one-story piazza across the front. Long, spacious halls cut through the center of the building on both floors, with high-ceilinged rooms on either side. The trim and woodwork, within and without, are handsomely carved. Beautiful, handcarved wooden mantels adorn the oversize fireplaces. Above the windows in the drawing room are the original red and gold cornices.

LONGLEAF

VI

Many pieces of walnut and mahogany furniture that were placed in the house when it was new still remain. One that is of particular interest is a small table that once belonged to Thomas Jefferson. This was brought to VALENCIA by Colonel William C. Preston. Mrs. Palmer's sister's husband, from Washington. Family portraits and priceless Parisian prints adorn the walls. A life-size bust of Colonel Preston rests on the Jefferson table.

Mr. Palmer was the first president of the Charlotte and South Carolina Railroad, as well as having been its chief promoter. He was most reluctant to sign a special "oath of Allegiance" after the Confederate War for President Andrew Johnson, and died a short time after so doing. This document is now framed and hangs on a wall in the drawing room at VALENCIA.

The plantation and house still belong to the Palmer family. The home is filled with priceless heirlooms, rare documents, and many hunting, lancing, and racing trophies that have been won by the sporting members of the family from several generations. Mr. and Mrs. Berkley Palmer and their family now reside at VALENCIA and live in the same gracious manner as did their forebears.

LONGLEAF

DAVIS — RUFF — MATTHEWS

LONGLEAF is situated just below Ridgeway between the Camden and Columbia roads. It is not imposing, but though it lacks in elegance, the unusual design, the history of the place, and the distinguished people who have resided here make it one of Fairfield's great old homes.

In the early 1850's young Henry Campbell Davis, a son of an old and revered South Carolina family, chose LONGLEAF for the site of his new home where he planned to build a large, comfortable plantation house in the true Southern tradition. A two-story building was erected, and the family moved into it before 1860. This was but one wing of the original plan, which the War Between the States interrupted and which was never completed due to the poverty-stricken days of the Reconstruction period that followed.

The little rectangular building is quite plain, with a large central chimney and a gabled roof. The ground-level first floor is built of brick, and the second story is constructed of the durable and famous longleaf pine timber which was cut from the plantation forests and from which the place took its name. A wide, two-story porch covers most of the front, with a shed roof supported by four square wooden columns with plain picket bannisters between them, giving it a balcony-like effect. Large brick pillars support the upper porch. The basement has a front, side, and rear entrance and also a door that opens out onto the balcony.

Born in Columbia on August 6, 1823, Henry C. Davis was the son of Doctor James Davis and Catherine Ross Davis. He took his A.B. degree at South Carolina College in 1844. For the next four years he served as librarian for the College and read law. On May 18, 1848, he married the beautiful Isabella Harper Means, daughter of the Reverend Robert Means, D.D., distinguished Presbyterian minister, and niece of Governor John Hugh Means of BUCKHEAD, Fairfield District, a signer of the Ordinance of Secession, who was killed in the Second Battle of Manassas.

CEDAR TREE

VII

A biographer of one of their sons, Professor Robert Means Davis, wrote in 1904, "about a century ago, the sturdy upcountrymen and the polished low-countrymen of this state here (Ridgeway) met and founded a settlement, and from their union proceeded a community of highminded, thrifty, independent and wealthy people. Imitating the ridge of land on which they settled and which gave the village its name, the people continuously threw off from themselves the accidental distinctions of rank and fortune and became year after year more tenacious of the real and lasting qualities of life."

With the Palmer and Thomas families, Mr. Davis was one of the builders of Saint Stephen's Church at Ridgeway in 1854. His mother, who had moved to Ridgeway from Columbia after Dr. Davis' death lived at IVEY HILL, and was herself a large landowner. She gave the property on which Saint Stephen's Church is built. One of her daughters was the wife of Edward Gendron Palmer of VALENCIA. Mrs. Davis' bachelor son, Edward William Davis (1816-1870), conducted a private school for boys at IVEY HILL for some years before the Confederate War. In the early part of this century, after IVEY HILL had been destroyed, Ridgeway Public School was built on the site.

Henry C. Davis served in the Legislature from Fairfield District from 1858-60, and from 1864-65. He was a member of the Secession Convention and signed the Ordinance of Secession on December 20, 1860. With the outbreak of the war he volunteered and was serving as Captain of Company C, 12th South Carolina Volunteers, Palmetto Rifles, when he was wounded at Sharpsburg. Following the war he was a Captain in the South Carolina Militia, attaining the rank of colonel in due time. In 1885 he was appointed postmaster at Ridgeway. He died of a sudden attack suffered on the train while he was talking on the coach with Miss Gabriella Marion Thomas of MOUNT HOPE. He is buried in Saint Stephen's churchyard.

One of Colonel and Mrs. Davis' sons was the distinguished Professor Robert Means Davis, of the University of South Carolina after an equally successful career as a teacher at Mount Zion, and as editor of the WINNSBORO NEWS. Henry C. Davis, Jr., another son, was one of the first Southern boys appointed to the United States Military Academy at West Point after the war, attaining the rank of colonel after a distinguished service in the Spanish-American War and later in the Philippines. A third son, James Quentin Davis, was a distinguished banker in Winnsboro. Catherine, a daughter, married Colonel David DuBose Gaillard, who also entered West Point from Fairfield and became one of the great engineers of the Panama Canal, where Culebra Cut now bears the name of Gaillard Cut in his honor. The last of the family was Eloise, who married William Herbert Ruff, a planter and merchant of Ridgeway, and died in her ninety-seventh year in 1957, one of the really great ladies of Ridgeway and of Fairfield County.

Doctor James Davis, the father of Colonel Henry C. Davis, was a highly educated man, a brilliant physician, and an extensive landowner. When a student, he studied and read medicine under Doctor Ross of Union, South Carolina, at that time one of the foremost medical men in the state. When young Davis asked to study under him, he was accepted but with two conditions. One was that he would not consider matrimony until he had completed his study; the other (and the old doctor was most emphatic when he stated it) was that, if he did consider marriage, he would not wed Dr. Ross' daughter.

MOUNT HOPE

VIII

Two young men who had preceded him had married two of the old man's daughters. The first condition was adhered to but not so for the second. When James Davis finished his course, he married Catherine Ross.

When the State Hospital or Asylum was established in Columbia, Dr. Davis was the first man to head the institution. He specialized in mental disorders and treatment for them, doing extensive research in other fields of medicine. He was one of the first men to recognize mosquitos, fleas, and other insects as being carriers of diseases.

During the Confederate War LONGLEAF was raided by Sherman's men. While they were pillaging the place and chasing the livestock and poultry about the yard, little Eloise, one of the younger children, ventured out onto the upstairs balcony. A Yankee soldier noticed her and called her a "pretty little Rebel." She did not like his words nor his attitude and would not answer him. Then he said, "Pretty little Miss, come down and give me a kiss!" Her response was a surprise; she spat down the stairs into his face and ran to her Negro mammy, burying her face in the protective folds of her nurse's skirts.

After the war the Davis family continued to reside at LONGLEAF until the family grew up, married, and moved away. The property came down to Mrs. Ruff. It is now owned by her granddaughter, Mrs. Palmer Matthews (nee Eloise Cork) of Winnsboro. The Matthews renovated and restored the old house and lived there for a number of years. They now reside in Winnsboro but still have a strong affection for the home of their forebears.

CEDAR TREE

PALMER — DESPORTES — BULOW — VAN EXEM

CEDAR TREE plantation house was built in about 1853 by Edward G. Palmer of VALENCIA for his son, Doctor John Palmer of Ridgeway. It is well-located on a high elevation a few miles from the town of Ridgeway.

This is a comfortable, roomy, one-and-one-half-story building with a gabled porch on the front, supported by well-proportioned columns. In the roof, on the front, and on the rear are attractive dormer windows. The structure is further embellished by a beautifully kept walled garden, containing boxwoods, rare shrubs, and blooming flowers for all seasons. The garden is entered through an intricately designed wrought-iron gate. The major portion of the wall around the grounds is covered by Cherokee rose vines that were planted more than one hundred years ago; they still bloom profusely in season. The lumber and eighteen-inch heart-pine siding of which the house is built were cut on the plantation. From foundation to roof the building is in an excellent state of repair.

Many of the original outbuildings are still in use. The smokehouse, kitchen, washhouse, and the old farm bell that used to call the plantation hands to work and meals are still a part of the place.

Near the house is an ancient cemetery containing the weathered gravestones and tombs of those who once lived here. Beneath one of these rests Colonel Dunbar, a soldier of the Revolutionary War.

[38]

CEDAR TREE remained in the Palmer family for many years, and since their ownership it has belonged to the DesPortes, Bulows, and Van Exems. Local tradition has it that one of the early owners was quite a gay and reckless sportsman and that he lost this lovely old place in order to pay a gambling debt.

The Bulows were Charlestonians engaged in the mining of phosphate. They purchased the place in the early years of this century. The property passed from them to Mr. Van Exem whose widow now resides here.

Mrs. Van Exem is one of South Carolina's charming great ladies. After the death of her first husband — a distinguished lawyer and statesman, who was Congressman from the Sixth District — Honorable Allard H. Gasque of Florence, South Carolina, she was the first woman from this state to be elected to Congress. Mrs. Van Exem is also a writer, dramatist, and patron of the arts.

MOUNT HOPE
THOMAS

by
CHARLES E. THOMAS

MOUNT HOPE, in lower Fairfield District about one mile west of the village of Ridgeway, was built by John Peyre Thomas, M.D., between 1835 and 1840.

The three-story brick-and-frame house is described as "plantation style," its first or ground floor of brick sometimes referred to as the "summer floor." The second and third floors of the house are entirely of locally grown heart-of-pine timber. Steps from the ground lead to the front and back porches of the main or second floor of the house. Each floor has halls or "passageways" running the full length of the building, with four large rooms on each floor, with two smaller rooms on the main or second floor at either end of the back or north porch. As was the custom at that time in order to take full advantage of the prevailing summer breezes, the house faces the south. It was presumed that the morning and evening breezes that generally were from the south to north would thereby cool the house through the long hallways.

The oversize bricks throughout the two-foot-thick walls of the ground floor, including not only the four exterior walls but the inside partitions between the ground floor rooms and along the open passageway underneath, were all baked in kilns erected on the plantation for the purpose of making bricks and tiles for the house. The ground floor is paved with square, red clay tiles, and all the hearths throughout the house are of the same tile. The four outside forty-foot-high chimneys are of the same large-size brick, most of which are in a good state of preservation after 125 years. There are no fireplaces in the ground or summer-floor rooms, as these rooms were designed for summertime use only. Each of the four rooms on the main or second floor and three of the four third-floor rooms have fireplaces. There is no fireplace in the "boys' room" on the theory that no fire in the winter mornings would make for faster dressing on the part of the boys of the household who slept in the dormitory-like top-floor room. The only other brick baked in the MOUNT HOPE kilns is said to have been that for Saint Stephen's Church at Ridgeway, referred to as the "Chapel" by Dr. Thomas, in his Diary, when it was built in 1854.

The pine timbers for the house were cut by slave labor with broad axes and crosscut saws. The irregular strokes of the axes and saws can be seen in the larger timbers supporting the second floor. These beams are spliced with a particularly interesting interlocking joint and fastened with round wood pins running through the twelve-inch-square timbers. The pine flooring throughout the ten rooms and long, wide hallways of the two upper floors is in continuous boards with none that do not run the width of the room or hallway. Another interesting feature of the flooring is that the boards of the hall floors run crosswise rather than lengthwise as in modern halls. This gives the effeçt of the floors of the rooms running through the hall into the opposite rooms, as only the thresholds of the hallway doors break this continuous pattern of the wide pine flooring.

Another architectural feature of the plantation-style house is the simplicity of the pine mantels. Above each of the large fireplaces is a high mantel of the simplest lines and undecorated design. The same lines are carried out in the doors and window frames, and in the chair-rail height wainscoting in each of the main floor rooms. The design is again repeated in the two large "presses" or wardrobe closets built in the master bedroom and in the top-floor hallway. These double presses were built in the house, for they are wider than the doorways.

All of the hardware used in the construction of the house, with the exception of the Carpenter English-made door locks, was handmade in the local blacksmith shop. Even the square nails used throughout the house were beaten out by hand, as were the door and window hinges, window-holds and latches. The large locks with their six-inch brass keys and brass knobs on each door, inside and outside doors, bear the English coat of arms of the lion and the unicorn. The same Carpenter lock was patented in the United States in 1840, and these bear the United States shield and eagle design. However, all of the MOUNT HOPE locks bear the English patent.

Dr. Thomas came to Fairfield in 1835, seeking a healthful climate for his family after the deaths in the lowcountry of two of his children and in Greenville that summer of his wife. The following year, 1836, Dr. Thomas married his wife's younger sister. Before his own death at MOUNT HOPE on January 1, 1859, Dr. Thomas had become the father of eighteen children, fourteen of whom survived him. When he was buried at Saint Stephen's Church, Ridgeway, his was the first grave in the newly opened churchyard. His second wife and thirteen of his eighteen children are buried there with him.

Dr. Thomas' carefully recorded "Diary of Weather and Occurrences," which covers the years 1827 to 1856, has been presented by his family to the South Caroliniana Society Library at the University in Columbia. Dr. Thomas had graduated from South Carolina College in 1816 before taking his M.D. degree at the College of Physicians and Surgeons in New York City in 1819. He interned at Bellevue Hospital, New York, before returning to South Carolina. His license to "practice Physic and Surgery in all their branches," signed by five members of the Committee of the Medical Society of South Carolina, Charleston, on October 2, 1821, is said to be one of the earliest medical licenses. At MOUNT HOPE are still Dr. Thomas' pharmaceutical scales, mortar and pestle, lancet, and other medical pharmacopoeia and instruments.

MOUNT HOPE was visited by many of the bummers, stragglers and soldiers of General Sherman's Union Army when the Federal troops sacked Fairfield County in February 1865. Everything that could be taken away by the foraging troops was hauled off in MOUNT HOPE wagons and carriages. The house was constantly pillaged and ransacked throughout that harrowing week following the burning of Columbia. Although the barns were set on fire and the house was frequently threatened, faithful slaves and brave women saved all the buildings from destruction. The four older sons of the family were away in Confederate service, Army and Navy; only women and children and frightened slaves were at MOUNT HOPE throughout the raids of February 1865. The family barricaded themselves in the parlor, cooked meagerly in the fireplace, and slept on the floor, fully dressed for several days and nights.

After the War, when there were no schools in South Carolina, the eldest daughter of Dr. Thomas, Miss Henrietta Eleanor Thomas, opened the MOUNT HOPE SCHOOL. Boarding students came from Columbia, and great numbers of day pupils from the area. It was the only school in the southern part of the county for twenty years before the state's public schools were reopened in 1885. Many local girls and boys received their entire education there, while others were prepared at MOUNT HOPE SCHOOL for colleges throughout the country, including the Southern boys to be admitted to the United States Military Academy at West Point following the War.

MOUNT HOPE is still owned by the descendants of Dr. Thomas, and is occupied in the summer by the sixth generation of the family to have occupied the 125-year-old plantation house.

LONGTOWN

by

CHARLES E. THOMAS

LONGTOWN, the easternmost settlement in Fairfield, and the oldest in that part of the county, is perhaps the least chronicled. It is probably due to its antiquity that much of LONGTOWN's early history has been lost, for many of its oldest and grandest homes have been destroyed by fire and other ravages of time and war.

"Through the wooded land ran a picturesque Indian trail" is the way one historian described the beginning of LONGTOWN. This was the Indian fur-trade route from North Carolina and the Piedmont area of South Carolina that followed the western slope of the Wateree River south to the Santee River and Georgetown, Charleston, and Savannah. LONGTOWN is said by Fitz-Hugh McMaster in the HISTORY OF FAIRFIELD COUNTY (Columbia 1946) to have first been known as LOG-TOWN because of the log houses built along the Indian trail, the name later becoming LONGTOWN. In any case it has been well named, for it is hard to define the limits of LONGTOWN.

The "town" of LONGTOWN is that area which borders the Ridgeway-Camden Road and covers the area from near Fairview, the old Ridgeway Hunting Club, southwest to the Kershaw County line, and east from the Wateree River to Dutchman's Creek, and west to the old Winnsboro Road.

The earliest settlers in LONGTOWN came from North Carolina and Virginia, and were Quakers, Episcopalians, French Huguenots, Presbyterians, and Baptists; about the same time came Swiss, Dutch, and German Roman Catholics, Dutch Huguenots, and Lutherans from across Broad River on the west side of Fairfield County. Printed records indicate that Nicholas Peay came from Hanover County, Virginia, to Pine Tree, now Camden, about the time of the Revolutionary War, and built MALVERN HALL in LONGTOWN. About the same time Charles Tidwell came down the Indian Trail to LONG-TOWN from the area of Jamestown, Virginia, and settled in the Bryant Hill section of LONGTOWN. His grave at Bryant Hill Cemetery, with his birth-date of 1690, might well be the earliest gravestone extant in the county.

LONGTOWN was also discovered by the German and Swiss settlers of Richland and Lexington Counties before the Revolution, for we have the record of Colonel David Myers of the Brick House, Bluff Road, near Columbia, owning plantations along the Wateree in Fairfield County soon after 1786 when his mother was reimbursed for a "black horse taken for public service" for the use of the Continental Army. His father, Jacob Myers, was paid for "144 days militia duty in 1787-88." Colonel Myers' son, John Jacob Myers, M.D., lived at SOLITUDE plantation in LONGTOWN, noted as a "luxurious and imposing structure and the scene of lordly hospitality, many celebrities being entertained there." Dr. Myers represented Fairfield County in the state House of Represntativs in 1840-41. He served as assistant surgeon to a regiment which escorted the Marquis de la Fayette from the North Carolina border to Columbia on his visit to South Carolina in 1824. It is reasonable to surmise that from this and the foregoing statement that General de la Fayette was entertained at SOLITUDE in Fairfield County, as well as in Camden and Columbia.

Other early LONGTOWN settlers were the Machettes, Wagners, and Zieglers from Holland, Germany, and Switzerland, and the Robertsons, Harrisons, Dixons, Picketts, Reeves, Stewarts, and Joneses through Virginia and North Carolina from England, France, Scotland, and Ireland. The Tidwells were English and the Peays French Huguenots. McMaster writes, "Before the Confederate War much wealth was accumulated, finer, larger homes were built, and so the name of LOG-TOWN became LONGTOWN." There was an academy near the Kershaw County line, with Professor McCandless (or McCandlers) in charge. He was said to have come from Georgia and was an "educator of high type." Boarding students came from Camden and Liberty Hill with day scholars from the entire LONGTOWN area. The professor had many visits from the irate mothers, whose sons he is said to have whipped on frequent occasions.

Austin Ford Peay, the son of Nicholas Peay of MALVERN HALL lived at FLINT HILL in Fairfield County. He was known as the "wealthiest man in that section." When he made a trip to Camden or Columbia ,he travelled at night with a mattress put in his carriage in order not to lose sleep and to be fresh for his day in town. This could well have been the origin of Mr. Pullman's first railroad sleeping cars. When in 1809 there was an embargo on the export of cotton, Mr. Peay decided to take his cotton to market. He went in his carriage, escorted by a long wagon train to Philadelphia from FLINT HILL. It is recorded that his cotton was sold for $25,000.00, a handsome price. He died at FLINT HILL in 1841 and was buried on his plantation, now flooded by the Wateree power development. The gravestones in this cemetery can be seen at low water. In the United States Census of 1860 the farms of the estate of N. A. Peay are listed at $253,000.00, by far the largest in Fairfield County.

MELROSE, called the grandest plantation house in upper South Carolina, was built at LONGTOWN above the Wateree by Austin Peay's son, Nicholas Adamson Peay. It has been described as a "massive structure of brick, stone, and marble of thirty rooms, broad piazzas and wide halls." It is said by descendants of his slaves to have had a garden on the roof with a ·pool in which fresh fish were kept for use at the table. The mansion was equipped with a water system supplied by fresh springs below the hill on which MELROSE was situated. Water was pumped to the roof by a hydraulic ram. Colonel and Mrs. Peay, the former Martha Cary Lamar, died before the Confederate War. Colonel Peay had served in the Seminole War in Florida in 1835. He represented Fairfield County in the state Senate in 1856, and died in office the next year.

When Sherman's Army invaded Fairfield County, MELROSE was one of the few plantation homes burned in the southeastern part of the county. The story is that a Union soldier rode his horse up the marble steps, through the piazza of MELROSE into the front hall. Tying his horse's reins to the ceiling candle chandelier, the Federal soldier rambled through the house and found the wine cellar where he lingered and imbibed too long. Soon other soldiers set fire to Fairfield's finest mansion, and the drunken soldier and his horse were consumed in the flames.

WISTERIA, the Tidwell-Myers family home, just across from the present Harrison-Dixon home in LONGTOWN, is said to have been saved by Nicholas Peay Myers, an intrepid Confederate son of the Peay-Myers families in LONGTOWN. Family tradition admits that Nick, a brave young man, acted as a spy for the Southern cause. He is reputed to have saved many helpless women and children, and even to have ambushed a few Yankees. He was wearing a Union Captain's uniform and insignia when he ordered the Yankee soldiers away from WISTERIA and saved his home from the torch. It is said that there were "Yankee skulls" in the attic at WISTERIA until Mrs. David William Tidwell (the former Mattie Myers) had them buried with the family and slaves at Bryant Hill Cemetery some time before WISTERIA was accidentally burned about 1935.

WISTERIA was one of the fine LONGTOWN plantation houses and was full of history, lore, and tradition. There were grease spots on the walls and even the ceilings of some of the upstairs closets where the Myers and Tidwells hid their hams and pork shoulders before Sherman's raid. These same bedrooms were papered after the war with Confederate money, it having become valueless, and paper being scarce.

LONGTOWN's Baptist Church was a great force in the early years when MELROSE commanded the area. It has been the burial place of some of the earlier families. The church building no longer remains, however, the Presbyterian Church which flourishes today has generally been supplied by the pastor of Ridgeway's historic Aimwell Church. Its cemetery is now the burial place of many influential LONGTOWN families, some of whom had been among the earliest settlers.

In 1854 when the Episcopalians in Ridgeway were building St. Stephen's Chapel, Colonel N. A. Peay offered to give $100.00 on the condition that the new church be built east of Ridgeway on the LONGTOWN Road "for the convenience" of his sister, Mrs. John Myers, the former Sarah English Peay. Colonel Peay was not an Episcopalian, and it was understood that Mrs. Peay was not to know of the gift as she, the devout member of another denomination, would not approve. Colonel and Mrs. Peay are buried in LONGTOWN's Baptist Cemetery, with one of the most imposing monuments in the state. Until the days of the Confederate War Mr. Richard Matchette of Dutchman's Creek and the LONGTOWN Myers attended Saint Stephen's in their colorful native Dutch costumes. Contemporaries describe them: "the men in knee-length pantaloons with big silver buckles and matching silver buckles on their shoes and belts; long flowing coats with wide leather belts and silver buckles; and broad-brimmed, low-crowned black and white hats. The ladies wore long skirts that touched the ground, colorful blouses with full sleeves, bright bonnets with flowing bows, under which their long, blond, tightly plaited tresses hung over their shoulders — and some below their waists, so long was their beautiful hair." The Dutch Episcopalians were devout and loyal Huguenots and Protestants.

WISTERIA was perhaps most noted for its fox hunts, although it is recalled that "the hounds disturbed Mrs. Tidwell's fine Wagnerian ear." Her descendants have inherited her ear for music. There were eight Tidwell sons, and more horses and hounds, and so with a few friends a fox hunt was easily organized at WISTERIA. It began with a pre-dawn breakfast served by Hence, a slave born at WISTERIA; the menu: steak, eggs, hominy, and biscuits, for the day would be a long one, especially if the fox happened to be a red one. The hunt crossed Tidwell Flats toward Wateree to the east of Dutchman's Creek to the north and west. If a grey fox was hounded around Bryant Hill Cemetery, the chase might be a short one, but if it was red, the hunt would go as far as FLINT HILL or BUCKHEAD or even across the river to Liberty Hill. However, no matter what time the fox, whether red or grey, was stopped by the hounds, the hunters returned to WISTERIA to find one of Mrs. Tidwell's and Hence's magnificent WISTERIA dinners ready for them.

Dutchman's Creek is another historical landmark of the early influence of the German-Swiss-Dutch families like the Myers, Matchettes, Zeiglers, and others who settled in this part of Fairfield County and gave their name to the creek.

History records the many wild animals of the Wateree-to-Broad-River area of Fairfield. They are listed as deer, foxes (red and grey), raccoons, wildcats, opossums (our only marsupial), cottontail rabbits (hare), grey and flying squirrels, wharf and blue rats, wood and muskrats, minks, weasels, leather-winged bats, moles, and mice. Among the one hundred or more birds mentioned, many are still native to the area; others are extinct or are today rare, like pileated woodpeckers, blue and white herons, and wild turkeys. Deer are said to have been common in the area until 1880, and about the same time Mr. Hugh S. Wylie is reported to have said that he saw "Not thousands but hundreds of thousands, possibly millions of wild pigeons in flight. They would darken the sky." He adds that wild turkeys were plentiful as well. Both the great naturalists, Alexander Wilson and John James Audubon, described seeing wild pigeons in such numbers as this earlier in the century in various parts of America.

But alas, WISTERIA burned in 1935 and the Tidwell lands are now a part of the extensive Bowater Paper forests. Time, war, and fire have taken many of LONGTOWN's ante-bellum mansions — and its finest, like MALVERN HALL, SOLITUDE, MELROSE, and WISTERIA. However, many of the descendants of these early Fairfield County families remain, some nearby and others scattered throughout the state and the neighboring states. LONGTOWN has a proud heritage and a long, rich history, full of thrilling facts and colorful fancy.

Among the families that settled at LONGTOWN before and during the Confederate War were the Rosboroughs, Walkers, Hunters, Parkers, Boyles, Rions, Edmunds, Ollevers, Mobleys, Stuarts, Spurriers, Boyds, Hamiltons, Rochelles, Crowders, Haynes, Mellichamps, Boulwares, Bolicks, Moores, Crumptons, Dixons, Gozas, Wilsons, and Martins. The above-mentioned families are only those who owned lands along the main roads that pass through the section.

BLINK BONNIE

JONES — ROBERTSON — KIRKLAND

BLINK BONNIE, in the Longtown section of Fairfield, commands one of the most majestic views in the county. From its spacious veranda portions of several counties, towns, and settlements may be clearly seen without the aid of binoculars. In the summer the varying shades of green melt away into purple tints where the heavenly blue of the sky meets the horizon. Several glistening creeks, the Wateree River, and Lake Wateree cut their own patterns through the forest. The panorama from this point is a challenge to any artist who might try to capture it on canvas.

In 1822 a Camden banker, Darling Jones, built this house for a summer residence. The design and construction of the commodious home show that the builder had all the good taste and hospitable traits of the era.

The main body of the structure is rectangular, with a wing to the left. Across the front is a wide, spacious piazza, supported by graceful, well-proportioned square columns. An outstanding feature of the house is the two enormous central hallways on the first and second floors. They extend all the way through the middle of the mansion. These served a dual purpose: first, they added greatly to the summer comfort of the three large, square rooms flanking the halls, and, secondly, they afforded ample space for entertaining on a grand scale. The decorations such as mantels, wainscotings, and cornices are simple but handsome. The walls and ceilings are plastered, and the formal rooms have elegant chandelier rosettes in the ceilings.

The left wing is off from the formal dining room and serves as a kitchen and family room. All the walls are paneled, and the cabinets are built of time-cured, mellow, red-heart pine.

In the back yard, to the left of the dwelling, is the unique old brick kitchen. This little building in itself is a gem. It consists of two rooms with large open fireplaces, ovens and warmers. One of the fireplaces still has its swinging cranes and spits. The floor is laid of brick. Due to the brick floor and the thick masonry walls, even on hot days the little house has a refreshing coolness, for it is well-ventilated with windows on the front and rear.

The little brick kitchen at BLINK BONNIE is still in use. Many discriminating South Carolina housewives, who pride themselves on serving rare delicacies, are well familiar with its trademark. Mrs. Kirkland, the present mistress of BLINK BONNIE, is a woman of many talents. She is not only a connoisseur of fine foods but also an artist in the preparation of them. Among her friends her artichoke relish and pickles became a legend. Now, during the artichoke season, the old kitchen on her plantation is a busy place, giving employment to several of the good cooks of Longtown, who under her careful supervision prepare the most delicious of all South Carolina relishes, Blink Bonnie Artichoke Pickles, Relish, and Iced Tomatoes. Some of the artichokes are raised on the place but the demand for her finished products has become so great that the farm people all over the county are planting artichokes to help meet the demand for this spicy side dish made famous by her recipe.

[46]

BLINK BONNIE

IX

After the death of Darling Jones the place passed to his son, Abram Jones, who continued to use it in the same manner as his father. The Jones' entertained on a lavish scale, and this fine old home was the social center of the community where the Virginia reels, quadrilles, and cotillions were danced. It was probably an inspiration for the fabulous Peay mansion, MELROSE, which was built in the 1850's.

When the Confederate War ended, there was a great change at BLINK BONNIE. The war had cost the Jones family their fortune. The plantation was sold at public auction and was bought by W. O. Robertson, who with his family occupied the place for many years. When the Robertson family moved away, BLINK BONNIE was used as a stage house or "station." Then it was rented to a long succession of tenants. Finally, after falling into bad repair, it became vacant for some time, a sad reminder of bygone splendor.

This deplorable plight ended in 1950 when the plantation was purchased by the M. A. Kirklands. Kirkland, a native of Camden and a descendant of the Kirklands who were among the first settlers in this section before the Revolutionary War, had long admired the old place. He and his talented wife began a restoration of the house immediately after they bought the property. Today BLINK BONNIE again stands proud and majestic in all the magnificence and grandeur that made her famous in the past. The present owners still have plans to further glamorize and embellish the house and grounds.

DIXON HOUSE

HARRISON — MOORES — HARRISON — DIXON

This old landmark is sadly in need of restoration but it still stands, defying time, in spite of its sad plight. The front doorway is still beautiful and outstanding in design, giving the old place a lasting semblance of dignity and refinement.

The place belonged to Reuben Harrison, a Revolutionary soldier. In the period before the war he was associated with Thomas Woodward, the "Regulator," in keeping law and order. He was twice married; Lucy Burge was the first wife and Nancy Kirkland the second. He died in 1835 and left each of his eight children two thousand acres of land. In addition to this he built homes for his three daughters, leaving the home place to his widow for her life.

One daughter, Frances, married a Brevard. Her home was behind the Darling Jones House and was built similar to it. It was razed a few years ago but the fine old mantels and woodwork were saved and are now still in use in a house near Camden. Nancy, the second daughter, married a Rochelle, and their big three-story house stood on a hill near what is now "Fairview," The Alcoholic Rehabilitation Center. It finally fell into disuse and was taken down a few years ago. The third daughter, Mary, married Charles Moore, and their house is the only one left standing of the many Harrison homes.

About 1830 all of the daughters and their families sold their property and moved West. John Harrison bought most of his family's estate as his brothers and sisters moved away. He was a very rich man, owning thousands of acres of land and listed as one of the largest slave owners in the upcountry. He

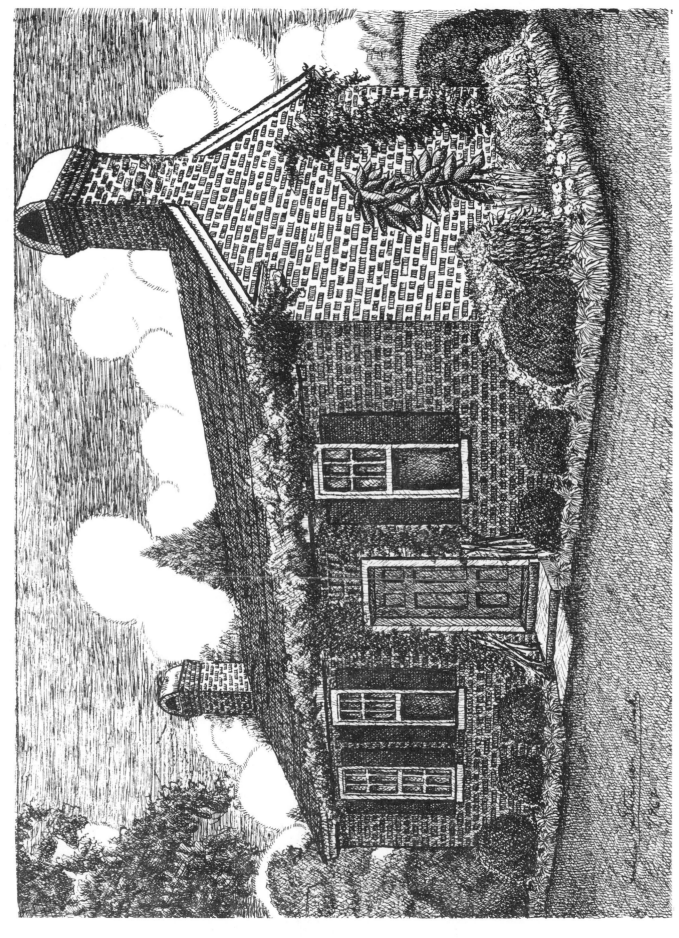

X

BLINK BONNIE KITCHEN

was also a sportsman and lover of fine horses. His animals were raced on all of the South Carolina tracks, taking many honors and trophies. His son, Eli Hunt Harrison, who married Elizabeth Fleming Douglass, became owner of the Moores' place. Eli and his three sons were all in the Confederate Army. His daughter, Lucy Rives, married Samuel Dixon, from Liberty Hill and owned and lived at the Moores' place which is now called the Dixon place. It is still owned and occupied by their daughters who are all well along in years.

John Douglass Harrison, Jr. came back by way of Washington, D. C. after his service in the Confederate Army. He was a barefooted, ragged, scantily clothed young man as he made the long homeward journey by foot. In passing through the nation's capital he encountered unusually large crowds of people on the streets. After inquiring he learned that they were waiting for President Lincoln's funeral procession which he waited for and witnessed.

When he finally reached home his mother saw that he had a proper hero's welcome. He was given a hot bath, fresh clothes, a wholesome, festive supper and a clean, soft bed in which to relax and sleep to his heart's content.

Before awaking the following morning a detachment of Federal troops rode up to the house. They told the inhabitants that they were looking for the notorious Nick Myers (his family's home was across the road from the Harrison place) and with no more ado entered and began to search the house. When they found young Harrison asleep in his bed they seized him, thinking that he was Myers, and dragged him into the yard with the intention of hanging him to the nearest tree. The boy's mother and others of the household pleaded for him and told the soldiers that they did not have the man that they were seeking. Finally the leader of the group agreed to send to a nearby plantation for someone to further identify the prisoner. When the good neighbor appeared on the scene he said, "For God's sake, John, what are they hanging you for?" This statement satisfied the Federals that they had the wrong man so they removed the rope from his neck, untied his hands and hurried on their way in search of "Old Nick."

Mrs. Robert Hayne McKelvey, the former Edna Dixon, one of the present owners of the old house, states that according to family tradition Cornwallis passed by and rested at the site of this place on his way from Camden to Winnsboro during the Revolutionary War.

GOZA HOUSE

TIDWELL — HARRISON — ROCHELLE — HARRISON — GOZA

This old house stood on a high hill below FAIRVIEW until it was razed during the past decade. This sketch is done from a picture that was made before the house was dismantled.

The property on which the house was located was a part of the original Harrison tract that was granted the first of that family to come to South Carolina from Virginia before the Revolutionary War. Reuben Harrison, a son of the first settler, owned this property after the Revolution. He built the house for one of his daughters who married into the Rochelle family. The Rochelles moved West with other members of the family in the 1830's and in 1835 Mrs. Rochelle's brother, John Harrison, purchased her property.

DIXON PLACE (DOORWAY)   XI

Little can be learned of the place from this point until after the War Between the States when the place was occupied by the Goza family. They lived here for many years and the plantation became known as the GOZA HOUSE. One member of this family who was reared in the old building was the late Mr. E. C. Goza, who was for many years postmaster at Columbia, South Carolina.

When the Gozas left the house several tenants inhabited it and the last to live here was a Negro family. After them it remained abandoned and vacant. It was a bleak, eerie-looking old building, with its porch gone, and rear wing falling in, as its empty windows seemed to peer down the road from the lofty perch on a rough hilltop. Many stories and legends became linked with the place and it finally became known as a "haunted house" or the "Ghosty House." The latter name probably originiated with and became confused in pronunciation with "Goza."

An interesting episode took place in this old house just after the close of the Confederate War.

A young Confederate soldier had but recently returned home from Lee's surrendered forces in Virginia. He was staying with an elderly uncle who had a plantation in the Lebanon community near old Jackson Creek Church. While defending his uncle's property and honor he shot and killed a Federal soldier. The soldier was a Negro who had formerly belonged to the uncle.

He reported the deed to friends in Winnsboro and asked for advice. Some told him to flee the country but others counseled that he surrender to the sheriff before he was apprehended by the military. At the time the sheriff was at his plantation at Longtown. The troubled youth rode out to find him but upon reaching Ridgeway he was informed that the soldiers were already looking for him. He was instructed to hide with a widow at her house near the town and not far from the sheriff's home where he should remain until receiving further word.

When he reached the place, the good lady had already received her instructions. She was to house the refugee for the night and at daybreak send him back to Winnsboro where the sheriff would be awaiting him at the jail to give him proper protection from the soldiers.

After a light supper he went upstairs to rest while his hostess remained on watch for the night.

The weather was rainy and disagreeable. The harassed young veteran was genuinely thankful for his haven and shelter in the warm old house. His peace and comfort was short-lived, for before he had time to sink into the warm featherbed, a Yankee officer and four soldiers arrived in search of him. When he heard them, he climbed out onto the porch roof and concealed himself under the sweeping, wet branches of a tree that grew near the porch. After the search was completed, he heard the officer tell the men that they would spend the night and renew their quest after an early breakfast.

Two of the upstairs rooms contained two double beds each. Three of the men occupied one of these rooms and the officer the other. The fourth man was left on watch for the night.

When the miserable and uncomfortable young man on the porch roof heard heavy breathing and snoring coming from the officer's room, he stealthily

GOZA PLACE

XII

crept back through the window, wrapt himself in a blanket taken noiselessly from the empty bed, and fitfully tried to rest for several hours. When he thought that all was clear, he opened the door, hoping to slip downstairs and make his getaway. He was astonished when he saw the man who was posted on guard, nodding on the narrow stairway.

Retreating again to the room, he realized that his only escape would be through the window. Climbing cautiously back onto the roof, he leaped to the rain soaked ground without hurting himself and made a dash to the stable. Leading his horse some distance from the house before mounting, lest its hoofs plodding into the wet mud and striking against the bare rocks might be heard. Once astride the animal he raced madly through the woods and country roads and reached the jail in safety.

Upon his arrival at the jail he was treated as a guest by the sheriff and his family until his trial was arranged and he was cleared. A romance developed during this interlude which ended in his marriage to the sheriff's beautiful daughter.

HUNTER HOUSE
FERGUSON — HUNTER — RION

Well back from the Old Camden road, peeping over an old-fashioned stile, is one of the most attractive old homes in the Longtown section.

Its proportions are pleasing but deceiving, for the house is much more spacious than it appears to be at first glance. The first floor is on the ground level and is built of brick. The second or main floor is fronted with a portico, supported by slender columns and enclosed with plain picket bannisters. The interior walls are paneled with wide pine boards. All of the trim and decoration is simple, and some of the old English-made locks are still in use.

One of the most attractive features of the house is the back porch, which extends across the east side of the rear wing on two floors. The second-floor porch commands an excellent view of the countryside. It is enclosed with turned pickets, and a flight of steps leads down to the first floor, which is covered with brick tile.

The house was built before 1820, for it was in that year that the will of the builder, Abraham Ferguson, was probated. He left the property to his adopted daughter, who at that time was attending the Chesterfield Academy. She later married a Mr. Hunter, and this became known as the HUNTER PLACE.

The Hunter family lived here until after the War Between the States. When the North finally emerged as the victor after this hard-fought contest, Mr. Hunter, a staunch Confederate, made the statement that he would never live in a country ruled by the Yankees. He was a man of his word, who was also true to his strong convictions. As soon as he could, after the war ended, he got his affairs in order and with his family moved to British Honduras. His descendants still reside there. Mrs. Hunter and one child are buried at St. Stephen's in Ridgeway.

Since the Hunters left the house, it has had many tenants, and in spite of the absence of tenant-owners it has remained in a good state of preservation

HUNTER PLACE

due to the superior materials used in its construction by Abraham Ferguson.

Several years ago Mr. and Mrs. Wallace Rion purchased the property. They have completely restored the house in a most charming manner and use it as a country home. The Rions reside in Columbia but they spend part of each week at the quiet, secluded little house on the old Camden Road near Ridgeway.

VAUGHAN HOUSE
VAUGHAN

Many years ago Simpson's Turnout was one of Fairfield's busy rural communities. It is located on one of the main roads to Columbia, between Winnsboro and Ridgeway. One of the centers of activities in the ante-bellum days was a large old house that stood near the road. It was known as the STATION or STATION HOUSE.

On the old stage route from Columbia to Winnsboro this building was the first stop out of Winnsboro and the last out of Columbia. Horses for the "fast stage" were changed here, and sometimes, when the weather was severe, the passengers would spend the night in the rambling old house. Mail for the community was taken to and dispensed from this building.

Little more can be learned of the old landmark other than it was the scene of many gatherings, parties and entertainments. Judging from the construction of the building, it has been in existence for about a century and a half. For a great number of years it was owned and occupied by the Vaughan family.

TOCALAND
WOODWARD — GADSEN — BIGHAM — JOHNSON

TOCALAND is just on the outskirts of Winnsboro, near the Rockton station. It is an interesting "Mosquito Cottage," a ground-level basement with a story and a half above. The basement walls are constructed of large granite blocks that were quarried on the property; their thickness makes these rooms delightfully cool in the summer. The pillars supporting the porch are tall granite slabs, quarried all in one piece. In the basement rooms most of the floors are tiled.

The second floor has a gabled porch across most of the front, supported with square wooden columns. A wide central hall bisects the second floor, with two rooms on either side and a quaint little stair against the left wall, leading up to the hall and two rooms on the third floor. There is also an inside stairway from the second-story hall down to the hall in the basement. The interior woodwork is refined but simple. Two massive inside chimneys afford fireplaces for each room. Originally there was a small wing on the right side of the house but in recent years it has been removed. This was used as a conservatory or greenhouse.

TOCALAND was built in 1854 by Major Woodward for his daughter, Regina, who married Christopher Gadsen of Charleston. Mr. Gadsen was

VAUGHAN PLACE

XIV

a son of the eminent Bishop Christopher Edwards Gadsen of the Episcopal Church, who was for many years rector of Saint Phillip's Church in Charleston. Bishop Gadsen was a close friend of John C. Calhoun. They were classmates at Yale, who continued a close relationship on through life. It is thought by some that Bishop Gadsen was responsible for the body of the famous statesman being buried in Charleston.

Young Christopher Gadsen, Jr. was a noted horticulturist and landscape gardener. Before coming to Fairfield he did work in several of the famous Charleston gardens. During his early years in the upcountry he designed and planted many of the houses and gardens in Fairfield County.

Needless to say, the grounds at TOCALAND were beautifully landscaped with boxwood, rare shrubs, bulbs, roses, and flowers for every season. Boxwood, privet, and native holly were used for the hedges that were laid out in formal geometric patterns. Some of the boxwood and holly hedges still remain and are in amazingly good condition. A rare tree, locally called "the Coffee tree," still retains its original position.

The orchards of this plantation were famous. Apricots, peaches, apples, pears, pomgranates, and figs were in abundance and were planted in patterns to carry out the general design of the landscaping.

Most famous of all were the vineyards. Grapes of all varieties were to be found but most favored of all were the Tokay vines, natives of Hungary, which were world-renowned for their sweetness and the excellent wines derived from them. From these the plantation took its name.

The Gadsens lived happily here until the War Between the States, with their sons, Frank and John. Mr. Gadsen went into the Confederate Army and was killed in action. In 1865 Sherman's men raided the plantation when they passed by but by some good fortune the old house was spared. The Woodward-Gadsen family burying ground is just across the Southern Railroad from TOCALAND on the highway.

After Mrs. Gadsen's death the place passed to her son, Frank. He and his wife, Lilla Rabb, lived here until his death. His widow kept the house and gardens in good condition as long as she was able to do so. She died in 1962 and is buried here.

In the 1930's or 1940 she sold TOCALAND to Mr. George Bigham whose family resided there until it was purchased in 1953 by Mr. and Mrs. John Johnson.

The Johnsons are proud of the old place and cherish it. They are in the process of modernizing and restoring the house, carefully retaining and emphasizing all of the charm and antiquity of the building. What is left of the old garden is being preserved and plans are to restore it in the manner of what it was in the past.

TOCALAND

PART II

WINNSBORO

HISTORICAL SKETCH
OF
WINNSBORO

by
BRYAN ROBERTS

The town of Winnsboro, county seat of Fairfield County, had its beginnings in the middle decades of the eighteenth century. Some estimates of a date of settlements near the present town site are as early as 1740, when Thomas Nightingale, the maternal grandfather of Judge William Johnston, had a ranch or cow pen about six miles away on Little Cedar Creek. By the 1750's there were numerous settlements in what is the present county area.

It was a land whose natural scenery was something to behold. There were rolling hills, undulating plains, and gushing springs, but much of the uncleared virgin forests was thick with high grasses, wild pea vine, and a wide variety of trees. The land was Indian territory, claimed by both the Catawbas and the Cherokees, and the settlers saw frequent visitors from these tribes. The Catawbas were kindly and generous; the Cherokees, hostile. Some accounts state that one of the Lyles settlers was actually killed by a Cherokee war party.

After the defeat of the Indians in 1755, the threat was lessened and many more settlers began to move inland, away from the rivers and streams. They became skillful hunters and trappers and were adept at raising stock. Before planting was begun, they brought in their bread by pack horse from the Congaree.

By 1757 the militia of the colony had three establishments within or just bordering the county area: two west of the Wateree River and one on the Broad. Since all men between sixteen and sixty were subject to military duty, these militia companies give a fairly complete picture of the number of people at this time. The three mentioned groups numbered about 235 men, but each probably had as many as five dependents. Fitz Hugh McMaster, in his *History of Fairfield County, South Carolina*, however, estimates the number of white settlers in the county proper as about two hundred in 1760.

When in 1761 the Cherokee War was brought to a close, the upcountry was open for settlement, and many more whites came into Fairfield. In addition to the French Huguenots and Irish from the coastal country, there came Germans, Swiss, and Scotch-Irish from Virginia and the mountains of Pennsylvania.

Now these began to take advantage of the mild climate and fertile soil by clearing large tracts of land and planting it. This was difficult work and, to add to the troubles, gangs of thieves began to steal their cattle and horses. There was little recourse to law and order since the nearest court, at Charleston, was nearly 160 miles away. Thus, to prevent these occurrences, a band of rangers, called "regulators," was organized among the honest, law-abiding citizens. These men, led in Fairfield County by Thomas Woodward ("Thomas the Regulator"), took the law into their own hands, punished the offenders, and petitioned the governor for redress of grievances. The Fairfield area had over forty regulators, more than any other territory in the colony, and many of them no doubt settled and owned lands near Winnsboro. (An excellent understanding of the movement can be gained from Richard Maxwell Brown's *The South Carolina Regulators,* just published in 1963, and from Charles Woodmason's journal, *The Carolina Backcountry on the Eve of the Revolution.*)

In the 1770's Winnsboro had its first notable progressions toward the establishment of a town. Colonel Richard Winn, from Virginia, had settled here. He was probably a younger son of Minor and Margaret (O'Connor) Winn of Fauquier, his father no doubt the same who obtained in 1774 a grant for eight hundred acres on Wateree Creek, near the present town. Richard, however, as a deputy surveyor, had purchased lands in the neighborhood as early as 1771. By the time of the Revolutionary War the Winn surname was so thoroughly associated with the place that "the Borough" adopted it.

Although many of the county's sons became soldiers in the Revolution, none had more glorious careers than Richard Winn. He was commissioned June 17, 1775, first lieutenant in the 3rd South Carolina Regiment, took part in 1776 in the Battle of Fort Moultrie, and the next year, as a captain in command, he made a spectacular defense of Fort McIntosh, Georgia. In 1780 he helped defend Charleston and as a major led a regiment of refugee militia to successful battle in York and at Hanging Rock in Lancaster. Later he was to have a distinguished political career, serving in the state legislature, as lieutenant governor of the state, and several terms in Congress before moving to Tennessee in 1813.

John Winn, another town father and brother of Richard Winn, also served in the Revolution, but one of his most significant achievements was first presidency of the famous Mt. Zion Society, an institution of learning chartered in 1777 "for the education and instructing of youth." Some accounts suggest that class instruction in Winnsboro might have been given nearly ten years before the charter was granted. At first the accommodations were of the rudest kind, log huts for the students' quarters and a larger log house for teaching purposes, but by 1787 there was a large, two-story building with an impressive tower. Later the success of the school brought about many enlargements to the building before its accidental destruction by fire in 1867. The Mt. Zion Society and the college can hardly be spoken of without the association of the Presbyterians, and its influence tended to promote the interests of this branch of the church as will later be seen.

The full dramatic impact of the Revolution fell upon Winnsboro in 1780. After Charleston fell, the college in Winnsboro soon stopped. Many of the townsmen had departed to battle, many never to return. After the Battle of King's Mountain revived the hopes of the colonists, Cornwallis, then at Charlotte, decided to withdraw from that vertible hornet's nest. Desiring a point that would permit contact with both Camden and Ninety Six, he was greatly attracted by Winnsboro with its relatively abundant supplies of flour, forage, and cattle.

The British Army arrived October 29th, 1780, and were to remain for the rest of the year. The encampment is said to have been on or near the present site of Mt. Zion Institute. His lordship's quarters might have been near this spot, although some accounts state that Cornwallis used the home of Richard Winn as his own quarters.

Apart from the heavy drain of food and supplies for British use, little damage was done to the town. However, it is related that Colonel Tarleton upon his retreat to Winnsboro had his men hang John Johnston, an old and respectable citizen with a large family, for no crime other than taking up arms on the American side.

Traditional tales of a plot to assassinate Cornwallis during his stay here are probably untrue. John and Minor Winn, who are said to have formed the plot, were supposedly arrested, tried, and sentenced to death, but pardoned. Richard Winn, in his notes, tells another story of his brother John's arrest. John was pardoned when Richard Winn sent word to Cornwallis that if he hanged John, one hundred British prisoners would pay for his life with theirs. The fiery Richard would no doubt have kept his vow, for later, when Lord Cornwallis asked him to give up and come in in exchange for restoration of his property, repayment of all losses, and protection of his life, Winn refused and returned an indignant reply, damning Cornwallis and all his protection.

British forces left Winnsboro early in January 1781, leaving in command of the Tories Colonel John Phillips, who was said to have been largely responsible for Cornwallis' leniency toward the Whigs. Phillips obtained a pardon for some seventy condemned to death at the court while his lordship occupied Winnsboro. One year later this same Phillips was condemned to the gallows but later had his sentence commuted to banishment to Great Britain where he is said to have held office under the crown.

The end of the Revolution began a period of growth and reconstruction in Winnsboro. The Mt. Zion Society met, reorganized, incorporated the school as a college in 1783, and graduated its first class four years later. Richard Winn had deeded the Society one hundred acres of land, and John Vanderhorst, a rich and influential townsman originally from Charleston, willed it one thousand pounds sterling.

The town of Winnsboro had its first plat officially recognized by an act of the General Assembly on March 8, 1785. The property where the town stood belonged to John and Richard Winn and John Vanderhorst. The streets and lots for a church and market place were made public property. No doubt the town had been laid out some time before the General Assembly enactment. This first plat included fourteen blocks or squares, with town boundaries on the south at Moultrie Street, on the north at Fairfield Street, on the east at Walnut, and the west at Garden.

The same act of the General Assembly established in the town two fairs annually, in May and October, for the purpose of selling horses, cattle, grain, hemp, flax, tobacco, indigo, and all sorts of produce and merchandise. Not only did this stimulate trade and commerce in the town but also it was a chief means of obtaining news from the outside brought by visitors whom the fairs attracted. These fairs were festive occasions and many liberties were granted, much crass behavior tolerated. No one was arrested except for treason, felony, other capital crime, or breach of the peace.

To be sure, the tavern was a popular spot, not only during the time of the fairs but also throughout the year. The county court regulated the price of drinks, meals, and lodgings. A featherbed with clean linen cost only sixpence, and a fine dinner could be had for one shilling, twopence. In the town several licenses to operate taverns were granted in 1785.

Within two years, in 1787, the town had prospered so much that it was ready for expansion. On March 27th an act in the General Assembly recognized the new town plat, which now included 26 blocks with 345 lots of various sizes. The town now surrounded the Mt. Zion property on three sides, and the northern town boundary was extended to a block beyond High Street. The streets of the town were wide and spacious: Congress, 100 feet; Washington, 90 feet; all others, except the 42-foot-wide Fairfield Street, were 66 feet. The town began to appear quite progressive after the public market was built on the northeastern corner of Congress and Washington Streets.

The next three or four decades saw important religious developments in the town. In 1787 the Mt. Zion Congregation of Winnsboro was incorporated by the legislature. It is assumed that this Presbyterian body was closely connected with the college and may have met in one of those buildings. It was not an organized church but at the turn of the century was titled a preaching or mission station by the South Carolina Presbytery.

Prior to 1808 almost all the church membership in Winnsboro was Presbyterian. In that year, however, Captain and Mrs. John Buchanan with the Rev. James Jenkins of the South Carolina Conference began work toward establishing a Methodist congregation and, in 1809, started a brick church on the site of the present Methodist Cemetery. When the church was completed the following year, it was the first church building in Winnsboro. The Presbyterians also had begun work in 1809 on their first church on Garden Street but it was not completed until 1811.

The Associate Reformed Presbyterian congregation in Winnsboro was organized about 1820. Their first church was built shortly thereafter on the corner of Fairfield and Vanderhorst Streets, in the northwest corner of the graveyard. It was originally an Associate Church and appeared on the roll of the Associate Presbytery of the Carolinas for the first time in May 1823.

When Robert Mills made his survey of Fairfield County some time before 1826, he spoke of the Episcopalians as having "a small church lately formed in Winnsborough." Miss Kate Obear tells us that a new church was built soon after the arrival here of her father, the Reverend Josiah Obear, in May 1841. The building, which stood in the present Episcopal Cemetery, was to be the site of shocking acts of desecration during the Civil War.

Some members of the Fairfield Church, which had been organized in 1820 and located about three and a half miles south of Winnsboro in the direction of Monticello, started the First Baptist Church in Winnsboro about 1855, shortly after the death of the Reverend Jonathan Davis, the organizer of the Fairfield Church. The construction of their church on the corner of Vanderhorst and Washington Streets was begun in 1858. Although this wooden building of Colonial design was not finished until after the war, it is said to have been used during the Civil War for classroom purposes by Mt. Zion students when their own building was taken over for a military hospital.

All religious activity increased throughout the nineteenth century, and the influence of the ministers of the gospel had a decided and notable effect upon the people of the town. It is said that all the members of the first graduating class of Mt. Zion College became ministers of the gospel, having come under the influence of the Reverend T. H. McCaule, a Presbyterian minister and first principal of the college.

Fairfield County's courthouse was built in 1823, designed by Robert Mills, the famous architect. Mills himself, in his notable and monumental *Statistics of South Carolina,* published in Charleston in 1826, gives a remarkable description of Winnsboro at that time:

"There are few, if any, more healthy places in the State than Winnsborough. The lands around are fertile, gentle undulating, and highly improved. It has a handsome court-house and jail, an academy, formerly a college, which is richly endowed and very flourishing; three churches, a masonic hall and a market house. The number of private houses, some of which are handsome, is about fifty, there are two houses of entertainment, and eight or ten stores."

The jail, a fine and handsome brick structure of which Mills speaks, stood on the lot at the southeast corner of Congress and Washington Streets. The spot had been originally intended for a church, but the congregation, considering the location too public, no doubt surrendered the lot to county authority.

Dr. James H. Carlisle, the "Grand Old Man of Methodism" and a member of the original faculty of Wofford College in 1853, was born here in 1825. Being a historian of note, he shed some additional light on the appearance of the town in 1832:

"Opposite (the courthouse) stood the old jail, 15 paces from the Main Street, and protected by a high board fence and iron gates. South of that stood a long wooden house kept as a tavern by Mrs. Baker. North of the jail . . . was the old market house, a strange looking, square, yellow wooden building, with a tapering roof and a belfry on top. Behind the market was a carriage shop and a blacksmith shop . . . while on Main Street beyond the market house were several law offices and shops of different kinds."

The incorporation of Winnsboro was enacted by the General Assembly in December 1832. At the same time it was stipulated that the town be governed by an intendant and four wardens. The following year saw the plans begun for the market house in the middle of Washington Street as deemed "most convenient to the inhabitants of the said town, provided, the said market house shall not be of greater width than thirty feet," thus leaving an additional thirty feet on either side in the 90-foot-wide Washington Street.

Through the years Winnsboro was blessed with outstanding teachers. Among the most notable was James W. Hudson, who became principal of Mt. Zion in 1834. Bringing distinguished teachers from northern centers of education to the school, Hudson made Mt. Zion's scholarship famous enough to attract students from the other parts of the state and from several other southern states. Many important men were "clay in the hands of this educational potter," among them Dr. William Porcher DuBose and Dr. James H. Carlisle.

The formal education of women in Winnsboro made a notable advancement when Mrs. Catherine Ladd, a native of Virginia and wife of the portrait painter George W. Ladd, opened the Winnsboro Female Institute in 1840.

[66]

Just a year before, she had heard that a building in Winnsboro had been erected for a girls' school but had never opened; she determined to give it a try." By 1850 she had nine teachers and about a hundred students, a notably successful school until the Civil War forced it to close. Mrs. Ladd had special talents for a great variety of artistic endeavors, spreading a knowledge and appreciation of music, art, literature, and dramatics.

Nor did the accomplishments of Mr. Hudson and Mrs. Ladd greatly overshadow those of a host of other dedicated educators, many of whom are duly remembered in Fitz Hugh McMaster's *History of Fairfield County, South Carolina.*

Our capable educators and their fine educational institutions instilled in the citizenry a keen respect for the printed word. To supplement the many private book collections already in existence, a public library was started in 1837. In the 1840's town newspapers were established to supplement the news from the papers of Columbia, Charleston, and Camden. E. H. Britton was largely responsible for this success. There are still preserved in the South Caroliniana Library in Columbia early issues of *The Fairfield Herald, The Register, The Winnsboro Daily News,* and *The Tri-Weekly News.*

The means of transportation were still crude at the time and Winnsboro was not a thoroughfare. The important stage lines were the Piedmont, through York and Union, and the central route, from Columbia to Camden and Cheraw. There was, however, through Winnsboro a tri-weekly stage line, these stops attracting much attention. In addition, there were private carriages, but travel farther than local points was very unusual. When David R. Evans went to Washington as a member of Congress in 1813-1814, it was estimated that the trip took about two weeks.

Fairfield mud, the natural deterrent of transportation, was overcome with the construction of the railway through town. Around the middle of the century the Charlotte and South Carolina Railroad began purchasing land for a right-of-way through the center of Winnsboro. Shortly thereafter the rails were laid for what was later one of the principal interstate railroad links of the Confederate States during the Civil War, used heavily in transporting troops and supplies.

The development of a bank in Winnsboro was delayed because of the financial panic of 1837, which had spread across the country. This paralyzed business, and the suspension of specie payments by the banks made the people distrustful. However, confidence was finally restored and in December 1851 application was made to establish and incorporate a bank here to be known as "The Planters Bank of Fairfield," with a capitalization of $300,000.00. First presidents were J. R. Aiken (1853-1860) and James H. Rion (1860-1865). Its cashier, H. L. Elliott (1853-1865), no doubt acted as president while Colonel Rion was on active military duty. The bank had its own Confederate currency, printed in six denominations from $5.00 to $100.00.

The outbreak of the Civil War brought to Winnsboro citizens the pains of apprehension. To be sure, there were still in many minds the memories of wars since the Revolution and the Cornwallis occupation. Winnsboro men had served in the War of 1812, the Seminole War, and the Mexican War, but the Civil War promised to be graver than any since the Revolution. By the census of 1860 Fairfield County had 1,578 white males between the ages of fifteen and sixty, but records show that Fairfield furnished nearly 2,000 men to the Confederacy.

The railway was most active, transporting volunteers out of town and later bringing in refugees from the coastal plantations as well as from distant places such as Vicksburg, Mobile, and New Orleans. As was to be expected, the casualty lists from battle were long, and so many of the families of the town were affected that the churches were frequently filled with mourners. To add to this deep sorrow, there was the problem of food. Flour was scarce and expensive; coffee and white sugar, almost unheard of.

Under these depressive conditions, the remaining citizens of the town received word on February 20, 1865, that Sherman's army was moving north from Columbia in a direction toward Winnsboro. As townspeople began to hide or bury all their treasures and foodstuff, the Reverend W. W. Lord, rector of St. John's Episcopal Church, and his four-hundred-pound vestryman set out to the Federal camp to beg protection for their village. Their efforts proved futile, for Winnsboro was to be visited by foragers before the main army entered town. These "Bummers" came early in the morning of the 21st, immediately turning to pillaging and burning. Laughing, shouting, cursing as they went, "these over-grown 'Boys in Blue' played snowball along the firelit streets with precious flour; made bonfires of hams and sides of bacon; set boxes and barrels of crackers afloat on streams of molasses and vinegar; fed horses from hats full of sugar," the Reverend Mr. Lord's son tells us.

In the burning itself between twenty and thirty buildings were destroyed, including homes, stores, and public edifices. The Reverend Mr. Lord's church even fell prey to these malicious burners. As some played "devils tunes" on the organ, which they had hauled out, others exhumed a recently buried corpse, setting it up in the clergyman's robes to witness the ceremony.

The Left Wing of the Federal Army, led by Major General H. W. Slocum, arrived in Winnsboro at 10 A.M., Friday the 21st. General John W. Geary's XX Corps division was in advance, and every effort was made to arrest the flames. Even the highest officers worked with their hands, burned their whiskers, and scorched their clothes in firefighting, but Geary's official report stated that "one square was burned before the fire could be arrested." By the time General Sherman arrived on the afternoon of the 21st, some progress had been made, but the conflagrations began again the following day.

The pillaging was another matter. General Geary placed Brigadier General N. Pardee in charge of the town to protect all private property, but much damage had already been done. The soldiers were quick to discover that water wells often held hidden treasures of silver and other valuables. Digging with shovels and bayonets, they soon unearthed other buried stores. Even the sacred silver of the church was not spared; Sion Presbyterian Church's elegant communion set was carried away and later presented as a "gift" to a northern congregation.

Pardee's brigade stayed on duty in Winnsboro on February 22nd, until all the troops of the XIV, XVII, and XX Corps passed through town. The march continued, the railway being destroyed just as it had been between Columbia and Winnsboro. Sherman thus fulfilled his objectives of isolating Columbia from the rest of the Confederacy, surrounding the Confederate forces in the northern part of the state, and misleading them into thinking that he was headed toward Charlotte.

Citizens of Winnsboro, fearing attacks from stragglers, secured General Geary's permission to leave behind several troopers for protection. A story is told that they were able to save Winnsboro from further destruction when a group of small boys warned them that six such stragglers were hiding in the market tower.

A detachment of Confederate cavalry rode into town the following day and relieved the guards of their duty. The people of Winnsboro openly expressed their gratitude to the Federal troopers, and they were permitted to join their command in safety.

Less than two months later the war was over and our 'Lost Cause' soldiers came drifting home. By May many refugees had left Winnsboro, but some remained. A company of Union soldiers was sent to control the town and stayed until the following spring. Making their camp just outside the town limits on the western side, these soldiers were generally considerate and respectful but took little interest in the town.

Brave townspeople bore the burden of reconstructing the town; the resumption of operations of the educational institutions was the first real goal. The places of worship were restored or rebuilt. Although the times were anything but prosperous, residences were soon constructed and gradually new stores began to appear in the burnt area. A secure confidence in the town's future had awakened in its people.

———

It is hoped that the drawings in this volume will evoke the imagination of the reader to relive these events in the history of the town. Many of the houses and public buildings erected during these times still stand and remind us of our heritage.

But these houses remind us of more than events. They are fitting monuments to one of the town's greatest assets, its people. For Winnsboro was a melting pot where the sturdiness of the Scotch-Irish, the elegance of the English, the refinement of the Huguenot, and the persistence of the German mingled to produce a blend finer than any of its ingredients. Dr. J. Chapman Milling in his introduction to Miss Obear's *Through the Years in Old Winnsboro* tells us:

> "While the whole State is historic, there are three or four communities which from early days have been outstanding — and interesting. Outstanding because of the disproportionately large number of worthwhile people they have produced; interesting because of the distinctive culture, slightly different from any other, which they have developed.
>
> Among these Winnsboro, and Fairfield County — for it is impossible to treat them separately — hold a high position. Go to any other section of the State and investigate the leading men and women. You will be more than likely to find that several of them were either born in Fairfield County or can point to Fairfield antecedents. And even outside of South Carolina it is astonishing how many really distinguished men there are, financiers, jurists, scientists, teachers, doctors, and clergymen, who are of Fairfield extraction."

HUNSTANTON

ROBERTSON — RABB — STRANGE

HUNSTANTON is located just beyond the city limits of Winnsboro, on the Columbia highway. It is built along the Colonial type of architecture which is locally referred to as a "mosquito cottage." However, this house is no cottage; it contains eighteen rooms in its three stories and wing. The front makes an impressive appearance. A two-storied, gabled portico extends over the center. The pillars of the lower porch, which is just above the ground level, support the floor above. Two flights of semicircular steps at either end lead up to the main floor, the gabled roof of which is supported by four large wooden columns, directly above the massive brick pillars below. The first floor or basement is built of brick while the remainder of the house is constructed of the very best and most durable heart pine. The main body of the house is rectangular and is covered with a gabled roof. To the rear of this is a large back porch and the kitchen wing.

The exact age of the building is not known but it is shown on a map of Fairfield County in 1820. At that time it was the home of Major Robertson, Esquire, who called the plantation SWEET BRIAR. The property remained in the Robertson family until after the Confederate War. At that time it was transferred to the Rabb family. In 1906 it was purchased by C. E. Strange, Sr. Mr. Strange changed the name of the place from SWEET BRIAR to HUN-STANTION, which was the name of the family seat of his people in Norfolk, England. He and his family lived at Hunstanton until 1922.

In 1946 his son, C. E. Strange, Jr., made HUNSTANTON his home. When he acquired the property, it had been suffering from neglect and "absentee ownership." The new owner had always admired the place and desired to restore it to its former dignity. He did this in an excellent manner, retaining all the charm and refined simplicity that had made it an outstanding landmark.

The rooms of the interior are large and square, with high ceilings and fine woodwork. They were all redecorated and furnished with many fine old pieces, family heirlooms.

Either Thomas G. Robertson or his father built the house. The family were natives of Halifax County, Virginia, having come there from Wales among the first settlers of Virginia during the Colonial period.

Their first home in Fairfield was about one and a half miles from this building, on a country road, between this and the Woodward estate.

At the beginning of the War Between the States Thomas G. Robertson was active in the maneuvers in the Charleston area. He was an old man and later during the war retired to his plantation for the remainder of the conflict.

In 1865, when Wheeler's men came through, retreating from Columbia, Mr. Robertson was told by them that the Yankees would be close behind. He proceeded to hide foodstuffs, hams, meat, flour, meal, and the family valuables between the heavy, hand-hewn sills of the basement ceiling and second-floor rooms.

Before this was completed, word was received that the enemy was fast approaching. Mrs. Robertson warned her husband that he should leave and

XVI

HUNSTANTON

hide because he might be recognized as one who had taken an active part in the earlier operations around Charleston. He responded that he would take her advice, flee to the woods, and hide in a place "where the Devil himself could not find me."

Shortly after he left the house, the invading Northerners appeared on the scene. They pulled down the fences, rode through the yard and gardens, trampling the rare plants and flower-beds. Some of the men dismounted to raid the place and to take toilet privileges in the yard without respect to themselves or the ladies of the household.

Young Thomas Woodward Robertson, a mere lad, had in his possession a precious bag of sugar that he was trying to hide away when the scavengers made their unexpected appearance. He threw the bag on the porch floor and sat upon it, using his large dog, who lay close to him, to help conceal his treasure.

Some of the Negroes welcomed the Yankees, among them a brazen young wench who readily accepted and returned the embraces and familiarities of some of the soldiers. She, with some of the other traitors, led the foe into the basement rooms and showed them where her master and his faithful people had carefully hidden the necessities and treasuers.

About that time Mrs. Robertson noticed from a window a body of soldiers leading her husband and his prized, matched grey carriage horses from the stables. She interceded for him and complained of the rank indignities and indecencies taking place, demanding the release of the old man and insisting that she be given a guard for the safety of her family. Her husband was released and a guard was posted, but the looting continued and the horses were confiscated along with all the other stock and supplies.

After ravaging the house, some of the soldiers brought in jugs of molasses and emptied them into the grand piano and onto the priceless Brussels carpets, but the building itself was spared from the torch.

The family carriage was pulled out from the carriage house, its top was torn off, and it was piled high with hams, meat, silver, and household treasures. Some of the plantation stock was hitched to it and, when last seen, it was being driven off by two bummers with jugs of liquor in one arm. The Negro girl who had shown them where the valuables were hidden was sitting between them, in high spirits, thoroughly enjoying their familiarities and obscene language.

After the departure of the army the only food that the family and faithful Negroes had for three days was excess corn left by the horses and scraps from the army mess.

RURAL POINT

ROBERTSON — DOTY

RURAL POINT is located on the eastern outskirts of Winnsboro. The house was built by Judge Robertson in 1852. In 1890 the property was purchased by William R. Doty, a native of Lancaster, Kentucky. Ever since that time, it has been the home of the Doty family.

XVII

RURAL POINT

It is a beautiful house, well located and elegantly landscaped. It is built twelve feet above ground level on thick brick walls that enclose the first or basement floor. The design of the building, like so many of its period in the Winnsboro vicinity, is that of the "mosquito cottage." A gabled porch covers the front entrance and a major portion of the front exposure. This is supported by hand-carved, square wooden columns and is approached by a flight of twelve wide steps. Seasoned heart pine, all pegged together, was used in the construction above the brick basement.

In the basement are a billiard room, an ironing room, and a wine-closet, with Italian tile on the floors. Above this, on the second or main story, are seven rooms, a wide hall, and a kitchen. The third floor consists of a hall, two bedrooms, and a storage room. Originally the kitchen was in the back yard.

All the wide pine plank flooring is in excellent condition and is kept brilliantly polished. Mantels, wainscotings, and cornices are all beautifully hand-carved. In the center of the parlor, hall, and drawing room ceilings are intricately designed, hand-carved rosettes from which hang the chandeliers.

The grounds and gardens are formally landscaped and are similar to the English gardens at Drayton Hall, near Charleston. Most of the plants were imported and were hauled from Charleston in wagons. Among them are many rare shrubs and some of the largest and oldest camellias in the upcountry. Walks are outlined with well-trimmed boxwoods, and hedges of cherry laurel enclose the garden. The old greenhouse is still in use but the "summerhouses" or "teahouses" which stood in the north and south sides of the grounds have been removed.

This place has long been known for its genteel hospitality. Many famous persons have been entertained within its walls; among them, General Chestnut of Confederate fame.

MOOSE HOUSE

HALL — CREIGHT — SARGENT — LOYAL ORDER OF MOOSE

The MOOSE HOME, long known as the Creight house, is located within the limits of Winnsboro but it is on the outskirts of the town and has all the character and flavor of a country home.

In park-like surroundings, the house stands proudly. It is large, built along classic lines, and could well be called a mansion. The wide corner styles are capped at the eave-line with Ioanian capitals, giving the effect of long tall columns. The oversized windows of the first floor are topped with cornices. Well-spaced decorative brackets, just under the eaves, support an extremely low, hipped roof, which gives the appearance of being flat. The central portion of the front extends into a porch with a flat deck and bannisters. This is supported by four well-proportioned columns.

The interior is in keeping with the outward character of the building handsome but not ornate.

[74]

MOOSE HOME

XVIII

This house was built in the 1850's by Mansell Hall, an architect and builder, for his second wife. After the Confederate War it became the property and home of the Creight family. At one time the grounds were beautifully landscaped in the formal tradition. Older residents of the town still recall them and the past elegance of the place.

After the passing of the last members of the Creight family the property fell into bad repair. It was later rented for several years. In 1937 Homer L. Sargent, an employee of the United States Rubber Company purchased the house site, including about ten acres. The grounds had attained a jungle-like appearance. He immediately had them cleared. Some of the shrubbery was salvaged and used in relandscaping along with other plantings which were done in the informal manner. At the same time he completely renovated the house which he later occupied and kept in excellent condition until his retirement. At this time he built a smaller house on the southern portion of the property and sold the old home and remaining acreage to the Order of the Moose. The old mansion now serves as a clubhouse and is quite an asset to the community.

FAIRFIELD INN

SHEDD — ERWIN — DOUGLAS — CLOWNEY — KILGORE

For almost four decades this charming old landmark has been known at home and abroad as the FAIRFIELD INN. Its accommodations, fine food, and atmosphere were highly praised and seldom surpassed.

The building was erected in 1861 by James N. Shedd, to be his private residence. It was constructed of brick. The outer walls, twenty-four inches thick, are plastered on the exterior with a weathered buff cement coating. The interior walls and partitions are also of brick and range from twelve to eighteen inches in thickness. They are covered with a thick lime plaster.

Originally the house was a two-story building with a square center hall. On either side of the hall, on both floors, were two large rooms, high-ceilinged and well lighted. The kitchen and service rooms were attached to the rear of the building.

Captain Shedd died about the time the house was completed. At the close of the war his estate was heavily encumbered, and by 1869 his widow had to sacrifice most of her property, her new home included. The house was sold at public auction and was bought by Thomas W. Erwin, the highest bidder at the sale, for only $3,000.00. He held it for less than a year and sold it to S. B. Clowney, a county official, for $6,500.00. Clowney occupied the place until 1878, at which time he moved to Texas and sold his house to Alexander S. Douglas.

The Douglas family made this their home for many years, and the old place became known as the DOUGLAS HOUSE, even after it was sold to Mary Kilgore in 1919, who, in turn, sold it to the United States Rubber Company in 1923.

The Rubber Company enlarged and completely renovated the place to serve the area as an exclusive inn. It was redecorated throughout and furnished

FAIRFIELD INN

XIX

in the most excellent taste, carrying out the motifs of the Colonial and Federal periods. Many of the handsome pieces of furniture were authentic antiques, selected with great care and expense. The smaller pieces and some of the adornments were all excellent reproductions and in perfect harmony with the period and atmosphere.

While operated as an Inn it became the social center of the town for entertainments of all kinds, including card parties, teas, receptions, luncheons, buffets, and drop-ins.

Recently this choice property was given to the Mount Zion Society by the United States Rubber Company. It was then leased by the Society to the Fairfield Country Club.

Now it is a most attractive and modern club with golf course and tennis courts, a large swimming pool, and other recreational facilities.

RION HOUSE

HALL — RION — RABB — STEPHENSON

Mansell Hall was a gentleman planter who had a flair for designing and building fine homes. Several of the houses that he designed, built, or helped with are still standing and bear witness to his talents and good taste.

Among his Negroes were several well-trained and highly skilled artisans. He used their talents and labor to execute his designs and plans, first for himself and later for friends and neighbors who desired his services.

The old mansion on Congress Street is one of his most impressive works. Originally it consisted of only two rooms and a hall on each floor, with a kitchen wing and outbuildings behind the main structure. It was designed so that it might be easily added to in the future. He built it in 1855 for his bride. She died shortly after they moved into the place, and in 1857 he sold it to Colonel James Henry Rion.

Colonel Rion was one of the most brilliant, interesting, and mysterious men ever to live in Winnsboro. He was foremost among the lawyers of the South, highly educated, a patron of the arts, and a philanthropist. He was a protege and a disciple of the illustrious John C. Calhoun, in whose home he was reared, and was reputed to be the son of the Dauphin of France. At the outbreak of the Confederate War he was made one of the first South Carolina colonels and threw his fortune into the Southern effort.

Colonel Rion's wife was the lovely and talented Mary Catherine (Kitty) Wier of Columbia. Her distinguished father was Samuel Wier, a native of Wiertown, Pennsylvania, a member of the family for whom the place was named and by whom it was made famous. This family owned and controlled the mines and steel mills in that area.

Mr. Wier, a talented writer and musician, broke with his family and espoused and wrote vigorously in behalf of the Southern rights. He moved to Columbia, South Carolina, where he established a newspaper and directed the music at the First Presbyterian Church until his death.

RION HOUSE

XX

Colonel John Preston (later General) became Mary Catherine's guardian, and after her father's death she made her home with the Preston family in the Hampton-Preston Mansion, the show place and social center of ante-bellum Columbia.

Aside from being a beauty, Mrs. Rion was a very gifted and talented woman. She inherited her father's musical and literary abilities and wrote several pamphlets and books. One of her books was on horticulture and was called "A Southern Lady Florist." When Clemson College was founded, her friend, Thomas G. Clemson, left it to her judgment to select the site for the institution and to approve the designs and placements of the first buildings.

The Rions had a large family, and before they moved into their home in Winnsboro, they enlarged and embellished the house and the grounds extensively. Wings were added to either side and to the rear of the building. Plumbing and gas lighting (then almost unheard of in Winnsboro) were installed. A French decorator was employed to supervise the painting and the carving of the medallions and woodwork that adorned the rooms. A handsome mahogany staircase was added, and the house was furnished with objects of art and beauty from abroad.

The original chandeliers with their exquisitely etched shades still hang from the ceilings. Thick, beveled, cutglass side lights, imported by Tiffany of New York for the house, still decorate the entrance.

A veranda and balcony front the house and are supported by six handsomely turned and carved Corinthian columns, which, with the wrought-iron brackets and rosettes, were imported. The bannisters are massive but beautifully turned and handsome.

In the garden rare shrubs, boxwoods, roses, bulbs, and cut-flowers for every season were planted, the landscaping being planned by Mrs. Rion personally. Some of the boxwoods and original plants still remain, as well as the wrought-iron gates and the fence which enclose the lot. Worked into the iron of the front gate is an "R" monogram.

This house was spared during the War Between the States. Mrs. Rion's powerful relatives in the North obtained and sent letters of immunity for her homes (the Rions also had a beautiful plantation house). Many of her friends brought their valuables to this place for safekeeping, and several families whose homes were burned found refuge here. Among these was the family of Sailing Wolfe, a well-to-do merchant, who was the grandfather of the renowned statesman and financier, Bernard M. Baruch.

In 1908, after Colonel Rion's death, the place was sold to William Rabb, and in 1931 it was purchased by J. W. Stephenson. The Stephensons restored and redecorated the house. They now occupy it as their home, and today it is one of Winnsboro's most beautiful ante-bellum mansions.

JORDAN HOUSE

LIGON — LUMPKIN — CONNER — JORDAN — HANCOCK
STEWART

This quaint little building has stood on the corner of Congress Street since 1851. The architecture of the building, aside from being quaint, is

XXI

JORDAN HOUSE

quite unusual. The heavy foundations and the first floor are of brick, on and below the ground level. The main structure is rectangular, with a hipped roof, heavy cornices under the eaves, and a wing on the rear. In the front center is a gabled room having two entrances and sets of steps that divide the two one-story porches, whose roofs are just below the cornice. The ends of the porches are supported by large, square columns and are enclosed with plain picket bannisters. The corner styles appear to be flat columns, and all the windows in the main body of the house are elongated.

The lot on which the house is located was originally a part of the Caleb Clarke property called CLARKEVILLE. James B. McCants, commissioner for the estate of Caleb Clarke, sold this property to W. J. Ligon in 1851. Ligon continued to own the place until 1863, and during his ownership the house was built. According to the records it must have been soon after he acquired the lots.

In 1863 Mannes Baum purchased the property from Ligon, ". . . Lots Nos. 15 and 16 . . . with buildings and other improvements." One of the lots was behind the one on which the house is located and fronts on Vanderhorst Street. The price paid by Baum was considerably more than that for which he sold it later. A. F. Lumpkin bought it in 1868 from Mannes Baum of the city of Camden.

In 1869 the same property passed from A. F. Lumpkin to John R. P. Lumpkin, trustee (for his daughter Marion Conner, for her life, and upon her death to be divided equally between her then-living children). Mrs. Conner died in 1906 and John R. P. Lumpkin, trustee, transferred the property to Rosa C. Jordan (Mrs. Thomas M.), a daughter of Mrs. Conner, who was living in the home with her mother. In 1917 Mrs. Jordan conveyed it to her son, Frank Jordan.

Frank E. Jordan continued to hold it until 1927 at which time he sold the house to Eugenia C. Hancock of Florida. M. M. Stewart, the present owner, acquired the place from the Hancocks in 1934.

CLARK HOUSE

MORRISON — ELLIOTT — KETCHIN — BUCHANAN — MILNOR
BOARD OF MISSIONS, PRESBYTERIAN CHURCH, U. S.
CLARK — STEWART

Although larger, the main body consisting of two full stories and no basement, this house is quite similar to the little building on the corner, next to it. The gabled rooms in the front enter between the porches; the square, column-like styles, the double steps, and the entrances are the same. The rear of the building, however, is different. Gable wings extend out to the side, and the porch rounds the corner and ends against the extended rear wings. The porch columns are square and paneled, rather than plain, and the cornices are not quite so deep.

This lot was originally a part of the property of the estate of Caleb Clarke, who died prior to 1850. The property was located on both sides of the public road from the Town of Winnsboro to Columbia and was divided for

CLARK HOUSE

XXII

estate-settlement purposes after the owner's death. The part located on the western side of the Columbia Road and lying south of Moultrie Street was divided into lots and was within the early stage known as CLARKEVILLE. These lots are shown on the old Town Map in the clerk's office and were later incorporated into the town.

In a deed dated January 13, 1851, James B. McCants, commissioner in equity (selling the Clarke property under order of the Court of Equity), sold the property to Mansel Hall for $240.00 and conveyed two lots (9 and 10) shown on the Clarke plat. Mansel Hall, by deed dated October 28, 1851, conveyed these lots, along with four others, to William A. Morrison for $300.00.

Morrison held the property until 1858. On December 16, 1858, he sold it to Henry L. Elliott for $3,000.00. This increase in consideration would tend to indicate that the lots were improved and buildings erected sometime during the Morrison ownership and that the house on lot 9 was built during this period.

On March 16, 1859, Henry L. Elliott conveyed lots 9 and 10, with the other lots, to Robert S. Ketchin but no price is shown. On May 12, 1862, Robert S. Ketchin bought a fifteen-foot by 420-foot strip from James B. McCants for $60.00. This strip was adjoining lots 9 and 10 and thereafter became a part of them.

Robert S. Ketchin conveyed this property to John M. Buchanan, along with other real estate, on May 24, 1862, for $4,500.00. A few days later, June 2, 1862. John M. Buchanan sold lots 9 and 10 (with the strip) to John G. Milnor. Milnor remained in possession until February 15, 1869, at which time he conveyed the above property to the Presbyterian Committee of Home Missions for $2,200.00.

The Board of Home Missions of the Presbyterian Church in the United States conveyed the eastern part of lots 9 and 10 and "a strip taken from lots 7 and 8 to the Board of Missions for Freedmen of the Presbyterian Church in the United States by deed probated June 12, 1886. The consideration was $5.00.

In 1888 the Board of Missions for Freedmen of the Presbyterian Church in the United States conveyed the property to Frank M. Clark for $1,200.00. During the War Between the States there was a split in the Presbyterian Church. The Northern Branch was known as the Presbyterian Church of the United States. The property was purchased by this Northern Branch for a home for a missionary sent to Winnsboro to build and operate a school. The lot continued through the block to Vanderhorst Street. The school was erected on the side facing Vanderhorst Street shortly after the purchase and stood there until the early 1900's.

The 1869 deed from Milnor to the Committee etc. shows the following as grantee: — "The Presbyterian Committee of Home Missions Inc., of the State of New York."

The Clark family lived here for a number of years and the place became known as the CLARK HOUSE. After the death of Frank M. Clark it was sold by his Executor, W. D. Douglas, to M. M. Stewart on November 15, 1926. M. M. Stewart and his family now occupy the attractive old home.

McCANTS HOUSE

McCANTS HOUSE
CLARKE — ELDER — PHILLIPS — McCANTS

The McCANTS HOUSE originally occupied the lot on the corner of Congress and Moultrie Streets. The grounds were beautifully landscaped, and it enjoyed a refined seclusion behind boxwood hedges and an unusually pretty picket fence of square, graduated wooden panels attached to granite fenceposts. The entire site was elevated and was encompassed by a three-foot granite wall. All the stone used in the landscaping and for the house was quarried on the adjoining plantation.

An outstanding feature of the yard was the profusion of white and yellow Banksia roses that had entwined themselves high up into the giant cedars. When these roses were in bloom, the sight was breath-taking.

This house was built in the very early 1800's, by James Elder, who sold it to George E. Phillips in 1845. It was the home of James B. McCants, one of Winnsboro's first lawyers, in 1855. Some sources say that the house was designed by the famous Robert Mills. Mansell Hall resided here at one time, and other sources credit him as being the builder. However, the design, the use of materials, and the character of the building do not follow the usual Hall pattern, and it appears to be of a much earlier period.

The house was a part of the once-connected plantation of James B. McCants, and it is now owned by his descendant, C. S. McCants, M. D., having been in this family for well over a century. Its foundation is of granite and brick. The basement ceilings are eight feet high, and this portion of the building was used as quarters for the house-servants. All the joists are of sixteen-inch hewn-oak timbers. The rooms in the main body are large, and they open into a hall from which the stair leads to a long hall and room in the attic. A covered passageway led to the detached kitchen. Excellent woodwork trims and adorns the rooms.

During the Confederate War several famous guests were entertained here; among them were General Beauregard and Governor Butler of North Carolina. General Beauregard, whose autographed protocal is in the hands of the McCants family, was on his way to rebuild the defenses of Charleston. General Kilpatrick, the Northern Cavalry leader, made this house his headquarters while he was in Winnsboro.

In 1954 the old house was moved to its present location on Moultrie Street by the "wheels of progress" to make room for the Winn-Dixie Supermarket. Ever since the building was moved, it has remained unoccupied, with boarded windows and no plantings or landscaping to show it off. Its pure lines and obscured beauty still show through to the lovers of old homes who pass by and dream wistfully of restoring the old place before it is too late.

BOYLESTON HOUSE
BOYLESTON — COLONIAL INN — REFO — BUCHANAN

In its prime the BOYLESTON HOUSE might well have been Winnsboro's most elegant and imposing mansion. It is a large, spacious house, designed along classic lines. The main structure is a three-story, rectangular building,

BOYLESTON HOUSE   XXIV

with a wing to the rear, and is covered by a gabled roof. It is fronted by a gable with deep ornamental cornices, dentil moldings, and carved brackets. The front gable is supported by four colossal Ionic columns, two stories in height. They rest on the floor of the veranda. Handsome, wrought-iron bannisters fixed into wooden rails enclose the porch except for the entrance area between the two center columns where the broad steps lead up from the terraced walk. Double windows flanked with slatted shutters light the front of the building. The entrance, with its double half-glass doors, follows the same grand pattern of decoration as that found in the cornice. The doors are set in a glass-paned frame capped with a handsome head cornice.

The interior, though in bad repair, is still beautiful and follows the same exquisite decorative patterns. Large, high-ceilinged rooms and hallways, and beautiful mantels and woodwork carry out the theme of elegance.

The grounds of this mansion were carefully designed and landscaped with terraces, walks, and exotic shrubs and trees. Tales of its beauty have been passed down for generations but as far back as the older residents can remember, quoting one, "The place has always had quite a fascination for children. The yard was always overgrown with trees and shrubbery and until recently was a wilderness. The shrubbery was lovely in the spring!"

In 1853 Robert B. Boyleston purchased four acres (eight lots) including this house site from Henry H. Clark and Robert B. Clark. Four of the lots fronted on Congress Street and the four abutting them fronted on Vanderhorst Street. This handsome old mansion was built by Colonel Boyleston. It remained in his family until 1905 when Samuel S. Boyleston, of New York, and Augusta B. Campbell, of Boston (his children), sold the place to Sabritt Dunn. Dunn did not live in the house and a year later, in 1906, sold it to Virginia Reynolds and Josephine M. Vanderhoof. Miss Reynolds operated the place as the COLONIAL INN, a high level winter resort for Northern visitors and sportsmen who hunted in the vicinity.

In 1910 the above owners sold the property to Gertrude H. Refo, who lived here until 1914, at which time it was purchased by Minnie A. Buchanan, the wife of Doctor John C. Buchanan. They moved here from the WOLFE HOUSE, which they owned, and lived here until after Mrs. Buchanan's death. Since the family no longer resided here the place fell into bad repair and is now suffering from neglect and emptiness.

The grounds, however, are no longer "a wilderness." Practically all the overgrown shrubbery and trees have been removed, and the old house now has a rather naked and deserted appearance.

BUCHANAN HOUSE

WOODWARD — BUCHANAN

The BUCHANAN HOUSE on Congress Street was built in the early 1850's by Osmund Woodward. He gave the house to his daughter, Claudia Rebecca Woodward, when she married Doctor Robert Augustus Buchanan.

The house was built along pure but simple Colonial lines. It is dignified but not pretentious. The main body of the structure is almost square and is covered with a hipped roof. An attractive low gable covers the front of

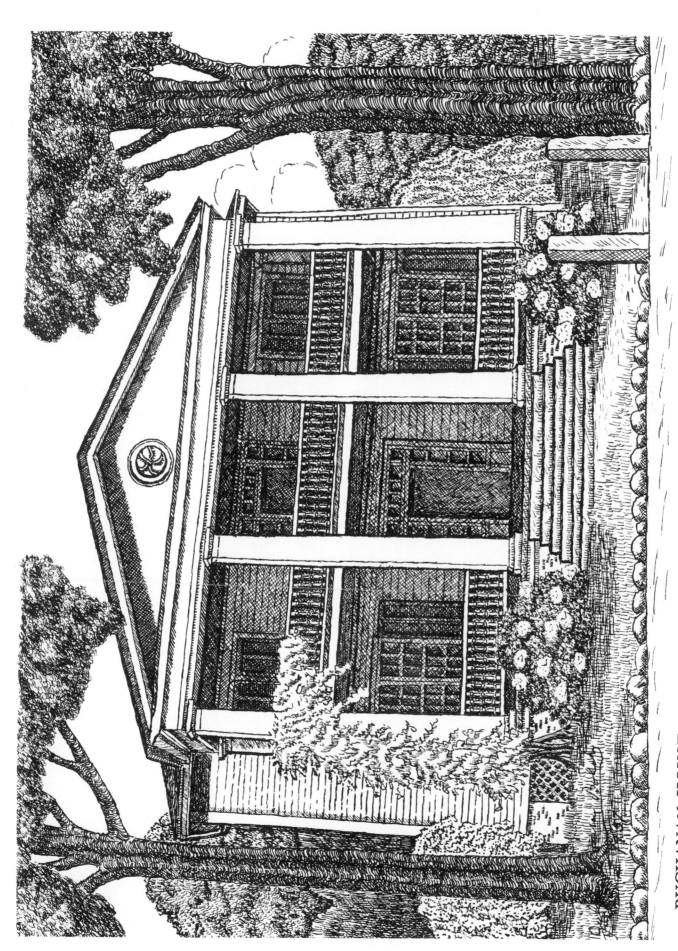

BUCHANAN HOUSE

XXV

the building and the two-story porch. In the center of the gable is a round "bull's eye" window. Four large, square wooden columns support the porch roof. Between them are delicately turned picket bannisters. Wide, graceful granite steps lead up to the front porch. The entrance doorways are flanked and topped with paned sidelights. On either side of the entrances are well-spaced, long double windows that extend almost from the ceiling to the floor, giving the place a patrician distinctiveness.

The house has belonged to the Buchanan family ever since it was erected, and until very recent years some of the family has resided here.

MACFIE HOUSE

CLARKE — NAYLOR — AIKEN — McCANTS — MILLER
CURETON — HEATH — TRAYLOR — MACFIE

The MACFIE HOUSE on Congress Street is a big, roomy, plantation-type home on Winnsboro's busiest street. Many people remark on the similarity of this and the Governor Gist home, ROSE HILL, in Union County.

The large, rectangular body of the building is fronted with a gabled double gallery or two-story porch, the bannisters of which are of an unusual sawed-pattern design. Large, round, solid wooden columns support both galleries, giving the house a classic appearance. The trim, bannisters, and blocked cornices are all beautifully executed. Large doors, surrounded by paned side-lights, center the house on both floors, opening onto the spacious piazzas. Old-fashioned louvred shutters, hung on hand-wrought hardware, give emphasis to the big windows.

In the interior the woodwork is simple but is ample decoration for the large, formal rooms and halls with their high ceilings and plastered walls.

This house sits well back from the street on a pleasingly landscaped lot. Large tea olives are prominent in the plantings, and when they are in bloom the whole area is perfumed by them.

Prior to 1850 Caleb Clarke owned the section of town in which this house is located. He sold lots and built several houses in the area, which was then outside of the limits of the town of Winnsboro and was called CLARKEVILLE. This was, perhaps, the town's first subdivision. The present MACFIE HOUSE was one of these earlier buildings.

In September 1863 Doctor Caleb Clarke, the son of Caleb Clarke, Esq., referred to above, sold this and the house next door to William Naylor of Charleston. From available records it appears that this house was built by the Clarkes many years before the sale.

After the War Between the States, in 1866, William Naylor disposed of the property to Mary G. Aiken, the wife of Colonel Hugh Aiken. Included in the sale were some other lots and a provision to apply to the house next door. The following is taken from that deed: ". . . eight lots as above . . . excepting from this conveyance the portion cornering on Congress Street and Depot Street . . . fronting on Congress Street fifty-nine feet and two hundred and fourteen feet on Depot Street . . .; also hereby reserving until June 1, 1867, the privilege of the tenant of residence upon said corner portion and of using the well water and the stable upon the premises hereby conveyed."

MACFIE HOUSE

XXVI

Mary G. Aiken transferred this property to D. W. Aiken, Trustee for her children, Gayle Aiken and Carrie Aiken, in 1869. In 1872 another transfer appears from Mary G. Aiken of Sewanee, Tennessee, and D. W. Aiken, Trustee, etc., to James B. McCants. The McCants family sold the place to Laura G. Miller of Shelby, North Carolina, in 1895.

In 1900 Laura G. Miller conveyed it to Ross B. Cureton, who was at the time living in the house. The Curetons lived here until 1917, and during that time the old home became known as the CURETON HOUSE. Mamie B. Heath (Mrs. S. W. Heath) became the next owner but never lived here. In 1919 she sold it to T. W. Traylor in January, and in August of the same year he disposed of it to R. R. Macfie. Since that time it has been occupied by the Macfie family and has become known as the MACFIE HOUSE.

The widow of R. R. Macfie, her son and daughter now live in the proud old home, which is still in excellent condition, for it has been well cared for down through the years.

BLAIR HOUSE

CLARKE — NAYLOR — GAILLARD — DWIGHT — OBEAR — BLAIR

Viewing this house from Congress Street, one sees the characteristics of a building of the late 1880's or early 1900's. This "front" is deceiving, for the house is of a much earlier vintage.

The character of the place changes when observed from Palmer Street (formerly called Depot Street). From this angle the original lines of the house are clearly defined, for it was designed to face this street. The original building was a small, rectangular, cottage-type house with a gable roof, out-side chimneys on either end, and a gabled portico protecting the doorway. The portico is flanked with a pair of steps on each end. This part of the house sits well above the ground and has a basement. In the early 1900's the size of the house was almost doubled when the front wings and piazza were added.

The property on which the building was located was a part of Caleb Clarke's CLARKEVILLE. This house was built prior to 1850 at the same time or before the large MACFIE HOUSE next door. Both of these houses were sold by Dr. Caleb Clarke to William Naylor of the city of Charleston in 1863. Four years later, 1867, Harriet G. Naylor of Charleston deeded this house to Harriet G. Gaillard, wife of Henry A. Gaillard ". . . in consideration of natural love and affection and also in consideration of the sum of $5.00 . . ." Later Harriet G. Gaillard passed title to Louisa C. Gaillard.

In 1893 Louise C. Gaillard had the property transferred to Elizabeth P. Dwight for ". . . $600.00 due by me to my daughter Elizabeth P. Dwight and natural love and affection. . . ." The Dwights lived here until 1907, and during their occupancy it became known as the DWIGHT HOUSE. Mrs. Dwight sold it to her son-in-law, Josiah J. Obear. The Obears sold the place to W. P. Blair in 1918. It is presently owned and occupied by Ernest P. Blair, a son of William P. Blair.

The house has been well cared for and makes an attractive appearance on the corner of Congress and Palmer Streets. The yard is enclosed with an old-fashioned picket fence, which gives it a distinctive, quaint, neat look.

BLAIR HOUSE

XXVII

KETCHIN BUILDING

CATHCART — LADD — PORCHER — EGLESTON — KETCHIN
CATHCART — WILBURN

The KETCHIN BUILDING on Congress Street is one of the most interesting, picturesque, and traditional landmarks in the town of Winnsboro.

It was built in the early 1830's as a private home by Richard Cathcart. Richard Cathcart was a well-to-do man and owned considerable property in the town and throughout the county.

This building follows the Charleston tradition in architecture and is similar to many of the town houses that were built in that city during and before this period.

It is a large, three-story structure, rather plain but dignified on the exterior. The only ornamentation is a fanlight over the double entrance doors (which are several steps above the street level) granite bands at each floor level, large granite blocks at the base of the building, and a cornice decorated with hand-finished wooden brackets at the roofline. The pattern of the brick work is interesting and is executed in a superior manner. Massive chimneys are built into the thick masonry walls with only their chimney pots exposed above the roof.

The plastered hallways and high-ceilinged rooms are decorated with hand-carved woodwork, mantels, and cornices in keeping with the refined dignity of the building.

In 1852 Richard Cathcart sold the building to George Washington Ladd, a portrait painter from Virginia, and his talented wife, Mrs. Catherine Ladd. The Ladds moved from the Feasterville Academy to Winnsboro where they opened a school for girls. Mrs. Ladd was a forceful woman with a winsome personality, a civic leader, and a devotee of the arts. Her school and her home soon became centers of culture and social activities for the community. She organized and promoted various clubs and organizations. Among them was a theatrical group composed of local talent which sponsored most of the dramatic entertainment of the town for many years. Plays, soirees, operettas, teas, art exhibits, lectures, dances, and balls were all under the direction of this capable woman.

During the War Between the States Mrs. Ladd's school had a full enrollment. Most of the boarding students were from other parts of the state. Young ladies from Winnsboro attended classes but lived with their parents or relatives. Part of the time and routine during the war period was set aside for work and means of raising money or supplies for the army of the Confederacy. This was done by both the school and the townspeople with Mrs. Ladd the leader of the projects.

As soon as the Yankees arrived in the town, Mrs. Ladd located one of the commanding officers and persuaded him to protect her "girls" by stationing guards around the school. The saving of the Masonic jewels from the plundering invaders has also been attributed to her diplomacy and efforts.

In 1862 the Ladds sold the property to Phillip E. Porcher of Charleston, Trustee for Martha Egleston, the wife of George W. Egleston, also of Charleston

KETCHIN BUILDING   XXVIII

District. Maria Porcher, in 1874, sold the building to Priscilla Ketchin, widow of Robert Ketchin, who lived here until her death in the early 1900's.

Since her death the house has changed ownership and tenants several times. For a time it became known as a hotel. In the 1920's it again reverted to a school and was a part of the public school system in which several of the primary classes were housed. When the buildings at Mount Zion were enlarged and increased, it again became a hotel and rooming house.

Now the imposing old building belongs to the Estate of John W. Cathcart and is occupied by Mrs. Gardner, who operates it is a boarding house. Mrs. Ella C. Wilborn, Nee Cathcart, a daughter of the late John W. Cathcart, owns and cares for the old building.

BEATY HOUSE

RAVENEL — STUART — LADD — McMASTER — BEATY

The design of this house is unusual. The main body of the building is situated almost on the sidewalk as are so many of the Charleston homes. However, this is not a typical example; a wing containing the main entrance and fronted with a porch extends to the left of the house and sits back from the street, allowing a small front yard that is enclosed with a neat picket fence.

The windows of the main body are outstanding. They are large and long, capped with gabled cornices and flanked with slatted shutters hung with hand-wrought hardware. Above the second-story windows, in the center of the gable facing the street, is a louvred window also carrying out the gable motif. The porch, too, is a decorative feature. It is covered with a simple shed roof just under the eaves of the one-story left wing, supported with square wooden columns, and, except for the entrance space, is enclosed with sawed "gingerbread" bannisters.

The decorations of the interior are simple but in accord with the style of the building. One of the main features of the interior is the oversized living room, which gives it an air of grandeur and spaciousness.

The house was built by the Ravenel family of Charleston some time after the Maria Porcher home next door. They lived here for several years, and after they moved away, a Mr. Stuart operated a school for boys in the building. Later, during the period preceding the Confederate War and for some years after, Mrs. Catherine Ladd used it as a part of her school, in conjunction with the large brick building next door. The grand living room (or salon, as Mrs. Ladd called it) was the scene of receptions, soirees, and dances. Mrs. Ladd was a gracious hostess, and part of the education of her "girls" included hospitality and the social graces necessary for a proper hostess. This, and the house next door, survived the Yankee occupation due to Mrs. Ladd's heroic stamina.

George Hunter McMaster owned the place prior to 1867. Later he and his family lived here. George H. McMaster conveyed the property to his daughter, Annie H. McMaster (Mrs. Beaty), in 1885. It is now the home of Miss Ella Beaty, a descendant, who lives here and cares for the old house.

BEATY HOUSE

XXIX

MASONIC LODGE

MASONIC LODGE – CATHCART – BRYSON – McCARLEY
KIRKPATRICT – KIMBRELL – MOBLEY – LIGON
STEWART – STEPHENSON

This is a quaint house and is distinctively different from the other old homes of Winnsboro. It is now almost obscured from view, for it has been moved back from its original position on Congress Street. Originally the long front piazza was almost on the sidewalk.

It is a rectangular building with a gabled roof and outside stone-and-brick chimneys on either end. The double porches are covered with a shed roof and extend across the front. They are both decorative and unique. The upper gallery is supported by four plain, square columns and enclosed with plain picketed bannisters and rails. The square columns of the lower piazza are fluted. Between them, just under the ceiling, are latticed panels about two and a half feet wide. Iron brackets attached to the sides of the columns support the lattice-work, evidently intended to shade the piazza. Between the brackets, attached to the bottom of the lattice, are wrought-iron decorations. Wrought-iron bannisters set in wooden rails enclose the porch except for the end to which the steps rise.

The lot on which the house is situated was sold by John McMaster to W. M. Moore and a group of several other gentlemen for the purpose of erecting a MASONIC LODGE on the site. The building was erected and remained in their possession until 1832, at which time it was sold to Richard Cathcart. It continued to be Cathcart property until 1872 when George A. White purchased it for his home.

Before the turn of the century Mr. White was the only baker in Winnsboro. His shop was located on Congress Street and was famous for the aroma that exuded from it on baking days. He also sold toys and candy, and his establishment was a favored haunt for the children of the town. After his death James M. Smith continued to operate the business.

In 1909 James L. Bryson bought the WHITE HOME and in the same year sold it at a slight profit to Annie L. McCarley. The McCarley family lived here until 1912 it was purchased by W. L. Kirkpatrick.

In 1920 the Kirkpatricks moved into another home and sold this place to A. J. Mobley and Earle Kimbrell. In 1923 Kimbrell deeded his interest to Mobley, who, in the same year, sold it to Walter W. Ligon. In 1944 the widow of W. W. Ligon sold the property to M. M. Stewart and J. W. Stephenson, who bought it for commercial development and moved the old building to the rear of the lot. An electrical company and a dry-cleaning plant now occupy the original site.

MASONIC LODGE

XXX

WINN-HANAHAN HOUSE

WINN — DUNLAP — NELSON — HANAHAN

The quaint little brick house at 119 Moultrie Street is one of Winnsboro's oldest buildings. It was built some time after the Revolution, and the first owner of whom there is any record was John Winn, the brother of Richard Winn, for whom Winnsboro was named. The above came from Edrington Historical Notes and was confirmed by Mrs. Mary Elliott Smith (Julian Elliott's daughter), whose mother was an Evans. Mr. Winn's wife was also a member of this family.

The house was originally built for a kitchen, and the main residence was to have been located in an oak grove on the corner of Congress and Moultrie Streets. Before its construction, however, the railroad came through and cut the property in half and so the residence was never built.

In the section intended for a kitchen there are two rooms and a hall on the first floor and two rooms on the second. The front windows of the second story extend to the floor. There is a large chimney on each side of the building, and a porch extends across the front.

In 1869 the property belonged to a Mr. Dunlap, who, during the same year that he bought it, sold it to a Mr. Nelson. Doctor Ralph B. Hanahan bought the place in 1880 from Mrs. Nelson. Until recent years the Hanahans continued to own the property. It was purchased several years ago by a Negro family who keep it in good repair.

EDRINGTON HOUSE

JACKSON — DUVALL — GROESHEL — LANDECKER — MOBLEY
STEWART — HAWES — BOYD — DOUGLASS
EDRINGTON — DOUGLASS

The EDRINGTON HOUSE is a well-constructed, beautifully designed building. It is unusually well-balanced and commanding in appearance, with a distinct flavor of the coastal lowcountry — the type house found in the salt-water, sea-faring towns of the Carolinas.

The actual design and construction is quite simple, but the pitch of the roof, the placement of windows, its lofty elevation, decorations, and embellishments set it apart, giving great dignity and pure beauty.

It is a two-story, rectangular structure covered with a gabled roof, having corniced eaves with a wide dado. Massive chimneys are at each end of the house. Right and left wings, with outside chimneys on the ends, flank the main body of the building and extend across the rear. A one-story porch dresses the front, with tapering, round columns supporting the roof and second-story balcony. Between the columns and enclosing the balcony are turned picket bannisters. The spaces between the columns are slightly arched, and dentil moldings decorate the dado. The entrance is a simple Colonial door set in a plain frame with four paned lights at the top. Four long, narrow

WINN-HANAHAN HOUSE

XXXI

windows are spaced across the front under the porch roof. A door from the upstairs hall opens onto the balcony, with only one window in the center of the wall on each side.

Throughout the building the woodwork and trim are of superior workmanship and are so much like that of the WOLFE HOUSE, next door, and MAYFAIR, at Jenkinsville, that they were probably done by the same craftsman. The front yard is enclosed with an old-fashioned spear-and-dart wrought-iron fence.

This house was built by a Mr. Jackson, a son-in-law of John Miller, the tailor, who built and lived in the WOLFE HOUSE, some time shortly after 1830. The same workmen evidently constructed both houses at about the same time.

The next owner on record is Mary A. Duvall, whose husband acquired the property in 1854. In 1883 she transferred the place to Joseph Groeschel. In 1884 another transfer appears — from J. N. Withers, Assignee of Joseph Groeschel, to Jennie Groeschel. Jennie Groeschel sold the property to Louis Landecker in 1898, and in 1900 he passed title to Emma A. Mobley.

The Mobley family lived here until 1905, at which time the house was sold to James Stewart and William V. Stewart. In 1907 it was sold at considerable profit to Leighton W. Hawes. Hawes continued in possession until he sold to Mary Boyd in 1919. Hawes never lived in the house during his ownership but rented it as an investment. Mrs. Boyd lived here for some time before she purchased the place.

The heirs of Mary Boyd sold the house in 1928 to J. E. Douglass, who held it as rental property until he sold to Lillie Crawford Edrington in 1934. It was during Mrs. Edrington's occupancy that the place became known as the EDRINGTON HOUSE. Mrs. Edrington operated a tourist home for many years, during which time it became well known and popular.

The Edringtons are listed among Fairfield's early settlers. They were Welsh people who originally settled in Virginia. Before the Revolutionary War one branch of the family came to Fairfield and settled, on lands previously granted, in the Blair's section on Broad River. After the war other members of the family came to the county. These people built several fine homes, but none of them are now in existence. William Edrington, who lived to be a very old man — almost a centenarian — wrote the EDRINGTON PAPERS or EDRINGTON'S HISTORY OF FAIRFIELD COUNTY, a very valuable and informative account of the early days in the county. His home, library, and the early records of the family were destroyed by Sherman's Army in 1865.

The EDRINGTON HOUSE in Winnsboro was vacant for many years and suffered from neglect. This, however, is being improved, for in 1962 the heirs of Lillie Crawford Edrington sold the house to Albert Douglass. Mr. Douglass now makes the lovely old house his home and is undertaking extensive restoration of the property.

EDRINGTON HOUSE

XXXII

WOLFE HOUSE

HAVIS — MILLER — McDOWELL — BAILEY — DuBOSE
WOLFE — BUCHANAN

This delightful old house, in spite of its beauty and elegance, seems doomed to a fate of prolonged deterioration from vacancy and neglect. It could well be one of the show-places of the community if it had but half a chance.

The house was built by John Miller, "the tailor," in the early ante-bellum period. It is well-designed, beautifully proportioned, and handsomely odorned and decorated. The handcarved moldings, doorfacings, mantels, cornices, wainscoatings, and trim, both on the exterior and on the interior, rank among the most artistic work of their kind to be found in the county.

The details and designs are strikingly similar to those of the ALSTON — COOK — CHAPPELL HOUSE in the Jenkinsville community and to those of the EDRINGTON HOUSE next door. It is quite possible that they were all executed by the same artisan, for they are of the same school of design, the ante-bellum at its best.

This is a large, two-story building, covered with beaded siding. It has a graceful hipped roof with a gabled portico extending over the center section of the front of the building.

In the portico gable is an unusually handsome fanlight window. The cornices and dados are edged with finely carved dentil moldings. Both porticoes are supported by graceful, hand-turned columns. The spaces between these columns are slightly arched, giving the house a lowcountry flavor. The porches are enclosed with heavy, well-designed bannisters.

The hall doors are most attractive. Paned and panelled sidelights adorn them, and over the doors are paned fanlights, a repetition of the gable window. The interior is spacious, with high-ceilinged rooms adorned with the same fine decorations as found on the exterior.

The lot on which the house is located was originally owned by Jesse D. Havis, Sr., who deeded it in 1823 to his son, Jesse D. Havis, Jr., along with other properties. In 1830 Jesse D. Havis, Jr., sold this and another lot to John Miller, who purchased other lots from him in 1831 and in 1838.

To satisfy a claim against John Miller in 1845, Shreiff J. Cockrell gave a deed to Robert Cathcart and John McDowell. In the same year Cathcart sold his part to McDowell.

The next transfer on record was in 1850, when David M. McDowell sold the place to R. S. Bailey. Bailey held it until 1852, at which time he sold it to Sarah F. DuBose of Lancaster. Samuel DuBose purchased it from Sarah DuBose in 1868, and in 1873 Sarah F. DuBose and Samuel DuBose sold the house to Sarah S. Wolfe, who at the time was occupying the residence.

Sarah S. Wolfe was the wife of Sailing Wolfe, a wealthy merchant and planter. Their home was destroyed by Sherman's troops during the Union occupation. The family took refuge with Mrs. James Henry Rion and later moved into this house. They made this their home, and it became known as and is still called the WOLFE HOUSE. One of their daughters, Belle, married

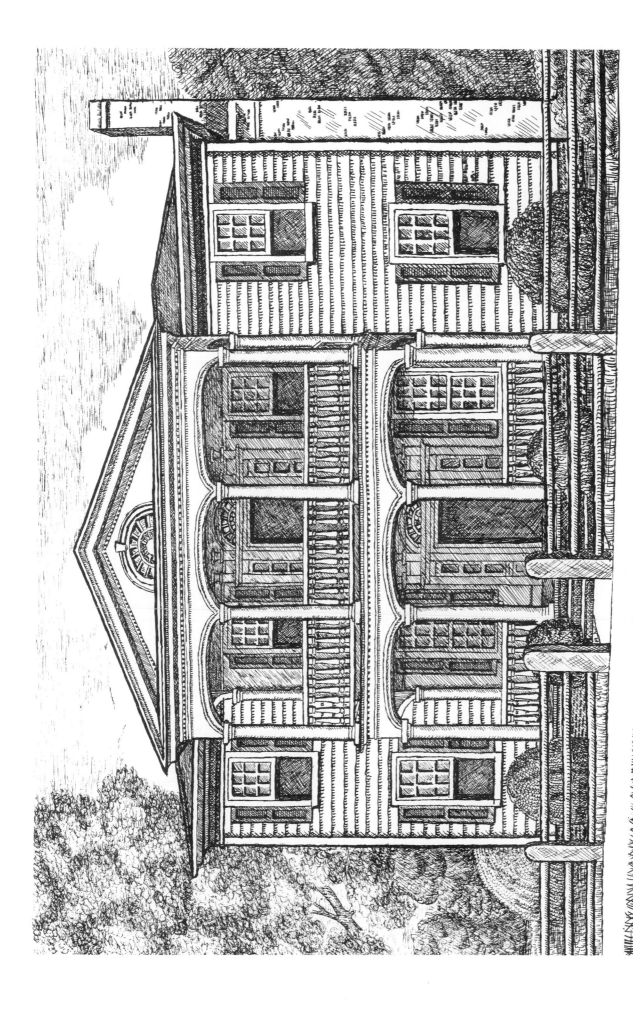

WOLFE HOUSE

XXXIII

Dr. Simon Baruch of Camden while they were living here. Dr. and Mrs. Baruch were the parents of the world-famous financier and statesman, Bernard M. Baruch, who has now passed ninety years and will go down in history as one of the greatest men of our time. The Wolfe's youngest daughter, Sarah was noted for her beauty and horsemanship. She married a DesPortes and became the mother of the "Winnsboro DesPorts."

This property passed from Sol Wolfe to Dr. John C. Buchanan in 1901 It is still owned by his estate. Since the Buchanans left the place, it has been inhabited by a long succession of tenants. Now it has fallen into very bad repair and for some years has been deserted and vacant, a sad fate for such a dignified old home.

FAIRFIELD COUNTY COURTHOUSE
1823

The FAIRFIELD COUNTY COURTHOUSE is one of the most stately and imposing buildings in the upcountry. It was designed by the famous architect, Robert Mills, and was built in 1823.

The classic building is executed in the true Mills tradition. It is a large, rectangular structure, covered with a simple but pleasing gabled roof, which extends over the building in the front and covers a broad, flagstoned portico. The four massive columns supporting the portico are well-proportioned and graceful. Originally two flights of wooden steps led up to the second floor but when the building was renovated and enlarged in 1939, the circular stairs of wrought-iron and brass and the landing balcony were added, much enhancing the original beauty of the building.

Ever since it was built, the courthouse and its "yard" have been a part of the heart of the town. Patriarchs gather here to play checkers, watch traffic, reminisce, and swap yarns in the shade of the big trees. Lawyers, business men, and citizens from all classes and walks of life exchange their views here and listen to the local philosophers and politicians.

A little-known story of interest is about the saving of the county, court, and jail records during the War Between the States. At that time Elijah Ollever, a small but stern man of French extraction, was sheriff of the county. When he was informed that the Northern army was moving towards Winnsboro, he made hasty preparations to save the valuable documents, papers, jail and court records. His home and plantations were in the Longtown section, near Ridgeway. Most of the records and books were hidden away in safety in remote places deep in the swampy, wooded areas near his home.

The most valuable of these he left at the house with his wife and sister. They sewed all one morning, making long cloth bags with draw strings and loops at the tops. When they finished, the papers were carefully packed into these sacks; belts were run through the loops and they were fastened securely around the waists of the women and girls in the household, concealed under their full skirts and petticoats.

The sheriff carried the jail records with him in his saddlebags and fled to the Wateree swamp for safety. On the way he was seen by a party of troops, who chased him to the river. To make an escape, he had to swim

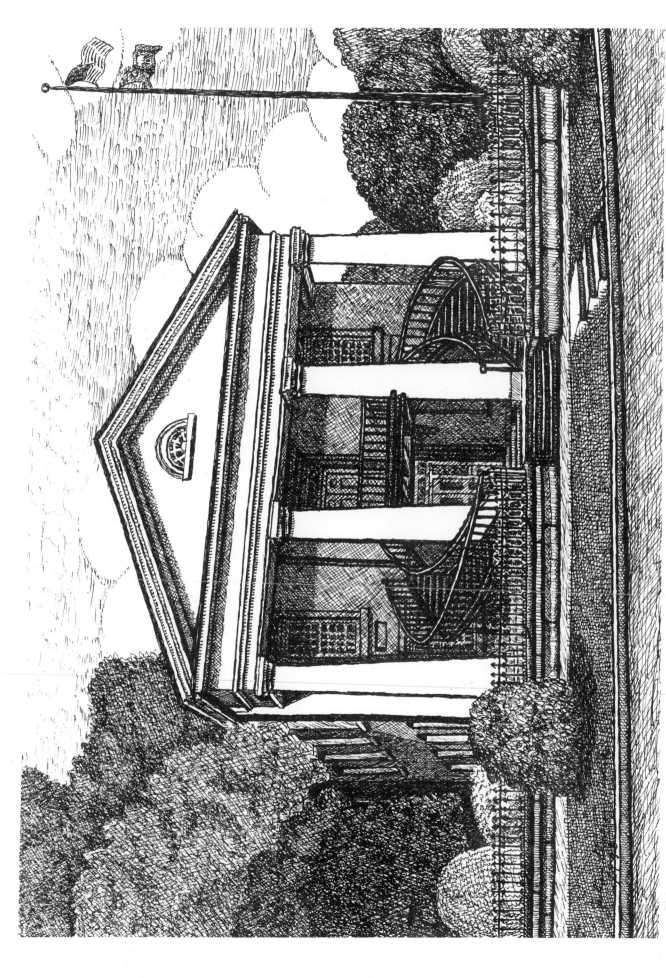

FAIRFIELD COUNTY COURTHOUSE

XXXIV

his horse across the swollen, icy stream while the soldiers on the bank showered bullets all around and over him. By some miracle neither he nor the horse was hit and he was able to escape.

When the Yankees entered Winnsboro, they liberated all the prisoners who were in the jail, regardless of their crimes, and set fire to the building The courthouse was also ransacked and marked to be burned, but one of the high-ranking officers who was a Mason entered the sheriff's office and when he saw the framed Masonic documents on the wall, he spared the place. A slate was on the desk. On this he wrote "Leave this building alone," signed his name, and placed it on the mantel where it was conspicious and could easily be seen by anyone entering the room. He then sent a detail of men back to the jail with orders to put out the fire and spare the building.

The slate that was left by the officer was kept as a relic of the war by the Ollever family for a long time but through the passing of the years it has been lost.

On court days the old building is a veritable beehive of activity. This place has been the scene of many famous trials, and on one occasion it witnessed a bloody riot in which several people were wounded and in which Adam Hood, a brave young sheriff, lost his life in the line of duty.

The courthouse has long been one of the landmarks of the community that it has served so well. The longer it stands, the more it will be revered and pointed to with justifiable pride by the citizens of Fairfield.

THE TOWN CLOCK
1833

The most familiar landmark in old Winnsboro is the TOWN CLOCK. The building is truly in the very heart of the community, being located in the town square near the courthouse. It was primarily built to house the public market, but because of the fact that its tower housed the clock and belfry, it soon became known to the citizens as the "Clock" instead of the "Market".

As early as 1785 there was a public market in Winnsboro. It was a square, wooden building with a tower at one end to house the bell which was used as an alarm for fires, danger, curfew, special announcements, and, last but not least, "butchering days" — to let the inhabitants of the village know that fresh meat was available. An old anecdote about this is still told in Winnsboro. In the olden times when the town bell would ring, the dogs from all over the countryside would make a dash to the market for their share of the bones and scraps. This old building was located on a corner of Washington Street.

During the 1820's Robert Cathcart purchased the old market building and with the deal donated his duck pond and some land in the center of Washington Street for the new market. The Town Council then petitioned the Legislature for authority to erect a new building which would house a Town Clock. The petition was granted on one condition, that being, "Provided the building be no more than thirty feet in width."

The new building was erected in 1833, and Colonel William McCreight, Intendant, ordered the works for the new clock in 1837 from Alsace, France.

TOWN CLOCK   XXXV

They were landed in Charleston and hauled to Winnsboro in wagons. The works are of superior quality, for this clock has run continuously for more than one hundred years and proudly holds the record of having been in constant use longer than any other town clock in the United States.

The bell for the clock was also made in France, with silver in its composition. It was used until 1895 when during a fire it was rung so vigorously that it was cracked and had to be sent to Philadelphia for repairs. When it was finally returned, the tone was so changed that it is doubtful whether or not this is the original bell.

The Lord account of the Yankee occupation of Winnsboro tells that after the Union troops began to move out of the town, some of the native boys spotted several "bummers," with oil-soaked torches prepared, hiding in the "courthouse tower." Since the Courthouse has no tower, the narrator must have confused it with the Market Tower which is located diagonally in front of the Courthouse.

The boys reported their findings to Doctor Lord, the Episcopal minister and one of the few men left in the town during its occupation by the invaders. Doctor Lord immediately took the matter to a Federal officer who was making preparations to leave. The man explained that he was already late in taking his men out after trying to round up stragglers and that they were already in danger of being captured by the Confederates who were in the woods to the east of the village. If he returned for the bummers, his risk would be too great. Doctor Lord argued with him and promised him immunity from capture if he would do his duty and get these renegades before they brought more terror to the already prostrate town.

The officer finally heeded his pleas and took a detail of soldiers to dislodge the drunken buzzards from their roost. He was later stopped by a party of Confederates but when he showed them the rector's letter, they gave him, his men, and prisoners an escort to the Union lines.

The public market occupied the ground floor of the building except for two very small rooms that served as the "guard house" for drunks and petty criminals. The second floor served as a Town Hall.

This grand old building is now the home of the Fairfield County Chamber of Commerce, and some of the other offices are used by various public agencies. It is still very much the heart of the community.

ELLIOTT HOUSE

CAMPBELL — ELLIOTT — SITGREAVES — ELLIOTT

Diagonally across Congress Street from Winnsboro's post office is one of the town's traditional landmarks, the old ELLIOTT HOUSE.

The building is another typical "mosquito cottage," a design that became popular in Fairfield County during the 1820's and was still used during the Confederate War era. The footings are massive granite blocks under the thick brick walls of the basement or first floor, which is below the ground level on the front but well above on the rear. Oversized chimneys afford fireplaces for all the rooms, from the first to the third floor.

ELLIOTT HOUSE

XXXVI

The interior is adorned with fine mantels and woodwork, adding much to the dignity of the high-ceilinged rooms and halls.

The front of the building is almost classic, with a gabled portico across the central portion, supported by stout, fluted, square columns. The gable of the portico is plain. It does not have the usual ornamental window or fanlight in the center. In the old days there was in front of this house a public well which supplied water for several of the buildings in the vicinity and was a popular watering place for horses and livestock.

In 1810 Reuben Harrison sold the lot on which this house now stands to William McCreight. At that time a house on the lot was referred to as "Lot No. 187 on east corner of Congress and College Streets where David Campbell formerly lived." The house referred to was later moved to the rear of the lot and enlarged. It is the house now owned and occupied by Mrs. Maymie W. Stevenson.

William McCreight sold the property to Cornelius Beard, "who was living there," in 1814. In 1824 Cornelius Beard transferred the same property to Robert Cathcart, and in December of the same year Robert Cathcart sold it to James Lemmon. This lot originally extended the whole way through the block, back to Vanderhorst Street, and included the property on which the GLADDEN and TIMMS HOUSES are located.

In 1833 James Lemmon sold the portion on which the ELLIOTT HOUSE now stands to John Campbell, who also "owned and occupied" the lot adjoining, which is now the location of the WILLIFORD HOUSE.

John or William Campbell built the ELLIOTT HOUSE some time after 1833, for in 1855 William sold the house and lot to James Elliott (the father) and James McKinney Elliott (son).

James Elliott was one of Winnsboro's pioneer citizens. He was a busy and active man in spite of being paralyzed from his waist down. He was a talented silversmith and for a period of eighteen years served as Clerk of Court for Fairfield County, from 1828 until 1846. Some of his silver work may still be found in Fairfield County and is treasured by those fortunate enough to possess it. Mrs. Carlisle McDonald Chappell has a spoon that was made by him, it was given to her as a wedding gift. James Elliott lived to be a very old man. He died in 1865 at the age of ninety-three.

James McKinney Elliott operated near his house a shop where cotton gins were built. Later this was converted into a coffin factory. His wife continued to operate the latter, after his death in 1896, until she died in 1907. After her passing, the house was sold to the Sitgreaves family, who lived there until the 1950's.

After the Sitgreaves moved, the house was renovated and divided into apartments. It now houses a suite of doctors' offices and an apartment.

Ever since its erection the old house has been well cared for. It is just as attractive today as when it was new, and it stands as one of the many witnesses to the good taste shown by the early builders of Winnsboro. The present owners are James M. Elliott of Virginia, and Joe B. Elliott of Villanova, Pennsylvania, grandsons of James McKinney Elliott.

WILLIFORD HOUSE

CAMPBELL — OBEAR — BACOT — ELLIOTT — LUMPKIN
WILLIFORD — McMASTER

The WILLIFORD HOUSE is one of the more familiar of Winnsboro's ante-bellum mansions. It is located on Congress Street, just one block removed from the business district, fronting on the main north-south highway. Its patrician appearance and character give the passing traveler a very good impression of the town.

The main body of the house is a large, three-story, rectangular building, covered with a gable roof containing three enormous dormer windows for the third-story rooms. The roof extends over a wide, two-story porch, supported by six colossal square columns which rise from the ground and extend upward to the eaves of the roof.

Large granite blocks are used in the construction of the walls of the first floor. The floor of the lower porch is laid with the same material. Wide clapboards are used on the second story as an outside cover while the gable and dormers of the third are covered with small, hand-hewn shingles. This contrast in the use of materials gives a pleasing effect.

The windows are large and well arranged, and wide entrances are encased in sidelights and transoms. On the first floor the porch is open, but on the second it is enclosed with heavy, beautifully turned bannisters.

A stone wall extends across the front of the lot.

When the house was originally built, there were two flights of outside steps leading up to a landing between the two center columns of the upstairs veranda. In recent times these have been moved, and the inside stair is now used exclusively.

The house was built by a Mr. and Mrs. Campbell. In 1856 it was purchased by the Reverend Josiah Obear. The Reverend Mr. Obear first came to Winnsboro in 1841 as rector of St. John's Episcopal Church. He was a native of Newberry, Vermont, and was of French descent. The name was originally spelled Aubert. He was a highly educated man and worked with several churches before coming to South Carolina for his health. He served at James Island and at Wilton before locating in Winnsboro. While he was here, the old church was built on the lot where the present Episcopal Cemetery is located.

He was married in old Saint Phillip's Church in Charleston. Soon after the completion of the church in Winnsboro, his health was much improved, and he and his family moved back to Vermont.

His old illness returned and he was advised to move south again. This time he came to Virginia for a short stay, then to Edenton, North Carolina, and finally back to Winnsboro where he and his talented wife planned to open a school.

He leased a house for three months from his old friend, Hugh McMaster, and later bought the Campbell property on Congress Street for the school. Before the building was ready for occupancy, the family resided with the DuBose family on their plantation, "Roseland," which was on the outskirts of the town.

The school proved quite successful and was filled with teen-age girls from out of town as boarding students and with girls and boys of Winnsboro as day students. Some of the Mount Zion students also took special courses such as music and French. Miss Susan Ann Finney, also from Vermont, was added to the faculty. She was a gentle woman and an excellent teacher. The reverend Mr. Obear's daughter Emily also assisted with the school.

During the first years of the Confederate War the institution continued to flourish but towards the end pupils, money, and educational interest began to wane. Miss Finney went to another school.

By this time Winnsboro was becoming a haven for war refugees. The family of W. Perroneau Finley came to Winnsboro from Aiken about the time that Miss Finney left. They numbered five in family and brought five servants with them — a driver, a butler, a cook, a maid, and a girl of twelve to help with the children.

Mr. Finley, a signer of the Ordinance of Secession, asked the Reverend Mr. Obear for lodging. His family was given Miss Finney's classroom, the family living room, kitchen privileges, accommodations in the third-floor dormitory, and servants' quarters.

Later, as Sherman's army drew nearer, the trains out of Columbia were loaded with refugees. On February 15th, 1865, Miss Hattie Gibbes, a daughter of the highly respected Dr. Robert Wilson Gibbes, arrived, having been loaded on the train by her father. She found refuge in Winnsboro with the Obears. (Dr. Gibbes was at that time Mayor of Columbia.)

The next day Chancellor Carroll, his wife, and three daughters arrived by carriage from the South Carolina capital en route to Abbeville but, on reaching Winnsboro, they learned that they had been cut off by the enemy. The Reverend Mr. Obear heard of their plight. By now everything in the little town was overflowing with refugees, and so the good rector made room for them. Chancellor Carroll was also a signer of the Ordinance of Secession from his section of the state.

On the evening of February 17th some of the many occupants of the grand old mansion noticed a reflection in the sky. With saddened hearts and low spirits they realized that their beloved Columbia was burning.

On Sunday Wheeler's men entered the town and told the people that the dreaded enemy was close behind. Mr. Finley and Chancellor Carroll took to the woods for safety before the Yankees arrived. All the Sunday dinners in Winnsboro, including the Obears', were consumed by the troops, and the inhabitants of the town did without their food.

The fires started as Wheeler's men left. Woodward's Gin House, the freight depot, and all the cotton in town were burned.

Monday, when the Yankees came, the stores were looted and fired. When the Obear household saw nearby McMaster's store in flames, they bolted their doors and took refuge in Mrs. Finley's room (the former living room) where her son was ill. There was no doctor. The child was covered with a crimson rash; it was not known whether the malady was scarlet fever, smallpox, or the measles.

In due time the Yankees arrived and broke into the house. On reaching the sick room in which the women and children were barricaded, they swarmed in with shouts and threats but on seeing the sick boy, limp with fever and

WILLIFORD HOUSE

XXXVII

covered with the scarlet rash, their leader halted them and ordered them out, shouting that the house was contaminated. This, perhaps, saved the grand old building from the torch, for a guard was posted around it to see that no one entered or left the place.

When things quieted down, the beautiful Lilla Carroll, dressed in her best, strolled out onto the piazza. She sang several popular Confederate songs but when she began singing OH, YES I AM A SOUTHERN GIRL, she was stoned by the Federal troops. Fortunately, she made a quick exit before any harm befell her. One rock was hurled so forcibly that it shattered a window and sent glass flying across the sick boy's bed and all through the room. Luckily, no one was hurt.

The household had no food that day. The Yankees took it all. Mrs. Finley was astonished almost to the point of fainting when she learned that her servants, including her treasured cook Rose, had left with the enemy. The next day the butler and the carriage driver returned of their own accord but the females had "jined up with the yankees."

In 1870 the Reverend Josiah Obear sold this house to Eunice A. Bacot, the wife of Pierre Bacot. She continued to own it until it was sold to Thomas K. Elliott at a Clerk's sale in 1887. The following year, 1888, Thomas K. Elliott conveyed it to Susannah A. Lumpkin.

Ten years later, in 1898, Mrs. Lumpkin sold the property to Quay D. Williford. Since that time the place has become known as the WILLIFORD HOUSE and has been retained by the Willifords and their descendants. The widow of Quay D. Williford (Mrs. Addie R.) lived here until her death.

The handsome old mansion is now owned by Mrs. Williford's grandson, Quay McMaster, but he does not occupy the place. It now houses suites of doctors' offices.

WOODLAND

JORDAN — TRAYLOR — CRAWFORD — LYLES

The WOODLAND house has not yet reached its century mark but that date is so near and WOODLAND is such a lovely home, so typical of those built during the ante-bellum period, that it is worthy of mention.

The house is beautifully located on a large, wooded lot and is shaded with spreading oaks and large, waxy magnolia trees that perfume the entire neighborhood when they are in bloom. It was built in 1870 by Samuel Johnson, an architect and builder, who designed and erected several outstanding homes in Winnsboro, for Captain W. G. Jordan.

Graceful, fluted columns support a classic portico on the front; this is the focal point of the building. The windows and doors are well proportioned and artistically spaced. A handsome, colonial-type stairway with delightfully carved bannisters dominates the interior.

In 1945 the property was acquired by Mr. and Mrs. Ernest Crawford from Miss Leila Traylor. They restored it in minute detail, retaining all its old-fashioned splendor. They lived here until after Mrs. Crawford's death. Several years ago it was purchased by J. M. Lyles, Jr., the present owner.

XXXVIII

WOODLAND

SION PRESBYTERIAN CHURCH

During the 1920's this old landmark of Winnsboro was razed. The new house of worship had been completed and was situated in another location. All that remains on the old site is the old-fashioned cemetery in which sleep many of Winnsboro's leading citizens of the past. This sketch of SION PRESBYTERIAN CHURCH was made from an old photograph which is now in the possession of a daughter of one of the former pastors.

The history of the church is quite complete. It was begun by a Revolutionary War soldier, Colonel William McCreight, who was one of the first elders and was clerk of the session for more than a half-century. His records are hand-written in beautiful script. They are concise and well expressed. In them he states that Sion was at first a preaching station or mission under the "First South Carolina Presbytery in 1799." The Reverend Robert McCollough was the first minister to serve the post regularly as a preacher.

In 1801 the Reverend John Foster came to Winnsboro to head Mount Zion College. He came from the Old Salem (Black River) Church, in Williamsburg County, which had its beginnings in the 1750's. He was a preacher of note, and as soon as he assumed his duties at the college, the congregation of Sion secured him as their regular supply. He was succeeded in both positions by the Reverend George Reid, who came to Winnsboro from York, South Carolina.

The Reverend Mr. Reid was installed as pastor in 1805, and it was during his pastorate that the congregation formally took the name of Sion. Up to and during this time all services were held in the courthouse.

In 1807 several of the members left the Presbyterian Church and organized a Methodist Church. Soon after, this group built their own brick house of worship, which was the town's first separate church building.

In 1809 the congregation of Sion numbered twenty-three. The three elders were William McCreight, James Beaty, and Thomas Russell. It was during this year that the little congregation began their church building, which was completed in 1811.

The original Presbyterian lot was located on a corner of the town square where the Bank of Fairfield now stands. This was not used; instead, the house of worship was erected on Garden Street on two lots that were deeded to the church by Major Thomas Means and his brother, Robert.

After the Reverend Mr. Reid severed his connections with the college, he continued as pastor of the church until 1810, at which time he removed to North Carolina.

This first building was a brick structure, fifty by thirty feet and twenty-one feet high on the interior, with galleries on three sides. In September 1811 the Reverend B. R. Montgomery held the first services in the new building. In later years the church was enlarged and the tower was added.

The Reverend Anthony Ross came to Sion in 1813. It was during his pastorate that the church divided again. This time the dissenting group organized the Associate Reformed Presbyterian Church in Winnsboro. The Reverend

SION PRESBYTERIAN CHURCH

XXXIX

Mr. Ross left in 1822 and was followed by the Reverend William Brearley, who came in 1825 and remained until 1841.

Under the Reverend Doctor Brearley the church prospered and grew in numbers and in spirit. During this period the spiritual needs of the slaves were emphasized, and many of them were received into the membership of the church. Too, a Sabbath School was established to serve the Negro children, who also received the rites of baptism. It was not until after the Confederate War and during the Reconstruction period that the Negro members pulled out and established their own churches.

The Reverend Samuel Hay of Charleston ministered to the needs of the church, following Doctor Brearley, and was with the congregation from 1844 through 1846 when he asked for a dismissal to return to Charleston.

Pastors following the Reverend Mr. Hay were the Reverends William E. Boggs, G. R. Brackett, E. M. Green, C. E. Chichester, H. B. Pratt, D. E. Jordan, Doctor S. C. Byrd (who was later president of Chicora College), the Reverends J. M. Holliday and G. G. Mayes. It was during Doctor Mayes' pastorate that the new building was completed and the old one was abandoned and finally razed.

MENG HOUSE

THOMPSON — QUATTLEBAUM — MENG

This attractive house on Washington Street was built by Osmond Thompson in the 1840's. It is one of the "mosquito cottage" types of architecture that was so popular in this section in the ante-bellum days. The first floor is on the ground level. The living quarters are on the second and third floors. An impressive gabled porch covers the front entrance. The columns on the porch are square and paneled. About halfway down, the steps divide at a landing. From the landing a flight of steps descends on either side, giving the building a very graceful front.

The ground floor is of brick and oirginally contained the kitchen and service rooms. On the second and third floors are halls and living quarters. A wing extends to the north on the rear of the house.

The stairway is one of the outstanding features of the building. It is beautifully paneled, and the newel post is quite handsome and in keeping with the formality of the main floor, which has exquisite woodwork, mantels, wainscotings, and trim. The high ceilings add not only to the beauty of these large rooms but also to their comfort during the summer months.

During the Confederate War the Thompson family was living in the house. They saved their silver and valuables from the looting soldiers by removing one side of the square columns and hanging the articles on nails that were driven on the inside carefully replacing the panels that had been removed.

The Quattlebaum family occupied the house for many years after the Thompsons. It is now the property of the B. B. Meng family. After the house was purchased by the Mengs, it was completely restored and remodeled, retaining all its old charm and elegance.

MENG HOUSE

XL

NEIL HOUSE

VANDERHORST — CLARKE — NEIL

In 1786 the site of this old building belonged to Major John Vanderhorst, a native of Charleston. The street on which the house is located is named for him, and it is shown as one of the original streets on the first plat of the town of Winnsboro.

In 1809 Caleb Clarke, Esquire, of Maryland, a highly educated lawyer and a scholarly gentleman, purchased the property and enlarged the house. In histories and accounts of old Winnsboro he is spoken of as one of the most honored and distinguished men in the town. His family continued to own the place until 1873. At that time it was purchased by John Jackson Neil, a native of Fairfield and the father of the present owners, Miss Nan Neil and Mrs. Harry Withers.

During the War Between the States the old house was a haven for refugees from Charleston, the Taft family.

The house is in a beautiful setting on a green lawn shaded by ancient giant oaks and enclosed with quaint, old-fashioned picket fences. The thick brick walls of the building are plastered over with tan stucco, and massive chimneys flank either end. It is fronted by a two-storied, gabled piazza, decorated with square, hand-hewn wooden columns and plain picketed bannisters. The general appearance is one of stalwart, refined simplicity. Long windows are shaded by wide, slatted shutters that are hung on their original hand-wrought iron fittings.

The interior is graceful and charming. All the rooms have a three-way exposure, and the old-fashioned, small-paned windows make them light and airy. All the woodwork is hand-carved. The fireplaces are large and are appropriately decorated with traditional, Adams-type mantels. All the trim matches the cornices and wainscotings.

The house is furnished in the manner of the old Charleston homes, with no definitely "period" rooms but with an accumulation of fine pieces and comfortable furniture that have been cared for and lived with for generations. Some of the silver was fashioned by James E. Elliott, an early Winnsboro silversmith, in 1807. A tea service of old Sevres dates back to 1758, and a Connecticut Queen Anne highboy graces one of the rooms. Several pieces of Revolutionary and ante-bellum slave-made furniture are still in constant use. Rare pieces of china and other decorative ornaments add tone and dignity to the gracious old rooms.

XLI

NEIL HOUSE

CATHCART HOUSE

CLARKE — KIRKPATRICK — CATHCART

The CATHCART HOUSE is one of Winnsboro's architectural gems. It was built in the 1820's by Caleb Clarke, the Maryland lawyer who settled in Winnsboro in the early 1800's, for his son.

The building sits high above the ground on massive masonry foundations. The main body is a rectangle covered with a gabled roof. An unusual porch graces the front and gives the house an air of elegance. The center portion of the porch is covered with a gable supported by square columns resting on bannister-height bases. Decorating the center of the front gable is one of the most magnificent fanlight windows in the town. This design is repeated over the front doorway, which is set between glass-paned sidelights. A long flight of broad, easy-rising steps leads up to the porch. The two corner sections of the porch give a terraced effect to the house, the corner posts of which match the paneled bases of the columns. Plain picket bannisters enclose the porch.

On the ends of the main body are two immense chimneys. Between the chimneys, in the upper section of the gables, are louvred windows topped with fanlights. The rear wing has a long, columned piazza on one side, enclosed with picket bannisters matching those on the front. A stone wall across the front and side of the lot sets apart this site and adds much to the attractiveness of the location.

For many years after the Clarkes ceased to occupy the building, it served as the manse for Sion Presbyterian Church.

Mrs. Margaret P. Kirkpatrick purchased this property in the 1920's and lived here until her death. During this time it became known as the KIRKPATRICK HOUSE. The old home is now owned and occupied by her daughter, Mrs. Evelyn K. Cathcart, and her family.

CATHCART HOUSE

XLII

McCREIGHT HOUSE

McCREIGHT — SMITH — QUATTLEBAUM

In Winnsboro there are many quaint, picturesque, stately, and homey houses. The old McCREIGHT HOUSE is a perfect combination of all the above objectives. It was built in 1774 by Colonel William McCreight, a Scotch-Irish cabinet-maker who was one of the first of his trade to settle in Fairfield County. Besides being one of the first, he was one of the best. Many of the old homes throughout the county contain fine pieces of furniture that were made by him. Wherever they are found, they are always pointed to with pride by their owners.

Before this house was built, all the houses in and around Winnsboro had been of log or stone construction. This home has the distinction of being the first "board" house in the town. It is a simple, comfortable, dignified building. The first floor is a little below ground level and is built of thick masonry walls. The tapering chimneys are massive, thus tying in with the solid foundation. The roof has a pleasing, gentle slope and extends on the front over a broad porch that is decorated with simple, square columns, rails, and pickets.

All the framing is hand-hewn, and the boards, both inside and out, are hand-planed and pegged. The few nails used in the construction were hand-wrought and are oddly shaped. The main body of the house is three stories, with two large rooms on each floor. The kitchen and dining room are in the basement, with the living and bed rooms on the second and third floors. The kitchen still displays some of its gifted builder's handiwork. On one wall is a quaint corner cupboard with butterfly shelves and glass panes in the upper doors.

The floors are of long, hand-hewn, hand-planed pine boards that are fastened with hardwood pegs. All the interior woodwork and trim is simple but refined in design. The mantels are wide, with high shelves and very little decoration. The original shutters still hang beside the old-fashioned, twelve-paned windows.

This old house has shared its hospitality with many of the great men who were in the area during the Revolutionary War. It witnessed and survived the Yankee occupation, and from all appearances this sturdy, well-constructed old building will have as many years ahead as it has had in the past.

After the McCreights, the James M. Smith family occupied the home. It is now the property of Mrs. W. M. Quattlebaum, a descendant of the Smiths, and the McCreights, who cherishes and cares for the old place which has remained in the same family since it was first built.

McCREIGHT HOUSE   XLIII

CALDWELL HOUSE

YONGUE — BONES — PALMER — ELLIOTT — CALDWELL

The CALDWELL HOUSE is one of the earlier cottage-type houses that were built in Winnsboro. Although similar to many others of the same period, it differs from them in its own unique architecture.

The main body of the house is rectangular, covered with a gently sloping gable roof. The roof of the house proper covers the porch which fronts it and is supported by four beautiful, fluted, round columns, two on either end. Jutting out from the porch is a gabled portico which covers the center portion. This is supported by four columns like those before mentioned, making eight columns in all across the front of the building and giving it a most impressive appearance. Plain picket bannisters enclose the porch, portico, and wide steps at the entrance. The step bannisters end against square newel posts, topped with acorn-designed caps. The floor level of this house is about four or five feet above the surface of the ground.

The Colonial door is set in a handsome frame decorated with sidelights and carved moldings. On either side of the entrance are two well-spaced windows flanked by handmade slatted shutters. A wing extends to the rear of the building. In the yard is an old kitchen with giant fireplaces, swinging cranes, and pot-racks.

Although this house is located in the heart of the town of Winnsboro, it was built in the order of a plantation house with a cotton gin (burned in the early 1900's) and other outbuildings that are necessary to plantation life. The interior is spacious and beautifully adorned with handsome doors, mantels, moldings, and trim. It is a splendid example of the better homes that were erected in Winnsboro in the early part of the nineteenth century.

The grounds are complementary to the building, well laid out and neatly kept. Large trees and quaint picket fences further enhance the beauty of the setting.

The CALDWELL HOUSE is on the corner of Zion and Hudson Streets and near historic MOUNT ZION SCHOOL. In 1834 the lot was owned by Mrs. Rebecca Yongue, who gave it to her daughter, Elizabeth P. Bones. The consideration was ". . . Natural love and affection to my daughter Elizabeth P. Bones . . ."

At that time Mrs. Yongue owned considerable property in this section of Winnsboro, including her home, now called the CATHCART HOUSE. Mrs. Bones built the CALDWELL HOUSE shortly after she received the lot and maintained it as her home until 1866 when she deeded it to Harriett W. Palmer. This is wording found in the deed, ". . . In consideration of my natural love and affection toward my grand-daughter Harriett Woodward Palmer, wife of Doctor John D. Palmer, and in further consideration of the care and attention which I am assured my said Grand-Daughter Harriett Woodward Palmer will bestow in providing for my natural wants and comforts during the infirmities of my old age . . ."

Harriett W. Palmer sold the property in 1884 to Henry L. Elliott, who in the same year gave it for ". . . love and affection to my daughter Marion E.

CALDWELL HOUSE

Caldwell . . ." The house was given to Mrs. Caldwell by her father as a wedding gift. The place is now owned by H. E. Caldwell, a son of Mrs. Marion E. Caldwell. He and his family reside here and keep the old house in excellent condition.

OLD METHODIST PARSONAGE

YONGUE — CATHCART — HAMMOND — DuBOSE — ST. JOHN'S CHURCH — McCAULEY — METHODIST CHURCH — WILLIAMS

The OLD METHODIST PARSONAGE on Zion Street ranks among the older Winnsboro homes. It is an attractive, small, cottage-type house, covered with a gable roof and fronted by a gabled porch. The original building consisted of four rooms and a hall on the first floor and two rooms and a hall on the second. The kitchen was in the rear.

This house has been enlarged by having a wing of several rooms added to the back of the structure. In the porch gable are small twin windows. The porch is supported by four hand-cut wooden columns and is enclosed with plain picket bannisters. It is built several feet above the ground and is entered by a flight of stone steps. The front door is of a plain Colonial design set in a paned frame surrounded by sidelights.

There is no record as to when the building was erected but, judging by early accounts it was probably built by the Yongues, who at one time owned considerable property in the area. The "Widow Yongue" deeded this place to her son, Alexander W. Yongue, who in 1840 sold it to Robert Cathcart.

From the Estate of Robert Cathcart the place was sold to J. B. Hammond in 1850. Later, at a sale by Sheriff R. C. Woodward in 1857, titles were taken by Theodore DuBose. At this time there is a skip in the chain of ownership. Mr. DuBose either sold or gave the little house to St. John's Episcopal Church for a rectory. In the years after the Confederate War his son, William Porcher DuBose, was rector of this church until he removed to Sewanee where he became one of the greatest educators of his day. In 1884 the church sold this property to Sallie F. McCauley, who in 1888 transferred it to her husband, D. J. McCauley.

The Methodist Episcopal Church, South, became the next owner in 1898, and from that time until 1957 it was used as the Methodist parsonage. Broadus B. Williams bought the little house from the church in 1957 and remodeled and restored it for his home.

A detailed description of this house and neighborhood is given in an article written for Harper's Magazine in 1910 by W. W. Lord, Jr., a son of Doctor Lord who was the Episcopal rector during the Federal invasion of Winnsboro. Doctor Lord and his family came to Winnsboro from Vicksburg, Mississippi, after it had fallen to the Union Army. The account is most complimentary of the people of the town and of their generosity to the family of the refugee clergyman.

When it was learned that the Northern Army was marching on to Winnsboro, Doctor Lord and the only medical doctor left in the town, an elderly man weighing over three hundred pounds, went out to meet the general

OLD METHODIST PARSONAGE

XLV

to ask that the village be spared from the torch and plundering. Young Lord stated that the departure of these gentlemen was most amusing, for the two men left in the portly physician's "dog-cart," of which the owner and driver occupied the entire seat and the dignified clergyman had to ride in the rear "box" usually reserved for canines.

When the Lords came to South Carolina, they brought their family silver and valuables with them from Vicksburg, where their treasures had been buried in a large, casket-like wooden box in the churchyard during the siege and occupation. Knowing from experience what was ahead for Winnsboro, Doctor Lord and his son spent a part of the night before the bummers arrived removing all the neatly piled wood from the woodhouse where, when empty, they placed the funereal-looking chest of valuables and restacked the wood around and over it.

The next day, when the Yankees arrived, an officer was quartered at the rectory, and a guard was placed there for protection of the property. After they left, the lady next door told the family that she was amused early one morning when she saw a neighbor's pig rooting around in the front yard and under the porch and steps of the rectory. Later the two men who were posted as guards saw the fresh dirt and assumed that treasure had been buried there during the night. They spent about two hours excitedly probing about and digging with their bayonets and bare hands in search of the nonexisting loot.

The young Federal officer who was quartered at the rectory was the man Doctor Lord implored and persuaded to remain in the town and round up the stragglers who were planning to burn and pillage after the army had departed.

The above episodes are but a part of the history and events that this little house has seen. It is still in excellent condition and will remain many years longer to bear witness to the historical parade of the grand old town.

ROBERT BRICE HOUSE
CATHCART — McMASTER — COAN — BRYSON — BRICE

The ROBERT BRICE HOUSE may be readily described as quaint, dignified, or homey, combined with a touch of elegance. It is in a perfect setting, surrounded by old neighbors of long standing, each unique in its own right and, with few exceptions, well over the century mark. This block and the neighborhood adjoining it are in all probability very much as they were when Sherman came to Winnsboro.

This is the "mosquito cottage" type of architecture but differs from others of the same type and period in and around Winnsboro. The thick masonry walls of the ground floor are like many others but the long, wide veranda differs by extending the full length across the front of the building and is covered by the graceful overhanging gable of the main body of the structure. Wide steps divide into two sets of narrower steps before reaching the ground. They are protected and decorated with wrought-iron bannisters, which are repeated on the front porch between the six supporting columns. Two enormous inside chimneys afford fireplaces to six of the rooms in the main body, which is covered with wide beaded siding.

ROBERT BRICE HOUSE

XLVI

The interior is spacious and is decorated with fine old mantels, beautiful trim and woodwork. The furnishings are in keeping with the house, with many fine old pieces that have been acquired through generations.

The earliest record of the place is a deed from James B. McCants, Commissioner in Equity for Fairfield County, to James and Richard Cathcart. It is dated November 6, 1849. In 1867 James and Richard Cathcart sold the house and lot to Doctor J. R. McMaster. Before this, the Cathcarts owned most of the property in the block. Evidently Doctor McMaster lived in this house for some time before he actually bought it. The place was later occupied by Mr. and Mrs. Coan and her brother, Tom McMaster, and became known as the COAN HOUSE. T. P. Bryson was the next owner.

It was purchased in recent years from the estate of Mrs. Bryson, by Mr. and Mrs. Robert Brice, who now reside there. They did an excellent job in renovating and restoring the place, which is now one of Winnsboro's more attractive old homes. The only changes on the exterior were in the front steps and the installation of the wrought-iron bannisters on the front porch and steps, which added greatly to the character and beauty of the old building.

HANAHAN HOUSE

ADGER — CATHCART — McMASTER — MARTIN — HANAHAN

The HANAHAN HOUSE at 100 Zion Street was built by a Mr. Adger, who sold it to Mr. Cathcart when he moved to his plantation home at Adger.

On June 15, 1844, Robert Cathcart conveyed the property to James Cathcart, Jr., for $1,000.00. In 1856 James Cathcart sold it for $2,500.00 to Dr. J. R. McMaster, who in 1860 conveyed it to Elizabeth B. McMaster for the same amount that he had paid Cathcart. The sum was to be paid by Hugh B. McMaster, her husband and trustee.

During the War Between the States the Hugh McMaster family lived in this house. At the time when Winnsboro was occupied, two small sons of this family had a pet game rooster. As Sherman's Army drew near, the little boys heard stories of how the Yankees destroyed all barnyard fowls and livestock. They swore to each other that the invaders would not harm their pet. As the smoke from the burning homes became heavier and the Confederate troops began evacuating the town, the children became more protective of their feathered friend and tied him to their bedpost, hiding him under the bed.

Before breakfast the next day the dreaded foes arrived. The children were still asleep when the soldiers came into their room. One of them found the cock and caught him. The little boys cried and pleaded with him not to take it away. To the pitiful pleas the trooper only grinned, wrung the fowl's neck, and threw the fluttering, bloody bird and its head into the bed with the small boys.

Needless to say, Creighton and Fleming McMaster never forgot the episode nor forgave the Yankees.

The old house in which this happened is a large, two-story building. Downstairs there are four large rooms, two on either side of the hall, which extends from the front to the back door. Between the front and back rooms are large chimneys, four feet thick, which afford fireplaces for each room. The staircase

XLVII

HANAHAN HOUSE

is on a side wall in the front hall and is open on up to the third floor. The kitchen was connected to the house by a runway. On the second floor the front rooms are large, with smaller ones to the rear. All of them open into each other and into the hall. The rooms on the third floor are large and ceiled with wide boards. A two-story porch extends almost the full width of the building.

After the war the property passed from the McMasters to J. F. Martin, from whose estate it was purchased in 1900 by Doctor Ralph Hannahan, Jr. It is now a well-kept, homey old place and is occupied by Miss Beck Hannahan.

MATTHEWS HOUSE
LAUGHLIN — MATTHEWS

THE MATTHEWS HOUSE is located on a large lot on the corner of Washington and Zion Streets. It has stood here for almost a century and a half. The house has been well cared for ever since it was built, and its charm has been enhanced by its age.

This is a large, two-story frame building, with big chimneys on either end, covered by a simple gable roof. The two-story gabled portico, with square wooden columns and unusual, saw-patterned bannisters, dresses the front. All the long, old-fashioned, small-paned windows are flanked with handmade, green slatted shutters hung on the original hardware.

The rooms and halls are spacious, with high ceilings and rather plain mantels and trim. The furnishings are well in keeping with the building, ranging from rare antique pieces to more recent furniture from several periods and generations that has been retained for comfort, sentiment, and beauty.

The high sawed-paling fence on its granite block base adds privacy and dignity to the property and is one of the attractive features of the old homestead. The gate is flanked by granite shafts that serve as the gateposts, and smaller granite fence posts support the palings.

The lot on which the house is built was purchased from John McCall by Charles Laughlin in 1824. The house was begun and finished during that year.

The Laughlins continued to own the property until 1870, at which time it was purchased by Mrs. Laura M. Matthews, in whose family it still remains. From Mrs. Matthews it passed to her daughter, Rachel R. Matthews, and from her to her brother, Palmer Matthews, Sr., whose widow and son, Palmer Matthews, Jr., and his family reside here now.

CARLISLE HOUSE
BUCHANAN — CARLISLE — MOBLEY — BRICE

Doctor James H. Carlisle has been acclaimed by historians as being one of South Carolina's most outstanding men. He was an educator, writer, and minister for many years, and before his death he became known as "Methodism's grand old man." During his long and useful life he taught and served

MATTHEWS HOUSE

XLVIII

in many places. At one time he was connected with Mount Zion College in Winnsboro and later with Wofford College in Spartanburg. He was there for so long and had such a dominant influence on the institution that his name and that of the college became synonymous. He also headed and directed publications for his church. He was born in Winnsboro in the year 1825. His birthplace is still a landmark on the corner of Washington and Zion Streets, 201 East Washington Street.

In the year 1819 John Buchanan, Sr., bought the lot on which the house is located, and several other lots, from Robert Means. The price of the lot was $100.00, and no mention is made of a house. In 1823 John Buchanan, Sr., willed the property to his niece, Mary Ann Carlisle, a daughter of his deceased brother, William Buchanan. Her husband was William Carlisle and they were the parents of Doctor James H. Carlisle and several other children. The following is taken from the Buchanan will: "I give and devise to my niece Mary Ann Carlisle all these lots or parcels of land situate in the Town of Winnsborough . . . (reserving for the use of the Methodist Church, twenty feet to be taken off the N. E. end of lot No. 102, and added to lot No. 115 on which the said Church stands). To the sole use and behoof of my said niece, Mary Ann Carlisle for and during the term of her natural life, and at her death, I give and devise the said last mentioned lots of land to the heirs of her body alive at my death, and to such as said Mary Ann Carlisle may have begotten of her body after my death, to them and their heirs forever. Provided nevertheless, and it is my will and intention that the said Mary Ann Carlisle, and her present or any future husband, shall have full power and authority to bargain, sell, alein, release and confirm to the Methodist Episcopal Church in the United States of America, all of the said lots of land last aforesaid described in fee simple should that Church at any time during the lifetime of the said Mary Ann Carlisle or her husband, desire to purchase, and the parties named agree on terms of Sale . . ."

A few years later the Carlisles planned to move to Alabama or Mississippi and petitioned the Court for a sale of the property, the proceeds to be invested either in land or Negroes in their new home.

The exact date and age of the house is not available but it is known and recorded that it was in existence and was improved by the Carlisles before they actually inherited the property. It is reputed to be one of the oldest homes in Winnsboro. Some sources state that it existed during Cornwallis' occupation of the town during the Revolution. The materials used in it and the methods of construction seem to bear this out.

Since the Carlisle family moved away, about 1835, several families have lived here. Mrs. Cattie Mobley and her family owned and occupied the house after the Confederate War. The house was not harmed during the Federal occupation.

Eugene Douglas Brice bought the property from W. D. Douglas, executor, in 1923. After the death of both Mr. and Mrs. Brice, the house passed to their children share and share alike. The place is now occupied by Misses Pauline, Maurice and Zelma Brice, their daughters.

It is a quaint, comfortable, and historic place and is still much as it has been for almost a century and a half. The only changes that have been made are the removal of a narrow hallway and the addition of a full second story.

CARLISLE HOUSE

XLIX

It is furnished with a number of rare and interesting antiques and heirlooms.

Doctor James H. Carlisle, aforementioned, married Margaret Brice but what her connection is with the present occupants of the home is not known.

CORNWALLIS HOUSE

BUCHANAN — HILLIARD — AIKEN & McCANTS — BOLICK STEVENSON — ROBINSON

The CORNWALLIS HOUSE is one of the oldest and most historic buildings in Winnsboro. By whom it was built or to whom it originally belonged cannot be ascertained. However, it is known that it is one of the buildings that was occupied by the British when Lord Cornwallis established his headquarters in Winnsboro. It is a locally accepted fact that this is the house in which the famous general resided during the occupation.

The house is built on a lot shaded with large old trees. The original portion of the house was built on the ground level and was two stories high. A wing and the third floor were later additions. This older portion of the house is enclosed with massive masonry walls and partitions that are coated with a hard plaster. The timber used in the framing is all oversized, and it is joined with mortises and pegs. The few nails used in its construction are hand-made. Inside stairs lead from the basement floor to the two floors above. Outside steps lead from the yard to the second-story porch. The first- and second-story porches are supported by columns. The lower porch is open but the upper piazza is enclosed with beautifully turned wooden bannisters.

All records of Fairfield prior to 1785 were kept in Camden District. Some of the Camden records were either lost or destroyed during the War Between the States so that now it is extremely difficult to go back any further. The first official record of this house is in 1797. At that time William McMorries, sheriff of Fairfield, deeded the place to Captain John Buchanan. This was the result of a Court action vs. Minor Winn, 1794, by Hugh Milling and Alexander Caldwell, executors of the estate of Alexander Millar, to recover a debt owed Alexander Millar. The judgment granted forty-two pounds sterling, plus expenses of two pounds, five shillings and six pence. The lots (including this house) were sold at public auction, and Captain John Buchanan was the highest bidder.

Captain Buchanan and his wife later resided here. Captain Buchanan was a distinguished soldier of the Revolution and a leading citizen of Fairfield. He was one of the first Americans to greet General de la Fayette when he arrived to assist in the struggle for American independence. Captain Buchanan and the French general became close friends, and Buchanan gave him one of his servants, a man named Fortune, to serve him during the war. After the Revolution, when la Fayette visited in this country he saw the Captain and Fortune again while he was in Columbia.

Captain John Buchanan owned much property in the town and throughout the county. Among his holdings was a tavern that was located on Congress Street almost directly behind this house. In 1807 he conveyed the tavern and some lots to his brother, Creighton Buchanan, but reserved the use of the well that was located on one of the lots for his use.

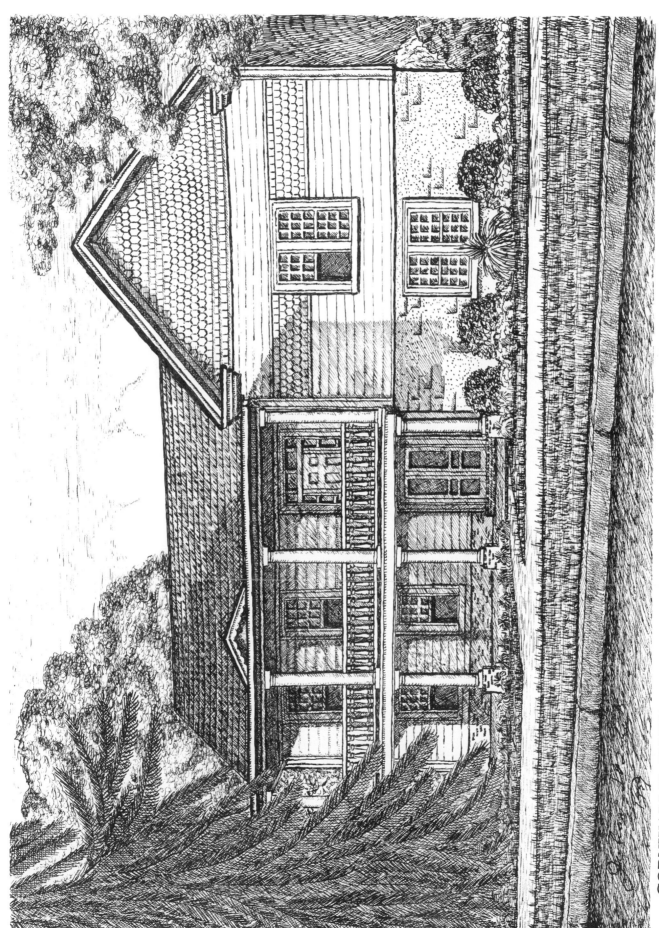

CORNWALLIS HOUSE

L

The Reverend James Jenkins was the first Methodist minister to preach in Winnsboro. While here he was entertained by Captain Buchanan and his wife. The Captain was not a church member but until that time he and Mrs. Buchanan had attended the Presbyterian Church. Mrs. Buchanan had relatives who were Methodist, and she had leanings toward that denomination herself. The Reverend Mr. Jenkins first preached in the Courthouse where the Presbyterian services were also held. The Presbyterian minister objected to Jenkins using the building. After that, the Methodist services were held in the Buchanans' home until the new Methodist Church was built in 1809. Captain Buchanan gave the lot for this and was instrumental in the actual construction of this, Winnsboro's first church building. He and his wife were among the charter members of the Methodist Church in Winnsboro.

At Captain Buchanan's death (1823) he willed the house in which he was living (the CORNWALLIS HOUSE) to his nephew, General John Buchanan. In 1862 the heirs of General John Buchanan sold the property to A. D. Hilliard, who at the time was living in the house.

In 1865 A. D. Hilliard disposed of the place to James R. Aiken and James B. McCants. The Levi M. Bolick family was living here at the time and later, in 1869, purchased the property from Aiken and McCants. It passed from Bolick to his daughter and only child, Elizabeth (Lizzie) B. Stevenson, who in 1909 sold it to J. Leonard Robinson.

The Levi Bolick family was living in the old house when Sherman's Army was in Winnsboro. When it was learned that the Yankees were approaching, the shutters were fastened and the doors bolted in hopes that the house would appear deserted and not be molested. The mother, the daughter, and two old servants did not even venture out for firewood, and when the supply was exhausted, they began burning the furniture in order to cook and keep warm. Two fine four-poster beds, tables, and chairs went up in the flames that warmed the frightened household.

In spite of all the precautions taken to make the place appear deserted, the house was broken into by the looters. The young daughter had a pair of pet Cornish hens that she treasured. When the bummers found them, the little girl begged the looters not to take away her hens. In response, the little birds were thrown into the air and the soldier and his companions shot at them with their pistols and left them dead in the yard.

This historic and beautiful old house is now occupied by the family of J. Roy Robinson, who inherited it from his father, J. Leonard Robinson, who acquired it more than a half century ago. It is a well-kept old landmark and is furnished with many fine old heirlooms, some of which are perhaps as old as the ancient building that houses them.

CATHCART HOUSE

YONGUE — McCLENAGHAN — CRAFTS — BRICE — CATHCART

One of Winnsboro's more handsome old mansions is the CATHCART HOUSE on Zion Street. From its beginning it has been in kind hands, and its refined dignity has never been subjected to misuse or neglect.

LI

CATHCART HOUSE

The stately residence sits well back from the street on a beautifully land-scaped lot. Boldly defined terraces with steps down to the lower levels add a touch of formality. Spacious green lawns shaded by carefully selected and placed trees and shrubs frame the house proper into a lovely picture.

It is a large building, constructed of brick which is covered with a time-mellowed tan cement plaster. The main portion is rectangular, covered with a gable roof, and fronted with two-story piazzas or galleries extending across the front of the house. Supporting each story are six hand-turned, solid, round columns, with plain picketed bannisters between them. This gives the building a majestic appearance.

The interior is spacious and elegant, just as would be expected. High ceilings, beautiful mantels and woodwork carry throughout the Colonial and early-American themes. In the house are handsome and priceless antiques that have been handed down for generations.

The lot on which the house is built is a part of the original Winn property that was acquired from Joseph Owen when the town was originally laid out. The home was built by Mrs. Rebecca Yongue or her husband in the late 1820's. Mrs. Yongue is sometimes referred to as "the widow Yongue." Her husband was known as "Parson Yongue."

In 1840 Mrs. Yongue conveyed the place to her son, Alexander Yongue, for $3,000.00. At the time of the transaction she was referred to as "a resident of Talladega County, Alabama." Alexander Yongue held the property until 1858, at which time he sold it to C. McClenaghan with the exception of a small plot in the garden where some of the Yongue children were buried.

George I. Crafts of Charleston bought the place three years later, in 1866, and held it until 1869 when he disposed of it to James A. Brice. The Brice family resided here until 1909, during which time it became known as the BRICE HOUSE. Janie K. Brice, the widow of J. A. Brice, sold it to John H. Cathcart. Mr. Cathcart and his family moved here from their country home near Adger, a few miles out of Winnsboro. Mr. Cathcart's widow lived in the stately old home until her death in 1961. It is now owned by the son of the Cathcarts, Doctor John H. Cathcart of Gaffney, South Carolina.

WYNN DEE

WINN — BRATTON — CATHCART

One of the most historic old homes in Winnsboro is a stately old house called WYNN DEE. Aside from being one of the oldest landmarks in the vicinity, it has always been the home of glamorous and prominent people who have ranked among Fairfield's great.

The land on which the building is located dates back to an original land grant from King George to one Joseph Owen. Owen came to South Carolina from Pennsylvania and settled in Fairfield in 1768. His lands were surveyed by Richard Winn, the man for whom Winnsboro was named. A few years

WYNN DEE

later Winn acquired the property, for in 1777 he gave the house and acreage as a wedding gift to his daughter Christina, who married Colonel William Bratton, a native of York County.

At the outbreak of the Confederate War WYNN DEE was the home of General John Bratton, Fairfield's ranking Confederate general, and his lovely wife, Betty DuBose, who was born and reared on nearby ROSELAND plantation. During the war several of the women of the Bratton and DuBose families refugeed at WYNN DEE. The troops looted the house and left the pantry bare. When they found a rusty old Revolutionary War sword in one of the trunks that they ransacked, they frightened the ladies of the house by telling them that since they had been caught concealing weapons, the house would have to be burned. An attempt was made to carry this out but the flames were successfully extinguished. Some of the troops rode their horses through the great hall and pulled down the original stairs that were in the center of the hallway. The base of the old newel post of these stairs is still visible in the floor.

WYNN DEE is a large and gracious house, in good taste but not pretentious. It is built of wood in the old "L"—shaped manner which was so generally used in the design of so many of the upcountry homes of this period. A wide, columned, one-story porch extends across the front of the building. The interior is ceiled with wide boards that run horizontally. The dados and trim were all done by hand and are quite handsome, particularly the Adam-type mantels, which are simply but pleasingly paneled up to the ceilings.

The small glass panes in the sidelights and arch of the entrance are of particular interest, alternating in circular and diamond patterns. The massive chimneys are another feature of the house. The bricks that were used in them were made in England, and they are laid in a Welch bond. In the basement is a cooling well. This was used in the old days as a storage place for foods and dairy products.

In the yard several of the old outbuildings are still in existence. The kitchen and well are of particular interest. Although they are no longer used for the purposes for which they were built, they are still a part of the landscape, remnants of the past that still add their share of charm to the old homestead.

The Cathcart family now owns and occupies WYNN DEE. Although family names have changed, the old house still shelters descendants of the Winns, Brattons, and DuBoses, for the Cathcarts are descendants of all the above families.

JOHNSON HOUSE

CRAWFORD — JOHNSON — JACKSON — TAFT — MARTIN — EGLESTON
ELLISON — FLENNIKEN — ASSOCIATE REFORMED
PRESBYTERIAN CHURCH — JOHNSON

The JOHNSON HOUSE on Liberty Street is outstanding in its serene, classic beauty. From the time that it was built it has been one of Winnsboro's finer homes.

This is a large, rectangular, two-and-one-half-story building, with a two-story wing extending to the rear. Two large inside chimneys come through the simple gable roof of the main structure. A smaller gable extends from the front of the roof covering the center section of the house which contains the front entrance, an impressive fanlighted frame trimmed and ornamented with hand-carved moldings.

The front door is repeated on the second story and opens onto an attractive balcony. In the porch gable is another repetition of the fanlights used over the doors. The front gable is supported by two tall, tapering columns and matching pilasters against the building. Tightly fitted tongue-and-grooved boards are used for covering between the pilasters instead of the standard clapboards that cover the rest of the building. The contrast in the use of these materials adds greatly to the decoration effect of the design.

Two large windows are on either side of the doors on both floors and are flanked with hand-made, green slatted shutters. On the right side of the building is a two-story veranda, supported by columns. Bannisters are used on each story and on the flat deck-type roof. The pattern of these wooden bannisters is the same used for the bannisters of the front balcony. In the ends of the main gable are handsome paladian windows.

The interior is spacious, refined, and hospitable. All the woodwork, trim, doors, and mantels are beautifully executed and give the large rooms that certain air of elegance that only the best of artistic craftsmen can accomplish.

The house is built rather low to the ground and close to the street but because of its size, height, and column arrangement the effect is pleasing. The front yard is enclosed with a low stone wall in keeping with the low foundation of the building.

Osmund Woodward sold the lot on which this house is built, along with several others, to John Crawford in 1833. In 1834 John Crawford sold to Samuel Johnson, who built the mansion about 1836-38.

The Johnson family continued to own the place until 1860. In that year John Adams and Rufus Porter, the heirs of David Johnson, sold the house and lot to Samuel Jackson at a rather low figure. Two years later, in 1862, Jackson disposed of the house at a much higher price. A. R. Taft of the city of Charleston was the purchaser. At that time the Confederate War was well under way, and many Charlestonians were leaving the coastal regions for the interior, fearing an attack on their city from land and sea. Soon after he bought the JOHNSON HOUSE, Mr. Taft transferred it to Serena Martin, an old friend. The Martins had been like parents to him; he named one of his sons for Mr. Martin. The Martins stayed here during the war and kept the property until 1871. Mr. Taft purchased another home in the vicinity of the JOHNSON HOUSE; in this other home his family lived during the war.

Mary Louise Egleston, the wife of DuBose Egleston, purchased the house in 1871. She kept it until 1874 and then sold to Robert H. Ellison, Jr.

During the same year it was purchased by D. R. Flenniken from Mr. Ellison. The Flenniken family kept the house for twenty years, until 1894, at which time it was sold to the trustees of the Associate Reformed Presbyterian Church in Winnsboro by Margaret M. Flenniken. The house then became known as the ASSOCIATE REFORMED PRESBYTERIAN MANSE for many years.

In 1946 Doctor Oliver Johnson, for many years the beloved pastor of the Associate Reformed Presbyterian Church and who had lived in the grand old house during his long pastorate, acquired the property from the church. Since that time it has become known as the JOHNSON HOUSE but still is referred to by old residents as the old A. R. P. MANSE. The original owner and builder of the house, Samuel Johnson, was no relation to the Oliver Johnson family.

The house is still one of Winnsboro's most beautiful old homes, and it is now occupied by the Oliver Johnson family, descendants of Doctor Johnson.

MOORE HOUSE

CAMPBELL — MURPHY — CAMPBELL — CRAWFORD — POTEAT
SMITH — McDOWELL — COPES — WINNSBORO BUILDING AND LOAN
TURNER — ELLIOTT — McCORLEY — MACKERELL — MOORE

This old house, once proud and fashionable, is suffering badly from neglect. It is located on the southern section of College Street and is not likely to be noticed by the casual visitor in seeking out the old homes of Winnsboro. Other smaller and inferior buildings have sprung up like mushrooms around it. In spite of this, once that it is discovered, a connoisseur will respect it and recognize the past dignity of the place.

Unlke most of the Winnsboro homes this house is built close to the ground level on the front. The main body is almost square, covered with a hipped roof, having outside chimneys on either end. The windows are large and well placed, with a large side-lighted doorway in the center of the building, opening upon the piazza and upstairs balcony. These porches are covered with a pleasing gable, supported by four round, solid wooden columns with hand-turned bannisters between them. Below it the roof of the piazza extends across the entire front of the house, the eaves out beyond the piazza floor. Originally six round columns on granite bases supported the roof but during some stage of remodeling the center columns were removed and the four remaining were cut off and rested upon square brick pillars.

The old house was built prior to 1843 when the first sale on record by Sheriff Richard Woodward for George Murphy was made to David Campbell. This place was probably owned and built by Campbell prior to this sale, for he owned most of the other property in the block surrounding it.

In 1856 Campbell sold the house and lot to Robert Crawford; in the next year Crawford passed title to Jacob Poteat, who remained in possession until 1870 when it was sold by Sheriff DuVall to R. B. Smith. In 1872 it passed from Smith to W. John McDowell. In 1874 the property changed hands again, Joel Copes being the purchaser. The Winnsboro Building and Loan Association took it over in 1878, then in 1879 disposed of it to Dr. W. K. Turner. At the same time, Dr. Turner bought an additional footage from Adeline Poteat. The Turners resided here for a number of years and then moved to Mrs. Turner's plantation in the Lebanon section. In 1886 Mrs. E. M. Turner sold the house to H. L. Elliott, who held it until 1901 when he sold to Mary A. McCarley. In 1904 it was sold again to Mary E. Mackerell. In 1912 Mary Jane Moore purchased the many-times-sold property and continued to own it for the remainder of her life. The house is now the property of Mrs. Bessie Moore McMaster (Mrs. Hugh B.), a niece of Miss Mary Jane Moore.

LIII

JOHNSON HOUSE

LONG HOUSE

McCAULE — BUCHANAN — THOMAS — AIKEN — DeTREVILLE
RABB — KETCHIN — LONG

The LONG HOUSE is one of Winnsboro's quaint, cottage-type homes. Its location is attractive, with the building sitting well back from the street on a high, sloping corner lot that has quarried-granite curbs around it on the sides facing streets. The walk entrance and the front corners are marked with low, pointed granite posts. Rock steps lead up to the walk, bordered with giant trees on either side. During the past several years deterioration and storms have made it necessary to remove several of these ancient sentinels.

The house is a modest one-and-one-half story, rectangular building with a gable roof and two massive inside chimneys. Another gable extends from the roof on the front and covers a porch supported by four slender columns. Double doors open from the porch into the hallway.

On the interior the woodwork, doors, and trim are very simple, almost primitive. The floor plan is a little unusual in that the hall does not extend through the building. It is wide and almost square, with two front rooms on either side. In the rear of the hall a cased opening connects with the large dining room of which two rear doors open into the kitchen and the back porch. A narrow stairway leads from the dining room to the hall and three rooms on the second story. Under the stair a door opens into a back room on the first floor.

The lot on which the house is situated originally belonged to Thomas McCaule, one of the founders and first principal of Mount Zion College. John and Creighton Buchanan acquired this and other lots at a sheriff's sale in 1811.

In 1818 Creighton Buchanan sold his interest to his brother John. Some time after this, the house was built. It is presumed that Mrs. Nancy Buchanan, sister-in-law of Captain John and Creighton Buchanan, occupied the house, for provisions were made for her in the will of Captain John Buchanan which said: ". . . also the lots of land in the said town of Winnsboro whereon I now live, with all the houses, tenements, and appurtenances thereto belonging, to him and his heirs forever; excepting and reserving the northeast half of the lot, parcel, or piece of land, on which stands the house wherein my sister-in-law, Nancy Buchanan during . . . her natural life and after death, or when she shall think proper to relinquish her claim to the said premises, I give and devise . . . the said lot of land unto my nephew John Buchanan."

In 1862 the heirs of General John Buchanan sold the house and lot to Stephen Thomas of the city of Charleston. At the time of this sale the place was occupied by James Hendrix. Stephen Thomas was a wealthy man. He was an importer and jeweler. His family refugeed in Winnsboro during the War Between the States.

Mr. Thomas continued to own this property until 1871, at which time he sold it to James R. Aiken, who in the same year transferred it to James Copes, trustee for James C. and Richard H. DeTreville "lately of the City of Charleston but now of Winnsboro—" It is assumed that these young men were minors

LIV

MOORE HOUSE

who were students at Mount Zion College. In 1874 they disposed of the property to Elvesa Rabb.

In 1884 William Rabb and Anna E. Brown (nee Rabb) passed title to Hattie M. Ketchin. The Ketchin family lived here for a great number of years, and the place became known as the KETCHIN HOUSE. Later it was rented to tenants until 1919 when it was purchased by Mrs. Julia S. Stevenson Long.

Mrs. Long was the widow of William S. Stevenson and of Captain James I. Long. She and Mr. Stevenson lived in the Lebanon section and reared a large family, two sons and nine daughters. Before the death of Mr. Stevenson the family moved to Winnsboro so that the younger children would have better educational advantages.

One of the daughters, Willie, married George Long. Several years after the passing of Mr. Stevenson his widow married Captain Long, the father of George. They lived at the Long plantation near Adger until Captain Long's death. In the meantime the daughter had also become a widow. Mrs. Julia S. Long bought the KETCHIN HOUSE and she, her daughter, and little granddaughter came there to live. The old house is still a part of her estate, and her two youngest daughters now reside there.

Mrs. Julia S. Long was a remarkable woman. Aside from successfully rearing her large family, she was a friend to anyone in need. She enjoyed company and her table always had room for one more. She was a woman who refused to gossip. Not only did she refrain from this human weakness but also she refused to listen by saying, "What a pity," "Disgraceful, say no more!" or "Poor thing," and then she would change the subject.

Her home was a haven for widowed daughters, grandchildren, and relatives who happened to be in town. Later the large family of children, grand-children, great-grandchildren, and great-great-grandchildren all looked forward to Mother's Day and other holidays when the family would gather at "Gran'ma's House."

Mrs. Long lived to be ninety-two years old, and at the time of her passing she was Winnsboro's oldest resident.

WILLINGHAM HOUSE

WHITEHOUSE — ROACH — BULGIN — DURPHREY — JOHNSON
CATHCART — CATHCART INVESTMENTS — McMASTER
WILLINGHAM — FREEMAN

The house on the corner of College and Vanderhorst Streets may well be one of the oldest in Winnsboro. Tradition places it in the pre-Revolutionary period, having been occupied by British soldiers during Cornwallis' stay in the town. Actual records go back to 1793, at which time it was sold by Thompson Whitehouse and William Roach to James Bulgin for 500 pounds sterling (the equivalent of $2,435.00). When it was built or how long White-house and Roach had owned it before the sale to Bulgin is not known but it easily may have been in use during the British occupation, which was less than ten years before the date of the sale.

LV

LONG HOUSE

From Bulgin it passed to William Durphrey of Rowan County, North Carolina, who in 1809 sold it to Samuel Johnson, merchant, for only $600.00. Johnson remained in possession of the property until late 1819 or 1820 when it was purchased by Robert Cathcart for $2,000.00. This old house remained in the Cathcart family for almost one hundred years.

The next deed on record was from James B. McCants, commissioner of equity of Equity Court, to James and Richard Cathcart. The price then was $1,500.00, and a right-of-way was reserved for the Charlotte and South Carolina Railroad Company. In 1859 Richard Cathcart sold his interest to James Cathcart, who during the next year, 1860, sold the property to Charles Cathcart for $1,800.00.

Charles Cathcart and his wife, Sarah Blain Cathcart, reared their family in this old house. Charles was not a young man when he married but he left a rather large family — James R., Andrew B., John S., Thomas M., and Charles Erving. Charles Cathcart came with his parents from County Antrim, Ireland. There were seven children in this family.

During the Union occupation of Winnsboro several homes that were in the block with this old house were burned — Doctor Boyleston's residence, the Millers', and John H. Cathcart's. The Alex Chambers' house was spared but the cotton stored in the rear of the Charles Cathcart house was fired "and by great exertions his house and that of Mrs. McCants was spared."

The Cathcart family lived here until after the death of Mr. and Mrs. Cathcart. It was then occupied by Mr. and Mrs. Dick Robinson. Until 1918 it remained in the Cathcart family; then it was sold to S. R. McMaster. At that time Mr. McMaster sold the house to Mr. Willingham who had the building removed to its present location on the corner of College and Vanderhorst Streets. The new location was about two blocks from the original site on Congress Street where Ruff Motor Company is now located.

This was a rather large building and when it was moved, it attracted much attention. The front was moved first and the rear wing, which had been severed from the main body, was brought down later.

In the renovation and remodeling after the "move" very little was changed but the general appearance of the house was greatly altered. In the original setting it rested on a high foundation and was entered by a flight of broad steps leading up to the long, wide piazza that extended across the entire front of the house. Now the building sits rather low to the ground level, and a two-story porch covers the front.

The Willinghams lived in the old house for a number of years, and it became known in Winnsboro as the WILLINGHAM HOUSE. In recent years it was purchased by Mrs. C. C. Freeman, who now makes it her home. The place is well kept and should be remembered as one of the original Winnsboro homes.

TIMMS HOUSE
LEMMON — BREARLY — DURHAM — BOGGS — COPES —TIMMS — DOVE

The TIMMS HOUSE is on the corner of College and Vanderhorst Streets. It is an imposing old home, built along simple, Colonial lines. The main body is a rectangle, containing two rooms and a hall on each of the two

LVI

WILLINGHAM HOUSE

floors, with a large chimney at one end and another near the center where the rear wing joins the main structure. The rear wing contains five rooms and an upstairs and downstairs porch. Covering the entrance, in the center of the front of the building, is a gable supported by four large square columns on granite bases resting on the front terrace or porch. Over the entrance door is a balcony. This is built in front of the door opening into the upstairs hall. (Originally this front gable was a two-story portico.)

The interior woodwork is simple but well executed. The rooms are almost square, and the ceilings are not so high as in many of the houses of this period.

The lot on which the house is built adjoins the property of the old Associate Reformed Presbyterian Church. The cemetery is still used but the church was moved to another location.

The exact age of the house is not known but it was built by James Lemmon some time between 1824 and 1836. The lot on which it stands was bought, along with several others, by James Lemmon in 1824. In 1836 James Lemmon sold ". . . a part of two lots . . . Nos. 179 — 178 . . . facing College Street one hundred and twenty-eight feet . . ." to William Brearly. Judging by the price paid by Brearly, there must have been a house on the lot. Mr. Lemmon was an extensive landowner, an excellent builder and cabinetmaker, and a successful planter and owner of several large plantations. The purchaser of the property, the Reverend Mr. Brearly, was pastor at Zion Presbyterian Church. He was a young man, an excellent preacher and pastor, and an organizer who was extremely popular while he was in Winnsboro.

Between 1836 and 1850 the house became the property of John W. Durham but no deed of the transaction is recorded. In 1850 John W. Durham sold the house and lot to the Reverend Mr. Boggs. In this deed Durham states ". . . on which I formerly lived."

The Reverend Mr. Boggs was a Presbyterian minister who served Zion Church for many years after 1844. He was a highly respected and well-educated gentleman who was born in India, a son of missionary parents. While living here, he taught a private primary school. In fairly recent years, during a renovation of the house, several well-seasoned switches were found behind the ceiling in one of the walls. Some of the old residents stated that the switches must have been left there by Mr. Boggs, who during his time often stated that he did not adhere to the old adage, "spare the rod and spoil the child."

In 1869 the place was purchased by Frederick Copes of the city of Charleston. In 1877 he sold it to Savilla C. (Die) Timms. Since that time it has been owned by her family and for most of that time occupied by them, except for a period in the early 1900's when Mrs. Julia S. Stevenson lived there. When she occupied the house, it was owned by her son-in-law, Andrew C. Timms.

Andrew Timms and his wife moved into the house later and spent the rest of their lives in the old home where he, his daughter, and his grandchildren were born and where he and Mrs. Timms celebrated their Golden Anniversary. This couple will long be remembered by their family connections and friends for their gracious hospitality and gentle personalities.

TIMMS HOUSE

LVII

This time-mellowed home is now owned and lived in by Mr. and Mrs. Fitz Dove and their family. Mrs. Dove is the former Marjorie C. Timms, a granddaughter of the former owner, Savilla Timms. Marjorie Dove is the only child of the Andrew Timms and a descendant of James Lemmon, who built the house.

GLADDEN HOUSE

LEMMON — JONES — GORDON — MAHON — ELDER — CATHCART NICKLES — BROWN — GLADDEN — STEVENSON — DOUGLASS

The GLADDEN HOUSE, as it has been called for so many years, is located on College Street. In its original setting it was a picturesque little cottage. Its small, gabled porch sat almost on the sidewalk and was entered by a set of steps on each end. The steps on the side facing Vanderhorst Street led down to the garden, which was enclosed behind a neat, white picket fence. The garden was formally planted with rose bushes, boxwoods, and bulbs, laid out in geometrical patterns and edged with bricks. Tall, colorful hollyhocks grew close to the house on each side.

The house itself is a simple rectangle, with a chimney at one end (originally there were two, one on each end of the building). The cornice below the gable roof is deep and is decorated with a simple mold. The porch gable, supported by four graceful, square columns, juts out from the center of the portico on the front. Long, narrow doors with one long, arched-top glass panel in each are set in an unornamented frame. Hand-turned bannisters are between the columns on either side of the steps (originally they enclosed the front leaving the sides open for the steps). Four well-proportioned and pleasingly spaced windows are on the front.

In 1839 James Lemmon sold this lot, which is really a part of two, to John W. Jones, in August. In September Jones sold it at a considerable profit to Thomas Gordon. There is no record of when Gordon gave title of ownership to the next owners, John D. Mahon and his wife Rebecca. The house was built some time between 1839 and 1860 by either Gordon or Mahon. In 1860 the Mahons sold the place to Francis Elder.

Francis Elder sold the house to John H. Cathcart in 1862. Some time during the Mahon, Elder, or Cathcart ownership, Hugh McMaster and his family moved into Winnsboro from the country and resided here until they went to what is now known as the HANAHAN HOUSE on Zion Street. This was in the 1850's or 1860's, before the Confederate War ended.

After the McMasters moved out, Samuel Cathcart, a brother of John H., and his family resided here. Mrs. H. E. Ketchin, who died recently at the age of ninety-four, was born in this house, and her family lived here for a number of years when she was a child. Mrs. Ketchin was a daughter of Samuel Cathcart.

In 1875 Samuel Cathcart, commissioner for the estate of John H. Cathcart, sold the place to J. L. Nickles. Here there is another gap in the title chain, for in 1887 A. Walker Brown sold the property to Sarah M. Gladden. The

GLADDEN HOUSE

LVIII

Gladden family lived here, and it became known as the GLADDEN HOUSE. Many residents of Winnsboro remember Mrs. Gladden, a loveable little lady, well advanced in years, who loved her garden and flowers and delighted in telling stories of the Revolutionary and Confederate Wars to the neighborhood children, who were always her eager and attentive listeners.

After Mrs. Gladden's death the Ernest Stevenson family occupied the house for many years, and it is still sometimes referred to as the STEVENSON HOUSE.

In recent years the place was purchased by John Douglass. He had the building moved back from the street and renovated it throughout. It is now an attractive, modern little house with a great deal of charm and appeal, painted Colonial yellow and trimmed with white.

STEVENSON HOUSE

HARRISON — McCREIGHT — BEARD — LEMMON — CAMPBELL ELLIOTT — LANDECKER — STEVENSON

The STEVENSON HOUSE on College Street is a quaint little cottage, built very close to the sidewalk. The lines of the building are completely plain and simple. The main body of the building is rectangular, covered with a gable roof, facing the street in a lengthwise position. One large inside chimney (far off-center) affords fireplaces for two of the rooms. A low, gabled portico with two supporting columns (also off-center), fronts the house. Steps enter it from either end, and the space between the columns is enclosed with plain picketed bannisters and a hand-turned rail. The doorway, too, is off-center, on the right of the portico. A kitchen wing and a porch extend to the rear.

This little house was originally located on the corner where the ELLIOTT or SITGREAVES HOUSE now stands. At the time that the house on the corner was built, this little building was rolled to the rear of the lot and faced on College Street. The first deed on record referring to this house was from Reuben Harrison to William McCreight in which it was mentioned as, ". . . where David Campbell formerly lived . . ."

McCreight held the property until 1814 when he sold to Cornelius Beard. At the time of the sale Beard was living in the house. The next owner was Robert Cathcart, who held it from June until December 1824, at which time he conveyed title to James Lemmon. James Lemmon sold the place to John Campbell in 1833. It was during his ownership that the older house was moved back and faced on College Street, leaving the corner on Congress for the large, new house.

In 1855 William Campbell sold both places to James Elliott and James McKinney Elliott. James Elliott, the father of James McKinney Elliott, resided in the smaller house. In 1890 James McKinney Elliott cut off this house and portion of the lot and transferred it to Laura McCants, Sallie M. Douglass, and James G. McCants. One month later the above-mentioned parties deeded it back to his wife, Margaret Anne Elliott, who owned it until 1897 when she sold it to Mary E. Landecker. During this time the house was enlarged.

STEVENSON HOUSE

LVIX

The Landeckers lived in the house until the early 1900's and were followed by the family of John B. Stevenson. Mrs. Alva Gladney Stevenson, the widow of John B., later bought the property and occupied it until her death in the 1930's. It was during this period that it became known as the STEVENSON HOUSE. After her passing it was purchased by Mrs. Maymie Wier Stevenson of the New Hope section, who was auditor of Fairfield County for many years, until her retirement. Mrs. Stevenson and her daughter now reside in the comfortable little house, surrounded by heirlooms brought with them from their country home.

McDONALD HOUSE
JORDAN — MATTHEWS — McMASTER — KENNERLY — McDONALD

This is one of the most attractive and best-preserved of the ante-bellum houses or cottages (as this type of architecture was called) that were so popular in Winnsboro and throughout the county for such a long time; some of these houses were built in the early 1800's, and they were still being constructed at the time of the War Between the States.

At first glance all these houses bear a striking similarity but each of them has an individual charm and differences reflecting the needs and tastes of the builder. The fluted columns of the portico and the triple windows in the two front rooms are unique to this particular building. On the interior a well-proportioned hall extends through the center of the house, with the stairway rising from the rear of the hall. Four spacious rooms are on the first floor in the main body of the house, with an additional room in the right wing on the rear, which also includes a porch. Upstairs are two most attractive rooms on either side of a small hallway. In these rooms inside chimneys pass through them in the center. Throughout the house the woodwork, trim, and mantels are typical of the era and are unusually well executed.

The lot on which this house is located was at one time a part of the Mount Zion College property. In 1850 Thomas Jordan purchased the three acres for $1,300.00. During the same year he built the house on its northeast corner. On the Congress Street corner he had his shop and carriage factory.

In 1898 Mary E. Creight, W. Glover Jordan, Nannie J. Jordan, Belle Des-Portes, Frances E. Jordan widow of Thomas M. Jordan, sold this house to John P. Matthews. R. H. McMaster (Colonel) bought the place in 1900 for his mother, who lived here until her death. Her daughter, Rachel Mc-Master Kennerly, acquired the individual interests of her brothers and sisters in 1920. She lived here for a long period, and the place became known as the KENNERLY HOUSE. In 1940 it became the property of Mrs. Kennerly's daughter, Sarah Law Kennerly, who sold it in 1950 to Charles E. McDonald.

The McDonalds have restored and renovated the old house completely, making it a much more attractive place than it was even when it was new. The beautiful, time-mellowed old flooring has been refinished, as have the doors, accenting the lustre of the natural wood and giving it a beauty that can only be acquired with age. The fireplaces, which had been reduced to accommodate coal-burning grates, have been reopened to their original sizes and now show off the finely designed mantels to the best advantage.

LX

McDONALD HOUSE

Dormer windows were added to the upstairs rooms to provide better lighting and more comfort. They accentuate the quaintness of the little building. Old brick steps with plain picketed rails replace the old stone steps and buttresses that were additions during a former remodeling and not in keeping with the place. The newel posts for the present rails are topped with an acorn design.

Wallpaper and paneling were carefully chosen for the decoration of the interior; period chandeliers were installed in the ceilings, all blending perfectly and affording an authentic background for the McDonalds' handsome antique furniture, portraits, and heirlooms.

PART III

LEBANON
and
NEW HOPE

LEBANON

by

ESTELLE STEVENSON B. DILL

One of the oldest settled sections of Fairfield County is in the area west of Winnsboro called LEBANON. The main roads through the community are the old Chester Road and the Newberry Highway. This is a rolling, hilly country watered by many springs and small streams, the largest of which is Little River. Originally these hills were thickly forested with pines and cedars. Later, when cotton became king, and the plantation system domineered, the forests were cleared and the hills and valleys were transformed into snowy fields of cotton. The people of the area have now reverted to cattle and sheep raising and to forest products. The old cotton fields have disappeared and the hills are again covered with lush, green, pine forests. The valleys and meadows produce fine grasses and grain for many herds of cattle and sheep that feed upon them.

In the days before the settlement of the country Indians hunted in the vicinity of LEBANON and at times made their temporary homes here. The remains of an old Indian cemetery is still on the lands of W. K. Turner near Little River. Arrowheads and other relics of this bygone civilization are often found in the Jackson Creek area of the community.

Deer, rabbits, squirrels, reccoons, opossums, bobcats, occasional wolves and mountain lions roamed these woods in the days past. McMaster's HISTORY OF FAIRFIELD COUNTY refers to the killing of an elk near Winn's Bridge (now Bell's Bridge), the antlers of which were presented to an English nobleman. Birds have always been here in abundance. In the ante-bellum days and up until after the turn of this century quail hunts were sporting social events for the young people of the neighborhood. On these hunts nets were carried by men, who, when the dogs found the birds, surrounded the area with them and the hunters on horseback would drive the birds into the nets where they were captured without having been shot. Another method was to use a cast net from horseback. Whole coveys were taken with these methods and since then game laws have banned this type of hunting.

Pioneers began coming to LEBANON in the 1740's. A Mr. Howell was among the first. He established a ranch called a "cow pen" on Little River, near Winn's Bridge. This was a similar establishment to that of Thomas Nightingale's, the first settler in the county. Howell came a few years after Nightingale and later these "cow pens" became permanent settlements. Some of the men engaged in these enterprises were rough and lawless and in the years that followed they had to be controlled by the Regulators.

Before the Revolution a number of Scotch-Irish emigrants came into this section direct from Ireland and Virginia. Their community centered around Jackson Creek Church which was founded by them. They were honest, hardworking, and thrifty and soon ranked among the leaders of the district. Among the families of this group were the Moores, Tinklers, Pauls, Wilsons, McMullens, Johnsons, Gladneys, Buchanans, Millings, Winns, Martins, Bells, and Phillips.

[167]

At the outbreak of the Revolutionary War these people were divided. They did not want to fight against their neighbors and neither did they want to be ingrates to the king who had made their new homes possible. This attitude of indecision was abruptly ended after the nearby Moberly's Meeting House fracas. After that, with the exception of the Phillips brothers, their entire interests and efforts were with the Colonies.

After the war the people of LEBANON prospered and multiplied. Many new settlers came into the community from elsewhere in America and another surge from Ireland during the 1780's and the 1790's. Among these families were the Turners, Stevensons, Brices, Camacks, Hardens, Kennedys, Clarks, and Herrons. It was during this period that the old stone church was built. The stonecutter who supervised this built other stone houses in the community. Two of them, the old MANSE and the BUCHANAN or HARDEN HOUSE still remain.

With the turn of the century larger and finer homes dotted the area, several of which are still standing. During this period and until after the Confederate War the fortunes of community increased, based on cotton. The emigrants soon became a part of the planter class, buying slaves and land, and more slaves and more land. When the war clouds gathered they were, with two exceptions, strong secessionists and Confederates. The two referred to were Pacifists who later espoused the Confederacy. Some of the families who were in the community during the war were the Pauls, McMullens, Stewarts, Stuarts, Stevensons, Gladneys, Millings, Aikens, Martins, Bells, Lemmons, Jordans, Turners, Brices, Camacks, Hardens, Harrises, Bolicks, Kennedys, Clarks, Popes, Herrons, and Whites.

During the war except in isolated instances the Negroes were faithful and loyal. Until the latter years of the conflict life went on as usual except for the absences of loved ones and the scarcity of manufactured and imported articles that had been cut off by the blockade. Clothing and shoes were among the scarce items. One planter in the community was so depressed over his Negroes having to go without shoes in the cold winter, with only rags to protect their frostbitten feet, that he took his own life rather than see his people suffer.

When Sherman's Army invaded Fairfield LEBANON was looted and some of the homes were burned. The plantation house of the Widow Brice was fired not knowing that her two small children were in the building asleep. When Aunt Camellia, the nurse, saw the smoke and knowing that they were in the burning house she rushed into the building at the risk of her own life, threw a quilt over her head and took a frightened child in each arm and brought them to safety. This house was about a mile from the present Lebanon Church. Another home, belonging to the Gladney family, farther up the road and nearer the church site was also burned. On the Old Chester Road the large old Tinkler house or "Post House" was sacked and destroyed. For years after the blackened chimneys remained as reminders of those horrible days behind the impressive old "Tinkler Gates." In the same vicinity but across the road James Stevenson's big brick home was looted and burned. The family was not on the place at the time. The cook's house in the back yard by some miracle was not consumed and after returning from the war a bachelor son, Hugh Stevenson, renovated it and used it as his home. For many years

[168]

to follow the bricks from this grand old house were carted away and used for foundations and chimneys in other homes that were built in the community.

After the war, in the Reconstruction period which followed, LEBANON had its share of hardships and tragedies. A scalawag was hung on the branch of a large oak in front of the present Earl Stevenson house and varied ghost stories of this sinister event still haunt the place.

On the road to Winnsboro from the old Jackson Creek Church a young Confederate veteran rode down and shot a former slave of his uncle's who had insulted the old man when he was ordered to leave the plantation on which he was a troublemaker and a member of the "Carpetbag Militia." In the same vicinity was the spot where the men of the community met to deal justice to culprits whose evil deeds were upheld by the Carpetbaggers who had taken over the government. The leader of the men of LEBANON was James Pringle Macfie, a former Confederate officer, who has now become a hero and legend of the county. It was due to his efforts that the Carpetbaggers and Negro Militia were discouraged from using their "drill ground" and terrorizing the neighborhood.

There is a hill near the present McClintock home where several Yankee stragglers were shot and later buried. Older citizens of the neighborhood still refer to this as the "Yankee Grave Hill" and in past years, after rains, occasional brass buttons from the long decayed uniforms of these unfortunate men have been found. Needless to say, this is a favorite spot for local ghost stories.

Not many years ago a giant pine was cut near the old stone church where the "Reconstruction Courts" were held. When it was being sawed for boards a great number of bullets were found imbedded into the wood. According to one resident some of these bullet-riddled boards are still in the community where they are treasured souveniers.

After the war several private primary schools were in the LEBANON community, the heads of families paying the teachers, furnishing room and board if necessary, and the school building. One of these was called the "Jane Turner School" deriving the name from the location. Another was the Manse Academy where the children attended classes in the Manse which was unoccupied for a number of years.

The first school under the public school system was known as the "Dave Stevenson School" and was located on his plantation near the Lebanon Church and the old post office which was called "Stevenson."

LEBANON has always been a pleasant place in which to live being noted for its hospitality, fine stock, and beautiful girls. The last mentioned became internationally known a few years ago when a Lebanon-bred daughter, Miriam Stevenson, became "Miss Universe." She is but an example of the beautiful daughters of old LEBANON who came before her and of those who will follow.

CLOWNEY PLACE

JORDAN — KIRKPATRICK — CAIN — CLOWNEY

One of the most stately old homes in the county is the old CLOWNEY PLACE. It is prominently located near the Newberry Highway. The house crowns a rolling hill and stands out beautifully against a landscape of green forests, fertile pastures, and ponds. The house proper is of pure colonial design, well built and handsomely adorned.

The main body is slightly rectangular but gives the appearance of being almost square with a wing extending to the rear. It is a two and a half story structure resting about three feet above the ground level, covered with a gable roof and fronted by tall columns supporting the gable extending over the porch or terrace. Massive inside chimneys afford fireplaces for the four large rooms on each floor and the two attic or third story rooms. Large, wide hallways with graceful stairs rising from them are in the center of the building on both of the main floors. The windows and doors are set in slightly gabled frames which gives the house a distinctive air of elegance. Spacious green lawns surround the building and set off the well kept driveway.

The exact age of the house is not known but it is definitely not one of the oldest although it has passed its century mark. Construction on this building was begun before the War Between the States but it was not finished nor lived in until afterwards when Mr. Jordan, who built a similar home in Winnsboro, had it completed by a talented Negro carpenter. He supervised the work meticulously and when the workmanship did not come up to his standards nor look to suit him he had it ripped out and redone. When the house was complete the Jordans made it the seat of one of the largest cotton plantations in the area. Fine horses and cattle were also raised on the place.

The house and plantation was sold by the Jordan Estate to Walker Kirkpatrick, an enterprising young planter from York County. He lived here for a number of years and then moved into Winnsboro where he went into business later selling the plantation to Doctor Cain of Columbia. Dr. Cain used the house as a summer residence. He was quite a speculator and in the early 1900's sold the place to Brice Clowney, a bachelor, who lived here until his death. The place passed from him to his younger brother, William C. Clowney, who now lives here with his family and operates a large dairy and cattle farm.

LXI

CLOWNEY PLACE

HARDEN PLACE

BUCHANAN — PHILLIPS — HARDEN

The HARDEN PLACE is located on a country road branching off from the Newberry Highway and continuing in the direction of old Jackson Creek Church. It sits on a hill and is shaded by tall old trees. The site is in a rather out-of-the-way place. This unoccupied old stone building with shuttered and gaping open windows and decaying stoop and porches is somewhat of an eeirie place. Ghosts and spirits of the past might well be hovering in and around the desolate old building.

In spite of neglect and disuse it is still sturdy in appearance and its thick stone walls stand square as though defying time and the elements. The building is covered with a hipped roof and on either end and built into the walls are giant chimneys.

This is one of the oldest and most historic old buildings in the community. It was erected about the same time or a little earlier than the Jackson Creek Church, the same stone cutter constructed both buildings. At the time of the Revolutionary War this place was the home of Captain John Buchanan, one of Fairfield's outstanding Revolutionary Heroes. He and his wife and other members of their families occupied the house until they moved into Winnsboro. At that time his friend, though a former Tory, John Phillips, moved in and lived here for a number of years.

Phillips was respected and esteemed by his neighbors in spite of their differences in political views. It must also be recalled that due to his and his brother's intercession with Lord Cornwallis on behalf of a number of captured Fairfield patriots that the lives of these prisoners were spared.

After the 1820's the Harden family occupied the house and it became known as the HARDEN PLACE. Since that time it has remained in the possession of that family.

Mr. Jeff Harden who once lived here came to an untimely and tragic death in 1894. He was tusselling in his buggy with a friend when he lost his balance and fell. In falling he became entangled in the reins and harness and was dragged to his death before the horse could be stopped.

Another member of this family, Mrs. Alice (Gladney) Harden will long be remembered by the other residents of this section with affection. She was one of the few nurses in the community. Her kindnesses and gentle care of the sick will not be forgotten by those who knew her.

LXII

HARDEN PLACE

BOLICK PLACE

CLARK — BOLICK — STEVENSON — HERBERT

Now delapidated and falling apart, this old house at one time the well-kept seat of a prosperous cotton plantation. It is built along the lines used in the design of so many of the Fairfield homes both in town and in the country during the early 1800's. The main body of the building is rectangular with large inside chimneys and it is covered with a gable roof. A gabled portico supported by wooden columns covers a major portion of the front. In the portico gable is a large center window flanked by sidelights. The double doors at the entrance are set in an attractive frame surrounded with glass panes. A long wing extended to the rear of the house and on one side was fronted with a long, columned porch. This wing contained a large dining room, kitchen, and store-room. In recent years it fell into bad repair and since then has been taken down.

The interior woodwork was well designed and beautifully executed but most of it has been removed or destroyed. The house is almost an empty old shell. This property adjoins the old stone Jackson Creek Church site and many fascinating and hair-raising stories are told of the old place.

It was built in the 1820's, or before, by the Clark family, early settlers in the old Jackson Creek community. It was in this old house that Lieutenant James Clark, the Mexican War hero was reared. The house was the home of his sister Mrs. Martha Clark Bolick and was bought by her husband, Levi Bolick, before the Confederate War. The Bolick's only child was a daughter, Elizabeth, who was better known as Lizzie. Mr. Bolick's brother Daniel and his wife died rather young and only a few weeks apart leaving several small children. One of these, Robert Daniel, was reared as a son by Martha and Levi.

Lizzie Bolick married William Stevenson who came to an untimely death shortly after their marriage. She never remarried but lived with her husband's people in the New Hope section and in Winnsboro for the remainder of her rather long life. Before her death she sold this place to Mr. Beverley Herbert of Columbia who is still in possession of the property.

OLD JACKSON CREEK CHURCH

David McCreight, William Hamilton, John and Alexander Robertson, James Gray, and John Phillips were among the first settlers in Lebanon (Jackson Creek) section of the county. All of the above mentioned men were from Ireland and were staunch Scotch-Irish Presbyterians; all of them having been elders in churches in their homeland.

Not long after the Revolutionary War, about 1780, these elders met and decided to form a church. They called an assembly of the people living in the neighborhood and the church was organized in the home of John Robertson by the Reverend John Simpson of Fishing Creek.

BOLICK PLACE

The early meetings continued to be held in the Robertson home and the Reverend Simpson usually preached for them. Some time later a church building was erected on the Robertson property. This log building was used until after the death of John Robertson. There was some sort of misunderstanding between his widow and the congregation which resulted in the church abandoning this building and erecting a similar one on the property of Joseph Chapman.

During the troubled years of the Revolution, the Reverend Mr. Thatcher, a northern minister, preached at Jackson Creek and the Wolf Pen Meeting House on the Wateree River. There were frequent Tory raids during this period and in 1780 Lord Cornwallis set up his headquarters at nearby Winnsboro. There was a skirmish at Moberley's Meeting House not many miles away. Due to this harassment, when services were held at Jackson Creek, men were stationed as sharpshooters and sentries in the trees and woods in the vicinity of the church so as to protect and warn the worshipers in the event of an enemy raid.

The exact date of the erection of the stone building is not known but it is thought to have been some time before 1800. This was one of the largest of the early churches in Fairfield. It was a tall rectangular structure built of native stones. The second story of the building was used exclusively by the Negroes whose masters paid rent on the pews that were used by their people. This gallery was entered by a flight of steps on the right-hand side of the main entrance to the building. The interior walls of the church were plastered over the bare stones and the furnishings were simple.

The old stone church was used until 1892, at which time it was in bad repair and considered unsafe for further use. Due to this condition and to the fact that the center of population of the congregation had shifted a new building was erected at another location. During the construction of the new building services were held at the Parsonage Academy at Stevenson, near the site of the new church. The Reverend D. E. Todd was pastor at this time and the new house of worship was completed in 1893.

Many pastors have served this old congregation. In the early days before the Revolution the Reverend William Martin, a Covenanter and a staunch Whig, preached here on occasions. The Reverend Mr. Simpson of Fishing Creek was the first regular supply and held regular services at Jackson Creek on a week day once a month for three years.

In 1784, the Reverend Thomas Harris McCauley, principal of Mount Zion, accepted a joint call to Jackson Creek and Mount Olivet. He served both churches until 1786, at which time he gave up Mount Olivet and devoted one half of his time to Jackson Creek for eight dollars per Sabbath. In 1792 he was released and the pulpit was vacant. During the vacancy Doctor McCaule and Mr. Gilliland preached here on occasions.

In 1796 Mount Olivet and Jackson Creek were again united with one pastor attending to the needs of both churches; The Reverend Samuel W. Yongue. In 1807 Mr. Yongue was also supply for Concord, Horeb, Aimwell, and Salem. He must have been a most energetic man for he was also Clerk of Court for Fairfield County. The records of 1813 show the combined membership at Mount Olivet and Jackson Creek at one hundred and twenty. It was during this period that Jackson Creek became known as Lebanon. The Reverend

OLD JACKSON CREEK CHURCH LXIV

Mr. Yongue died in 1830 having served Lebanon for thirty-four years. He was followed by the Reverend C. L. R. Boyd in 1838.

After the Reverend Mr. Boyd the churches had no regular pastor but were supplied by the Reverend G. W. Boggs. In 1841 the Reverend Malcomb B. Frazier of Alabama was called and remained until 1846. He was followed by the Reverend Edwin Cater who stayed until 1849 to be followed by the Reverend T. A. Hoyt until 1851.

The records from 1851 until 1866 were destroyed in a fire at the manse but from information given by some of the older members two pastors served the church during this period, the Reverends Mr. Smith and E. P. Palmer.

After the Confederate War the Reverend W. E. Boggs was pastor from 1866 until 1868. During his pastorate the Reverend G. W. Boggs and the Reverend G. R. Brackette preached for the latter part of 1868, until the Reverend W. W. Mills came and remained until 1884. Mr. Mills was followed by the Reverend J. C. McMullen and Mr. T. H. DeGraffenreid, a seminary student.

The other pastors to serve the church before the turn of the century were, the Reverends John Marion, H. G. Gilland, Doctor D. E. Jordan, the Reverends H. B. Garris, Douglass Harrison, W. G. White, J. L. McLin, M. R. Kirkpatrick, W. K. Boggs, D. E. Todd, James Russell, and A. M. McNaull.

The ruins of old Jackson Creek still stands majestically in its granite walled churchyard among the tombs and monuments of the great and the humble who worshiped here in the past.

MONUMENT

to

LIEUTENANT JAMES CLARK

In the granite-walled old Jackson Creek Churchyard are many ancient and interesting monuments and gravestones. The largest, most impressive and historic is one that stands to itself on the left of the ruins of the old building.

It is a tall granite shaft mounted on a tiered base. It is a memorial to a national hero who lost his life in the service of his country, Lieutenant James Clark. James Clark was a native of the Lebanon section of Fairfield County, a member of the old Jackson Creek Church and was reared in the very shadow of the ancient house of worship. He was an outstanding example of the type of manhood produced in this proud old Scotch-Irish neighborhood. He died a hero's death at the Battle of Cherubusco in Mexico during the Mexican War in 1847.

The impressive marker to his memory was erected by his fellow comrades and the day that it was unveiled was one of the memorable events of its time. Great statesmen, heads of state and local government as well as representatives of the national government attended the ceremonies where his bullet-pierced flag, side arms and swords and a national medal of valor were presented to his sister, Mrs. Levi Bolick (Martha Clark), a member of the old church and whose home adjoined the church property.

MONUMENT TO LIEUTENANT JAMES CLARK

Below is the inscription which was placed on a marble slab set into the base of the giant granite shaft.

To The Memory Of
Lieutenant James Clark
Of Company G. Palmetto Regiment
South Carolina Volunteers In Mexico
He Was Born October 1st 1815
In 1836 He Served As A Volunteer In Florida
And In 1847 In Mexico
In The Memorable Battle Of Cherubusco
On The 20th. Of August 1847
As Commander Of His Company
And While Leading It On to Victor He Received
A Shot In The Forehead And Fell Exclaiming
"Onward Men, Onward
Remember Where You Came From"
Thus Ended The Brief Though Brilliant Career Of One
Of Fairfield's Bravest Sons.

This inscription and monument stood proudly in the lonely churchyard to bear witness to valor for generations and men to follow until about a year ago. At that time for what reason we we cannot imagine, the slab bearing the inspiring inscription was pried from its embedment in the granite marker and broken into many pieces. It now lies scattered incoherently at the foot of the monument.

THE OLD MANSE

LEBANON CHURCH — STEVENSON — POPE — STONE

The OLD MANSE is one of the best known buildings in the Lebanon section. It was built about the same time as the old Jackson Creek Presbyterian Church and has served that church as a manse and school for more than a century.

The unique old house is located less than two miles from the present Lebanon Presbyterian Church. It is a rectangular two story building with thick rough, stone walls, towering chimneys at each end and covered with a steep gable roof. Across a portion of the front is a porch supported by square wooden columns mounted on granite bases. The lines of the building are simple and rather severe but the house has a sort of austere dignity about it.

The interior is in keeping with the outward appearance, simple, plain, and unpretentious, a suitable home for a Puritan clergyman. It is typically early-American and could well have been imported from England, Scotland, or Ireland.

Many of the patriarchal old pastors who served the church before the American Revolution and almost until the present century have resided here. At times they lived in their own homes or in other communities. When such was the case the old building was used as a Session House, a temporary home for newcomers until their own homes were built, a home for some unfortunate

THE OLD MANSE

people whose homes were burned, and, last but not least, it served as a school house for children and young people of the neighborhood.

For over a century this old house remained the property of the Lebanon Presbyterian Church and served in the above mentioned capacities. In the 1890's it was no longer needed for a manse nor a school and the Session decided to sell the property. William Stevenson, a deacon in the church, bargained to buy the place and moved his family here from his plantation. He had a large family and this old house had more room than his home and had the great advantages of being near the church and the school in which his oldest daughter was teaching and which was attended by several of the younger children. This family lived here for more than a year. The old place was perhaps gayer then than in any other time of its history. The older daughters, now young ladies and noted for their beauty, were fond of dancing and it was in the large parlor of the OLD MANSE that the "two-step" was first introduced to the community amid a great shaking of heads among the chaperones.

All was not gaiety for this family for while they resided here; the oldest son (there were two boys and ten girls), a student at Clemson College died. After this William Stevenson forfeited his option and moved back to his old home.

In 1898 the property was purchased by David L. Stevenson, William's younger brother, whose plantation surrounded the OLD MANSE property. He bought the house and small tract for protection and to be able to choose his neighbor. A short time afterwards he disposed of it to Jason Pope who lived there for a number of years. The historic old house is now owned and occupied by Wilbur Stone whose parents lived in the old home before him.

The house and grounds are kept in good repair and condition for the Stones take a pride in their ancient home and are always hospitable to stangers who are interested in seeing in it.

JANE TURNER PLACE
TURNER

This large, comfortable, old frame house in its neat surroundings has long been a landmark in the Lebanon community. It is located at crossroads, sitting well back from and facing the Winnsboro-Newberry Highway, which is crossed by the road to the old Jackson Creek Church in one direction and Adger in the other.

It is a typical upcountry plantation house, two stories high, covered with a gable roof, and fronted with a long, wide, one story piazza. To the rear is a wing and the kitchen. Neat outbuildings are in the background surrounded by acres upon acres of rolling green pastures.

The approach to the house is attractive. It is well back from the road and is framed with beautiful trees and shrubs and several well-trimmed, thick hedges which set off the yard and gardens. An attractive gate is at the entrance to the yard.

The history of this place is rather obscure but within the memories of old neighbors it has always been known as a TURNER PLACE, members of

JANE TURNER PLACE

LXVII

that family having owned and occupied it. J. B. Turner is the first known owner. He gave the place to his grandson some time after the War Between the States. The wife of the grandson (Yongue Turner) was named Jane. She was a widow for many years and during that time the plantation was referred to as the JANE TURNER PLACE. The school which was across the road and also on Turner lands was called the JANE TURNER SCHOOL-HOUSE.

In later years and even to the present time it is often called the SARAH BELLE TURNER PLACE for the late Mrs. Sarah Belle Lemmon Turner who lived here for so long. The friendly old house is now owned and occupied by her children and is still one of the best kept and neatest places in the community.

THE DOCTOR W. K. TURNER PLACE
WINN — PALMER — LEMMON — TURNER — BLAIR

The DOCTOR W. K. TURNER PLACE as it is often called, has long been known for its classic and dignified beauty. It is one of the most impressive plantation houses in the county. The design, location, and setting are all complimentary to each other.

This house is on the Winnsboro-Newberry Highway not far from Little River. It is entered by an avenue through neatly fenced green pastures to the yard which is enclosed with another wooden fence. In the background are rolling hills and green forests. In the yard, directly in front of the entrance steps are two graceful, wrought-iron urns on either side of the walk. They are mounted on brick bases and have been here for generations. The house is a large two-and-a-half story building with a gable roof, outside plastered chimneys and a wing extending to the rear. The front is beautifully adorned with a gable extending over the open porch or terrace. This is supported from the full two story height with two large, gracefully tapering, solid wooden columns set on classic bases and capped with Doric capitals. Over the handsome doorway is a lower gable supported by two smaller columns of the same design. The windows are long and well proportioned and are set off by the old fashioned slatted shutters that flank them.

The rooms and hall-ways of the interior are spacious and well decorated with hand-done woodwork.

Before the Revoluttionary War this was a part of the vast Winn Estate. The old Winn home which has long ago disappeared was on a hill behind this house. The exact spot can easily be distinguished by the large trees that still shade the old site. Behind this and in the woods is what is left of an old Indian burying ground.

The present mansion was built by the Palmers who bought the property from the Winns in the early 1800's. They sold it to James Lemmon before the Confederate War and he in turn gave it to his daughter, Elizabeth, when she and Doctor W. K. Turner were married. Since that time it has been known as the DOCTOR W. K. TURNER PLACE or later, the W. K. TURNER PLACE. It passed from Doctor and Mrs. Turner to their son, W. K. Turner,

DOCTOR W. K. TURNER PLACE

who is still living although well over ninety years of age. Until a few years ago this remarkable old man still rode horseback regularly.

In recent years Mr. Turner has transferred the place to his daughter and son-in-law, Mr. and Mrs. Frazier Blair of Hendersonville, North Carolina. The Blairs are planning to retire here in the near future.

LEMMON PLACE

This large, old house is situated near Little River and Bell's Bridge on the Newberry Highway. Although close to the road it is almost obscure to the casual passerby. Shaded and secluded by giant trees and enclosed by an old-fashioned picket fence it is a comfortable and homey old place once it is found. The shrubs and flowbearing trees in the yard are somewhat over-grown but they bear evidence to the dignity and charm of the old place.

The house is built along the same lines as so many of the Fairfield plantation houses of its time. It is large and comfortable with four rooms and a hall on each floor of the main body of the building and it has a wing extending to the rear. In the attic is a dormitory type room that has always been used for storage and overflow. A portico fronts the building. Originally this consisted of two open porches but some time during the history of the old house the upper portico was enclosed for a room.

James Lemmon bought the plantation on which the house is located from a Mr. Trapp in 1829. Immediately after purchasing the land he constructed the house and made it the seat of his large estate. Mr. Lemmon's wife was the former Mary Ann Lauderdale, the daughter of a prominent early settler of Fairfield. Their son, James Thomas Lemmon, inherited the place. Mr. Lemmon Senior was one of Fairfield's leading and wealthier citizens during his life. He owned several plantations, much property in Winnsboro, and was an excellent builder and cabinet maker. Before his death he gave each of his children a home and slaves.

This plantation with its grand old house now belongs to Miss Lillian E. Lemmon a daughter of James Thomas and Mary Ann Lauderdale Lemmon. Miss Lillie lives here alone with many family heir-looms and cares for the old place, keeping it much as it has been for almost a century and a half.

CLARK PLACE
ROBINSON — CLARK

This old house no longer exists except in the memories of those to whom it was dear but since it was standing when the sketch was made it will be included in this book for it was one of the older homes in the Lebanon section.

It was a long, large, rectangular building with huge brick chimneys on the ends, covered with a gable roof, with a one story wing extending to the rear of the building. A broad piazza stretched across the front of the building and was covered with a one story shed roof. This porch was enclosed with plain picketed bannisters. The roof extended over the porch and was supported by six square wooden columns mounted on granite bases, all in one

LXIX

LEMMON PLACE

piece, about five feet above the ground. The cornices of the main structure and of the porch were decorated with block patterns. Double doors framed by paned side-lights made an attractive entrance.

The rooms were spacious and were decorated with handcarved woodwork and trim. Two of the mantels, in particular, were well executed and quite handsome. The easy-rising stair with its bannister and pickets of walnut was one of the main decorative features of the house.

This house, from all appearances, must have been built in the very early 1800's by one of the Winns. The second owner on record was Ed Robinson whose family lived here for many years before the War Between the States. Ed Robinson married Elizabeth Bolick and they had two daughters. One of the daughters, Lizzie, married Moses Clark. She and her husband purchased this place from her family and lived here their entire lives. It was occupied by their descendants for many years and the property still belongs to this family.

Older residents of the community recall the place as always being hospitable, one in which many of the parties and dances of the community were held. The site is not far from Little River in one of the oldest settled portions of the section. It is near the Bell, Winn, Palmer and Lemmon homes.

THE BELL PLACE
BELL — LEMMON — HENRY — WILKES

The BELL PLACE is one of the older of the pre-Revolutionary houses in the county. It occupies the site of one of the first settlements or "cow pens" in the upcountry.

Originally the BELL PLACE consisted of more than three thousand acres of land. The house was built in the 1750's, and is probably the oldest house in the county that is still in use. The original portion consisted of two rooms and a hall on the first and second floors and two partially finished rooms in the attic. These rooms were floored and ceiled with wide, heart-pine planks, some of which were hand-planed. None of the lumber was tongued and grooved. In this old portion of the building loop-holes for sighting and firing on the Indians and holes used as candle holders are still to be seen in this pioneer house of which the entire framework is put together with pegs.

The doors in this part of the building are of particular interest and are of authentic, pre-Revolutionary design, now reproduced and referred to as "colonial doors." In each is a distinct cross, indicating according to tradition, the religious belief of the household. The Bells were Scottish Covenanters, in this country referred to as Associate Reformed Presbyterians.

Many years before the War Between the States the old house was enlarged and remodeled. A two story, seven room wing was added to the back of the building and was fronted with a double-decked porch. During this time the three big mantels with their straight panels and beautiful handcarvings were added. This work was done by highly trained plantation hands who used only their pocket-knives to carve the intricate designs. The kitchen was in the yard a distance behind the house.

CLARK PLACE

LXX

The Bells owned many slaves and the quarters for housing them was about one quarter of a mile from the main dwelling. Across the road from the plantation house was a large slave cemetery. A few of the marked graves still may be seen. The inscriptions are quite interesting. Near this burying ground, on a peninsula jutting into the Little River swamp, is a large grave. It is evidently the tomb of a person of some consequence. A heavy granite base supports the stone tomb which is above the ground and covered with a heavy slab of granite. This is enclosed with a low rock wall. In recent years this grave has either been desecrated or badly damaged by storms and floods for the slab now lies half buried in the ground beside the open grave. The wall is broken and the massive base has been upset in several places. Time and weather seems to have erased all traces of an inscription. Old timers say that they can remember when the inscription was still legible and that this is the grave of a Winn, probably the Richard Winn for whom Winnsboro is named.

Another story that is told but is sometimes contradicted is about a daughter of the family who eloped with her father's northern born overseer. The ambitious young man thought that he would be received as a member of the family and of the gentry of the neighborhood and would live in the "big house" with his bride and her people. When they returned to the plantation he had a rude awakening. They were met by the master who horse-whipped the groom and later built a small four room house in the yard for the couple to occupy. Whether this is truth or legend is not known but it is a fact that there was a four room building near the house that was removed a few years ago because it was not only useless but a fire hazard, as well as an eyesore.

This old place is heavy with tradition and many stories are told about the old house being haunted. One of these is based on an unfortunate accident that occurred many years ago. Mr. Martin, a Presbyterian minister, and several other men, were riding up the avenue of trees leading to the house. The men were joking and cutting at each other with their riding crops. As the play grew rougher some of them lost their tempers. One struck the preacher, who dismounted and picked up a rock to throw at his assailant. John Bell had also dismounted and had hidden behind a tree. Just as the clergyman threw the rock Mr. Bell peeped from behind the tree. The hurling stone struck him with full force on the head and he died soon after he was brought to the house for treatment. His widow continued to operate the plantation for a time and then it was leased.

Walker Kirkpatrick, a young man from York County, managed the place for the Widow Bell and later rented and planted it for himself. He was an affable and popular bachelor and married a Lebanon girl, Maggie Pope. Later his brother, Robert Kirkpatrick married Maggie's twin sister, Mattie. When the Kirkpatricks lived here they were young and gay and the old house was a center of the social activities of the neighborhood. Dances and parties, quail hunts and picnics were held here often.

In the early 1900's the place was sold by Mrs. Bell to James T. Lemmon who bought the house and a one thousand acre tract of land. At his death the plantation was inherited by his daughter, Mrs. Lambert Henry, the mother of the present owner, Mrs. Myrtle Henry Wilkes.

THE BELL PLACE

LXXI

NEW HOPE

by

MAYMIE WEIR STEVENSON

NEW HOPE is in the northern section of Fairfield County. It is a very old neighborhood and is steeped in history and tradition. The people are predominantly of Scotch-Irish and English extraction, most of them strong adherents of the Associate Reformed Presbyterian Church.

A few families lived in the community before the Revolutionary War and had established substantial homesteads. Among these were the Simontons, Roseboroughs, Taylors, McLurkins, and Weirs. Jeanne McLurkin, a pretty daughter of the section, was one of Fairfield's Revolutionary heroines.

When the war ended several families of newcomers from Ireland settled here. They landed in Charleston and secured their grants at the seat of the government before actually coming to Fairfield. Among these families were the Dunbars, Thompsons, Brices, Douglases, Douglasses, and Stevensons.

These people were hard-working, honest, thrifty, and fairly well educated. They were poor but proud and they took great pride in the fact that they had paid their passage from the old country, bought their lands, and still had means to tide them over until they could become established in their new surroundings. They were charitable in their speech and were always friendly to the poor and needy.

In NEW HOPE the observance of the Sabbath was the strict law of the land. Guests, either expected or unexpected, never interfered with the church-going or family worship. Those of them who later owned Negroes treated and cared for them in a kindly manner and attended to their religious as well as they physical needs.

The people of NEW HOPE prospered through their industry but held fast to the old religious beliefs and customs. They built homes in accordance with their prosperity. Some of these were spacious and dignified but none were ornate nor pretentious. During the Ante-Bellum period NEW HOPE became one of the most prosperous communities in the county.

During the War Between the States the NEW HOPE plantations were looted but not many of the homes were burned. The stamina and fortitude of the women and the loyalty of most of the Negroes were responsible for this.

After the war several families moved away and times were harder but this community still held to its old standards and put its emphasis on religion and education. Many prominent men and women came from this neighborhood. The ministers were numerous; among them were, the Reverends R. W. Brice, J. R. Castles, E. E. McDonald, R. M. Stevenson, D.D., J. C. Douglas, J. W.

Douglas, R. B. Miller, and one student, J. B. Chisolm, who died while attending the seminary.

Among the lawyers were: Charles S. Brice, A. S. Douglas, Scott Douglas, W. B. Douglas, C. A. Douglas, J. E. McDonald, and John Means Simonton. The physicians from NEW HOPE were: Walter Brice, W. S. B. McLurkin, Henry Castles, Jr., J. Micheal Brice, J. L. Thompson, J. C. S. Brice, W. F. Mitchell, J. E. Douglas, Sr., J. E. Douglas, Jr., John W. Douglas, and Eugene Brice. The dentists were: R. T. Douglas and C. M. Douglas.

W. Banks Dove, one time Secretary of State for South Carolina, was from NEW HOPE. Miss Macie (Mary P.) Stevenson served her church as a missionary to Mexico for fifty years and during that time was instrumental in the establishment of a girls' school in Tampico. Her brother, Doctor R. M. Stevenson, was a publisher and for many years was a professor at Erskine College in Due West, South Carolina.

NEW HOPE CHURCH
ASSOCIATE REFORMED PRESBYTERIAN

NEW HOPE Associate Reformed Presbyterian Church is one of the oldest congregations in the county. Originally it was a part of the area served by HOPEWELL CHURCH which is in Chester County. HOPEWELL was about seventeen miles away. In the olden times this was quite a distance to have to travel to church. Due to this inconvenience another meeting place was made at NEW HOPE in 1796.

Carnaham's (Kerneyham's) Stand was where the services were held, the name being derived from that of the family on whose lands the meetings were held. For the first few years this church was merely a brush arbor. It was located near and adjoining to the present NEW HOPE Cemetery. The early ministers who preached here were the Reverends John Mushat, William Blackstock, and John Hemphill.

Later a log building was constructed about a quarter of a mile from where the present house of worship is located and the Reverend Doctor Hemphill was pastor. Doctor Hemphill served this congregation from 1796 until his death in 1832. During this period his time was divided with the Hopewell and Union Churches. He was succeeded by the Reverend James Boyce, D.D.

Doctor Boyce was a brilliant, highly educated man and was a great force and power for the good and improvement of the community that he served from 1832 until 1870. In 1870 he was elected president of the Theological Seminary at Erskine College. Doctor Boyce was followed at NEW HOPE by the Reverend Laughlin McDonald who came in 1871 and remained until his death in 1874.

Other pastors who ministered to this congregation since that time are the Reverends R. G. Miller, D.D. (1874-1886), H. H. Blakely (1887-1890), A. J. Kirkpatrick (1891-1896), R. E. Johnston (1897-1900), B. G. Pressley (1905-1907), W. W. Parkinson (1916-1922), W. H. Stevenson (1922-1926), and W. A. Kennedy (1926- _____).

With the above regular pastors several supplies were sent to the church during the periods when there were no regular ministers. Some of the supplies were the Reverends G. R. White, John A. White, C. R. Birnbach, R. L. McCown, W. A. Blakely, and G. W. Hanna.

Many of the pastors and supplies at NEW HOPE also served other churches in the area while they were at NEW HOPE. Doctor Hemphill served Union and Hopewell; Doctor Boyce served Ebenezer until 1843 and NEW HOPE alone until 1870. The five pastors following him served NEW HOPE exclusively. Then the Reverends McCowan, Parkinson, and Stevenson served NEW HOPE and White Oak and Doctor Kennedy NEW HOPE and Hopewell.

The present church building is the second house of worship for this congregation since the log cabin days. The land for the first was donated by Doctor Walter Brice and the site for the present church by S. G. Brice.

This building is a modest but dignified frame structure with a small bell tower on the front. The cemetery is but a short distance away. It is a beautiful secluded spot and is kept in excellent condition. Within its walls are the graves of many of the pioneer settlers of the community.

NEW HOPE CHURCH   LXXII

BALWEARIE

DOUGLASS

BALWEARIE takes its name from the Douglass castle of Balwearie in Scotland, the ancestral home of the Douglass family that settled in the New Hope section of Fairfield County in South Carolina. The land on which this house is located was granted by George III of England to the Douglasses.

When the house was built or by whom has not been determined. The first known owner was James Douglass, a bachelor and a man of wealth. He owned much land, many slaves and was evidently a devoted horticulturist as well as a successful planter.

In the ante-bellum period the gardens and orchards of BALWEARIE were known for their beauty and neatness — and — well must they have been beautiful and well tended, for, according to the Douglass records, twenty Negroes were assigned to the task of keeping them. On either side of the broad walk' in the front of the house was a boxwood hedge behind which were intricately laid out mazes of smaller-growing, well-trimmed English box-woods, embellished with bulb and flower-beds. To the rear of this and around the house were lilacs and rare shrubs, all well-pruned and geometrically-shaped.

Across the road, in front of the house, were the stables, carriage-house, and Negro quarters, surrounded by the fruit orchards. The nut orchards screened the barns and outbuildings outside of the gardens on one side of the house. On the other side was the kitchen, smokehouse and cook's house with the vineyards beyond them.

The manor-house itself was a rectangular building on great granite foundations, rather low to the ground, with thick, plantation-made brick walls. It was covered with a gabled roof from which a front gable extended over the porch supported by square wooden columns and enclosed with hand-turned bannisters, entered by broad granite steps. The chimneys are built inside and affords a fireplace for each room. On the sides of the building the bare red (some of which are burned almost black) brick, while the front and rear walls are covered with a heavy white plaster. A broad entrance composed of large double doors framed with glass panes and a glass-paned gable above them is one of the distinctive features of the decoration. Elongated, double windows with four panes over four further dress the front. On the rear there was originally a porch which protected the double back doors and the windows.

As before stated, James Douglass was a large slave owner. During the stormy days preceding South Carolina's secession from the Union he was also one of the few Unionists in the county, although a staunch supporter of slavery. This made him unpopular among his kinsmen and neighbors. After South Carolina seceded, the Confederacy was organized, and the war ensued, he still advocated "preservation of the Union." When Columbia fell and Sherman's greedy hordes were moving on Fairfield and New Hope he was ridiculed but stood firm to his convictions until the Federal troops appeared at his very doorsteps. He told them that he was a Union supporter and should be respected as such but to his dismay they paid him no attention and looted his property. This in itself was a shock to the old man but when the soldiers

LXXIII

BALWEARIE

began to abuse him and demand that he give them his gold and silver he became stubborn and irate, giving them no satisfaction. Before leaving they completely wrecked his home and furnishings, set fire to the house and hung him by his thumbs to a tree.

After the war the house was repaired and when James Douglass died he left this property to his nephew, Doctor Thomas Douglass. During the "cyclone of 1886" the old house was damaged again. The second story was completely demolished. Portions of the roof of this house were found later miles away.

The house was repaired again but this time only a half story was added, with a large gable with an oversized window in the center.

Doctor Thomas Douglass' son, another Doctor Thomas Douglass, inherited the place. He lived in a house nearby and later his family moved to Winnsboro. This old house was vacant for a long period. It is now owned by Doctor Douglass' children, Doctor John Douglass and Miss Maude Douglass of Greenville, South Carolina. They are now in the process of restoring the old place and have done much to bring it back to its former dignity. Green pastures and ponds spread to the front, sides and rear, where once the orchards flowered, but are now the habitat of a fine Black Augus herd of Scottish origin.

ALBION
DOUGLAS

ALBION is the largest and most elegant home in the New Hope section. It is the ancestral home of the Douglas family having been built about 1840 by Alexander Douglas, who was a grandfather of the late Albert Douglas, whose widow now owns the place.

The house is beautifully located on an elevation at the head of an avenue of ancient trees. Its appearance is commanding; a true Southern plantation mansion in the best tradition. Green lawns and larger trees set it off. This tall, three-story manor house is built along simple Colonial lines. The main body is covered with a gabled roof and extends over the upstairs veranda. In the center of the roof is a beautiful gable. The mammoth chimneys are built in the house. Two-story piazzas extend across the entire front and each porch is supported by ten large square columns and are enclosed with picketed bannisters. The windows are long and well placed. The entrances are simple but decorative, surrounded by glass side lights. The decorations of the columns, doorways, windows, and trim are beautifully designed and executed.

As would be expected, the interior is spacious with elegant mantels, rosettes, cornices, and mouldings. A graceful stair of three flights domineers the front hall. A narrower stairway rises from the rear hall.

The original owner of this old house employed a builder from York to construct his home. The best of materials were used. The original locks and hardware are still in good working order. Alexander Douglas was a slave owner, a successful planter and a builder of good wagons. His wagon shop was located on the main road near the avenue leading up to his home.

Down through the years this place has remained in the Douglas family. It has been well kept and is still in good condition and with a little redecoration, proper furnishings, and landscaping it could well be one of the show places of the Upcountry.

LXXIV

STEVENSON PLACE
STEVENSON

This imposing old landmark has been standing in the New Hope section for long over a century. It was built in 1856 by Robert Murdock Stevenson on lands that he inherited from his father, John Stevenson. John Stevenson came to this country from County Antrim, Ireland about 1785. He and his wife Janette (Murdock) Stevenson, and three children, William, James, and a little girl left their home in Ireland to settle in the New World. The daughter died on the long, stormy voyage and was buried at sea. The family landed in Charleston, South Carolina and secured lands in Fairfield County. They had other relatives who had settled in Charleston and in the Rocky Creek section of Chester County, the latter place not far from their new home.

Before John's death in 1808 he acquired considerable property. He had land in Lebanon, Feasterville, and the Dark Corner neighborhoods as well as this tract in New Hope. Before his death his son, James, married Eleanor Weir, a daughter of David Weir and his wife, Jeanne McLurkin Weir (a heroine of the Revolutionary War days). When James was married his father gave him a tract of land in the Lebanon community where James later built a large brick home. This house was destroyed during the Confederate War.

In his will John bequeathed to his son, William, the lands that he had acquired from Joel Butler. The home tract was divided between Robert, Andrew, and Samuel. This acreage extended from Avon to the Dark Corner. Robert's portion was at Avon and included the home place. Samuel took the upper portion and Andrew the mid-section.

John Stevenson was a small, frail man but his wife, Janette, was a tall, handsome woman. Their original house stood a short distance to the rear of the present dwelling.

After John's death his widow and unmarried children lived together at the old homestead. When a young man Samuel married Cynthia Yongue and moved to his own place where he built a large frame house. Hugh had a beautiful home called WHITE HALL near Monticello but still spent most of the time at his mother's residence. Hugh, Andrew and Margaret were never married. In 1848 Robert married Elizabeth Brice. They had no children and she died in 1851. In 1855 he married Rebecca Margaret Hartin and they raised five children to maturity.

One of the sons, William Hilliard Hartin Stevenson, married Elizabeth J. Bolick. He came to a tragic death not long after his marriage. His widow never remarried but lived with his family for the remainder of her life.

William's death brought sorrow into the old house but there were gay days, too. Margaret Eugenia Janette (Nettie) Stevenson married Doctor James Douglas. Her wedding was in the home and was a lavish affair that was talked about for years. There were so many guests in the house that she and the numerous bridesmaids had to dress in the big attic and descend three flights of stairs for the ceremony.

STEVENSON PLACE

LXXV

Another son, Robert Milton Stevenson, married Emma Christian. He was a distinguished minister in the Associate Reformed Presbyterian Church, a publisher, and for many years a professor at Erskine College in Due West.

Robert Stevenson's daughter, Mary Permelia, was never married. She spent fifty years of her adult ilfe in Mexico where she was a missionary. While she was there she helped to establish and taught at a school for girls in Tampico.

Robert Murdock Stevenson was called "Long Robin Stevenson." He was a large man, six feet and nine inches tall. As a young man he excelled in athletics. He was a promoter and stockholder of the first railroad from Columbia to Charlotte. When the road opened he made a trip in a private coach with the young ladies of his family. Along the way he jokingly told the spectators that he was the biggest man and had the prettiest women on the line.

Much of the original furniture is still in the house. Some of it was built to order for the oversized owner. A walnut couch and chair are still in the hall. Among the other interesting pieces in the house is a handsome swinging cradle, drop-leaf walnut table, walnut bedroom suites, rosewood piano, and several crayon portraits of members of the family done by Macie (Mary Permelia).

The house has a large reception hall from which a graceful walnut stair winds for three stories to the attic. On the first floor are two large rooms with walnut cornices, chair rails, mantels, and window cornices, and two smaller and simpler rooms to the rear. On the second floor there are three rooms and a hall. None of these have closets but in each is an oversized walnut wardrobe. The attic is one big room. All of the floors are of wide heart pine boards all in one length. The walls are still coated with the original plaster and are free from cracks. All of the wood used in the building was cut on the place and the bricks were plantation-made. Originally the kitchen was detached from the house. It was a two-story building in the rear with a covered walkway connecting it to the main structure.

A German builder was in charge of the construction of the house and had plantation labor furnished by the owner to help him. He was given strict orders to do no work on the Sabbath but being a most industrious individual he did not heed his instructions. After his work was completed he told the owner that he had carved the mantels, cornices, and the elaborate rosettes for the chandeliers in an outbuilding to keep from being bored and idle on the day of rest.

The beautiful old place still remains in the family. Mrs. Maymie Weir Stevenson, the widow of Long Robin's youngest son, James Ebenezer Stevenson, still cares for it. She and her husband lived here and reared a large family. He was the Auditor of Fairfield County at the time of his death. His widow filled his unexpired term and kept the office for over twenty years until her retirement in 1954.

Mrs. Stevenson still occupies the old house on occasions and during the summer months. The family assembles here for Christmas and the clan holds a reunion once a year when the stories of Long Robin and the hospitality of bygone days are recalled and relived.

DOCTOR WALTER BRICE PLACE

LXXVI

DR. WALTER BRICE HOUSE
BRICE —MACFIE— JOHNSON

This attractive old house was built by Doctor Walter Brice in the 1840's. For many years Doctor Brice was a beloved physician in the New Hope section. The house he built was stately, commodious, and comfortable and a much visited place in the community. It sits back from the road and is approached by an avenue of beautiful trees.

Among the original outbuildings was a picturesque little structure similar in design to that of the residence. It was known as the "Doctor's Office." Here it was that he kept the herbs which he compounded into medicines and pills for the sick. The patients who came to him were treated in the "office."

During the War Between the States a wing of Sherman's Army came this way. When Mrs. Brice heard that they were approaching she and her faithful butler gathered all of the family silver and valuables and buried them under the flagstone floor of the Doctor's Office. This was done with great care and secrecy for some of the Negroes on the plantation were known to be eagerly awaiting the invaders and were willing to help them in any way that they might.

When the dreaded day finally came the Yankees swarmed all over the place, ransacking as they went, madly searching for gold, silver, or jewelry. When nothing of any value was found they were greatly disappointed and angry for they had been told by Negro informers that there would be much loot in this house. When this proved false they told the soldiers that the butler must have hidden it away. They immediately seized the frightened man and demanded that he reveal the hiding place. When he refused they threatened him and later flogged him but still he kept the secret. Finally they turned to methods of torture and he was hung from a tree in the yard by his thumbs. His agony was so great that his mistress commanded the men stop and ordered the good butler to take them to the office and get the loot for them. After this was done the man who took a bag of flat silver for himself began taunting and talking disrespectfully to the young mistress of the plantation. She told him coldly that he had taken what he had come for and suggested that he leave, adding, "This will be the first time in my life that I have not had a silver spoon with which to stir my tea."

The soldier reached into the bag containing the silver, pulled out a spoon which he bent and twisted all out of shape and with an outburst of oaths threw it at her feet. A descendant of this lady still has this memento of the horrible day and all that was left of the family silver.

After the bummers had departed it was whispered that the rebellious Negroes were planning to raid and take over the plantation for themselves.

LXXVII

TOM "SHANTY" BRICE PLACE

Members of the Brice family and their faithful people gathered at this house to protect themselves. The raid was staged on a moonlight night and those within the house could see and hear the angry mob approaching. Just before they reached the dwelling they noticed the figure of a large black man in the road between the building and the marchers. He raised both long arms into the air above his head and motioned to them to go back. Strangely enough they did; some of them at a trot!

The people within the house thought that this big man was the stranger who had been inciting the Negroes to riot and that for some unknown reason he had changed his plan for the night. He was never seen nor heard of again and the once defiant Negroes ceased to cause or talk of further trouble.

Some time later those who witnessed the affair learned that the big man was no man at all but the ghost of a faithful servant. The insurrectionists had recognized him and had heeded the spectral warning, fleeing in terror. He is still talked about in the community and is referred to as the "Big Black Ghost."

This place has remained in the Brice family for many years, passing from them to the Macfies with whom they intermarried. A few years ago it was sold to Henry Johnson who has modernized and restored the house and now makes his home here.

TOM "SHANTY" BRICE PLACE

BRICE

The old house known as the TOM "SHANTY" BRICE place is one of the oldest buildings still standing in the New Hope section. Very little of its history can be found. It is known to be the home of T. S. Brice who was quite a colorful figure and politician in his day. He served Fairfield in the Legislature in 1890.

An amusing story is told about him and his campaign speeches. He would always close his orations with an invitation to all of his supporters to come visit him any time that they were traveling his way and that they would always be welcome and have room made for them in his "little shanty." Some of these people were later surprised when they paid him a visit to find the "little shanty" to be a large, spacious, rather elegant home. From this episode he was given the nickname of "Tom Shanty."

PART IV

JENKINSVILLE
and
MONTICELLO

MONTICELLO–JENKINSVILLE

by

KATHERINE PEARSON TOMLIN

"What comes over a man, is it soul or mind
That to no limits and bounds he can stay confined"—

This bit of poetry from Robert Frost, universal in application, is particularly apt in summing up the restless, questing spirit of Fairfield County's first settlers, seeking new horizons, new freedoms, and new meaning to their lives. The vicinities now known as Monticello and Jenkinsville, in western Fairfield, were among the county's earliest settlements. In the 1740's groups of Scotch-Irish, Dutch, and Germans from the northern frontier colonies settled along the creeks and rivers of these sections; from the Low-Country and Charleston came a few Englishmen and French Hugenots. The fortuitous blending of such diverse extracts has produced a fine type of citizen, imbued with solid character and strong intellect.

This spot in the wilderness of Fairfield (originally an undivided part of Craven County), was both a challenge and a temptation to these first few souls, neither of which they resisted. They willingly undertook to accommodate themselves to their strange, new environment — the lush lands and virgin forests, dripping with promise, were incentive enough. But to possess these treasures and to reap their gold were to be difficult endeavors. A firm foothold on this new land had to be secured, and with its accomplishment went severe hardship and gruelling labor. Existence, for them, was precarious and capricious at best. Lifelong habits and the orderly structure of society which they had known in the old world, had to be abandoned and forgotten. An indomitable spirit sustained by a firm faith in God carried them through several decades of such harsh existence. Thus, did their new life unfold, and their dream take on the shape and substance of reality.

An ancient map, undated, but stained and darkened with age, delineates the "plan of the village Monticello." This original map, now in the possession of Charles Burley of Monticello, contains a memorandum which reads: "The plan includes forty-eight acres of land, and is situated on the ridge which divides the waters of Broad and Little Rivers in the District of Fairfield, sixteen miles southeast of Winnsborough, and thirty-five miles northwest of Columbia. The said fifty-eight acres of land is laid out into sixteen squares of two acres each; each square containing four square lots of half an acre each." The two streets bisecting the village were named Drayton and Winn, the former being 160 feet wide and the latter 121 feet wide. The other streets were: Warren, Wooster, Montgomery, Haynes, Laurens, De Kalb, Campbell, and one other whose name is obliterated. Apparently all of these streets were not developed, although a few of them did become permanent avenues; some of the houses which they fronted are still standing.

This, of course, is only a description of the village property. The entire Monticello-Jenkinsville territory originally comprised all that land from Scherrer's Ferry (now Strother), extending in a southerly direction along Broad River for approximately eighteen miles. To the east of the river the vicinity covered roughly five miles. Within this section were the communities now known as Strother, Rock Creek, Dawkins, Monticello, Alston, Long Run, Jenkinsville and Wallaceville. Little River marked the eastern and southern boundaries of the area.

Authentic records of names and holdings of the pioneers of this section are scarce and difficult to unearth. However, with a little deduction and a few gleanings here and there, one is able to piece together a fairly accurate picture of their settlement and its development. Wilkinson's Creek, running to the west of Monticello, is described as having settlers along its course as early as the 1740's. People by the names of Conoway, Alder, Owens, Free, Conomore, and Handcock were among these first adventurers. Along Little River men with the names of Gibson, Carey, Hughes, Rees, McGraw, Spencer, Leslie, and Andrews formed a settlement. Their livelihood was hewn out of the wilderness, like those of other early settlers in Fairfield. Corn, planted along the fertile creek-lands, furnished their chief source of food. Cattle pens were established for the purposes of augmenting their food supply and of marketing skins and beeves to the coastal areas. A mill was erected on Wilkinson's Creek in 1752; the first in Fairfield, it was owned by Thomas Owens and solved the problem of corngrinding for the tiny settlements. The site of another mill on a creek running through "Mills Place" near Monticello, gives evidence of the initiative and industry exercised by these first settlers. Also, it was incumbent upon them to use ingenuity in constructing forts for protection against Indian attacks. Meriwether, in his "Expansion of South Carolina, 1729-1765," states that the early forts were rather flimsy affairs. However, John Pearson asked the government to send some swivel guns "to place in each of our flankers." On Wilkinson's Creek forts were built on the places of Philip Pearson and James Andrews. Nixon's Fort and Raiford's Fort on Little River were numbered in the chain of forts continuing down to McCord's Ferry. Besides the arduous tasks of wresting a living from the land and trying to stay alive, our forefathers had time for little else except religion. In their extreme isolation it was necessary to practice piety along with industry; it brought them comfort and the confidence which they needed to carry on.

The first organized congregation in Fairfield was in this section. Its members were Thomas Owens, Jacob Conomore, Lawrence Free, Richard Gregory, and a few others, who formed the nucleus of two Seventh-Day Adventist groups. As there was no ordained minister available, John Pearson, who was then living in the district which is now Richland County, assumed the duties of lay preacher, serving both churches. The church meetings no doubt provided their only social intercourse.

A few new settlers came after Braddock's defeat in 1755, among them, the Rogers. They owned headrights to tracts along Wilkinson's Creek, and Little and Broad Rivers. In addition to corn they planted indigo and some hemp. With the advancing decades came still more settlers, possessing larger and more numerous land grants. A few slaves were brought up from the Low Country, and as their number multiplied the labor situation was eased somewhat. Increased profits stimulated the purchase of more slaves; a prosperous era which eventually would reach significant proportions was about to begin.

The remains of a few large pre-Revolutionary plantations in this section are still in evidence. A crown of lovely liveoaks, hung with Spanish moss, marks the hill-crest site of an imposing plantation mansion built nearly two hundred years ago by James Alston. Situated between Monticello and Broad River, the house was destroyed by Sherman in 1865.

A small section of the house of Phillip Peter Pearson, who located near Wilkinson's Creek after leaving the Congarees, is still standing. His gardens were reputedly among the lovliest in the state, however nothing remains of them today. History records that this gentleman, who was the first Clerk of Court of Richland County, once furnished supplies to Colonel William Washington's calvary corp for one week without compensation. The latter had halted at Inglemen's Mill to watch British Colonel Innes posted at Scherrer's Ferry (now Strother). One of Pearson's sons was Philip Edward Pearson, author of the "Pearson Manuscript" and of the appendix to "Mill's Statistics of South Carolina."

In the Saint Barnabas Community, the Episcopal Mission for colored people, which was organized by the late Bishop Finlay, stands the remnants of the once-handsome residence of General Thomas McMeekin. A certain charm still lingers about this old house, graceful even in its ruin. Near here, the stately skeleton of another house, still standing in tall-columned symmetry, was the Holley House.

Scattered brick, granite steps and cellar are all that remain of the splendid home built by General John Pearson. On the crest of a hill at Parr Shoals, these fragments and a granite wall inclosing the family's graves, remind one of the renowned Revolutionary War General, who served with Sumter under the command of the "Gamecock." A momument placed by the Richard Winn Chapter of D.A.R. marks his grave.

A folorn and faded-yellow depot bearing the sign "Strother" (now abandoned as a railroad station) is all that bears witness to the fact that along here was the river plantation of General William Strother. Prominent in the affairs of his country, General Strother was a delegate to the Continental Congress of 1776, one of the founders of Mt. Zion Institute, and a hero in the War of 1812.

These bits from a vanished past remain to remind us of the particular charm of our heritage. History lives on in its relics.

By the beginning of the Revolutionary War farms in the Monticello-Jenkinsville vicinity were expanding into larger plantations. The war halted this expansion, but some years after the Declaration of Independence it was resumed. Some of these plantations were owned by men of independent means, who also possessed land grants. Although several of the following names were in evidence before the Revolution. Those listed in the 1790 Census of Fairfield as being from this locality, are: Aiken, Alston, Arnat, Andrews, Beam, Blair, Bradford, Chappell, Cook, Curry, Dawkins, Ederington, Elkins, Frazier, Free, Gibson, Gladney, Glenn, Hancock, Hawthorne, James, Jenkins, Kincaid, Kirkland, Martin, Milling, McGraw, McBride, McGill, McMeekin, O'Neal, Owens, Pearson, Powell, Rabb, Raiford, Robinson, Rogers, Shedd, Trapp, Turnapseed, Strother, Willingham and Yarborough.

A desire for the production of money crops to be exported as staples led to the introduction of cotton into the Up-Country. European connections were still intact, so that access to a sure market was provided. These developments, along with the advent of the cotton gin, inaugurated here a period of affluent prosperity comparable to that of the Low-Country.

The inhabitants of this district, eager and able to share in this imminent cultural awakening, lent their efforts, talents, and wealth toward fostering its development. Prime consideration was given to the nature of intellect and spirit, as well as to achieving and diligently maintaining a high level of material prosperity. Outstanding, and often lasting, contributions were made by these citizens.

The Rev. James Rogers, coming to Fairfield from Ireland in 1791, a few years later helped establish here an academy of learning, over which he presided for twenty-five years. Built from individual contributions of citizens, it was first known as the "James Rogers Academy." There are conflicting reports as to whether this academy was a school for boys or girls, or perhaps for both sexes. However, the weight of evidence would establish more or less conclusively that it was at first a male institution, but by 1800 was known as "The Monticello Girls' School." Thomas Jefferson, whose ideal of an educated citizenry led to the public school system, made a generous donation to the school through General John Pearson, then a member of the legislature. Its name was then changed to "The Monticello-Jefferson Academy." Still later, reports indicate, this school was attended by students of both sexes, and enjoyed a sound reputation as a noteworthy institution of learning.

Many persons who distinguished themselves in later life obtained their backgrounds of knowledge here. William Harper, the first student to enroll at South Carolina College when it opened January 10, 1805, was an alumnus of the Monticello-Jefferson Academy. He later became Chancellor of Mississippi, and then of South Carolina; he was also author of the Ordnance of Nullification. His brother, John Wesley Harper, was the second enrollee at South Carolina College.

Another man of eminence, who first studied here, was Dr. James Bolton Davis, the leading agriculturist of his day. Descended from Captain James Kincaid, Revolutionary War hero and legendary inventor of the cotton gin, Dr. Davis introduced the first Brahman cattle (sacred cow of India) into this country in 1849. Also, he brought with him from Turkey, where he had been United States Minister of Agriculture, several pairs of Cashmere and Thibet Shawl goats. His father, the Rev. Jonathan Davis, who was chairman of the first board of trustees of Old Furman University (then located three miles west of Winnsboro) had also attended this school. Dr. Davis' home in Monticello was one of the most elegant in Fairfield; today it is an historical landmark, and is owned by Mr. and Mrs. Ross Robinson, who recently restored it.

One cannot always be certain of how one's forebears came to this country, and when it can be definitely established that they came over in the "Mayflower," perhaps, in passing, it is worth noting. Lydia Waters, a student at the Monticello-Jefferson Academy about 1810, had ancestors on this maiden voyage. She later married Robert Boyce of Newberry and became the mother of William Waters Boyce, outstanding state legislator, member of United

States Congress prior to the War Between the States, and member of the Confederate Congress. His report on "Free Trade and Direct Taxation" created worldwide attention. He was esteemed as a man who possessed superior moral courage. Mr. Boyce married the daughter of Dr. George Butler Pearson of this section.

Judge O'Neal, distinguished jurist, states in "Bench and Bar," of which he was author, that he was born in Monticello in 1786 and attended the "James Rogers Academy."

Attendance at the Monticello-Jefferson Academy was perhaps at its peak in 1822. Among students who later attained significance in the south were Gov. John Hugh Means, Silas H. Holler, lawyer and legislator, and William Ederington, author. Other names on the school's roster in that year were: Hutchinson, Dansby, Davis, Means, DeGraffenreid, Woodward, Powell, and Nyers. A Mr. Hodges was headmaster.

At the start of the War Between the States this institution underwent still another change, becoming "The Zealy Academy for Girls." The Rev. John T. Zealy, whose descendents still live in Fairfield, was then in charge of the school. When Sherman's Army passed through Monticello Village this academy became the focus of attention for a brief interval. Two stories are related in this connection, one being that when General Kilpatrick learned of the girls' school, he decided to personally guarantee that no harm be done it. However, two officers, Captains Horton and Estes had the same idea, and beat the General to the draw. They filled an ambulance with foodstuffs and went to the academy, where they were most cordially received, and stayed on for a gay and festive dance that night. Music was furnished by the cavalry band. Another story relates how a local boy knocked a yankee soldier unconscious, put on the latter's uniform, and walked the school's front porch all night to protect the girls.

After the war this school became the "Monticello Public School", where Captain Hayne McMeekin of Monticello taught; when no longer needed the building was converted into a home for Captain McMeekin. His son, the late Gus McMeekin and his wife (Nancy Chappell), continued to live there until it was burned in 1932.

Another school projected in the original plan of the village was operated by a Dr. English, and was known as the "English School." It faced the Monticello-Jefferson Academy, occupying the spot where the Charles Burley house now stands. It was destroyed by fire when Sherman's forces passed through the village.

That emphasis was placed on learning is further demonstrated in this section by the establishment of "Broad River Academy" at Jenkinsville in 1824. According to the Appendix of "Mills Statistics of South Carolina," it was in operation in 1826, but since no other records can be found pertaining to it, it is assumed that it eventually closed due to a lack of funds.

Though not in this area, "Shurley's Institute," near Winnsboro, had as its Assistant Principal in the 1820's R. Y. H. McMeekin. A newspaper article of that day describes the school as being in a "neighborhood noted for its health and morality and furnished with philosophical and chemical apparatus and every convenience necessary to aid in imparting thoroughness of instruction. Students here are greatly shielded from temptation to vice and extravagance."

[212]

While Furman Institute, at first a Manual Training School, was maintained near Winnsboro, one of its best-known professors was Dr. James C. Furman, who lived and preached near Monticello.

Along with education in this section, religion was regarded as a vital cornerstone of society. And religion of one's choice was indeed a goal which was realized spiritually and tangibly; this is borne out by the early establishment of churches. The Little River Baptist Church, the oldest in this section, was originally organized as "Gibson's Meeting House" in 1768 on Little River near Gibson's Ford, the old stage crossing. Jacob Gibson, from whom the Monticello McMeekins are descended, was its first pastor. The present building was dedicated in 1856, and is located half-way between Monticello and Jenkinsville, in the Brick Church neighborhood.

Ebenezer, or "Brick Church," on the banks of Little River. is the birthplace of the Associated Reformed Synod of the Carolinas. Originally a log cabin before the 1780's, the present church was built in 1788 of hand-moulded brick by its own congregation, who called this work a "labor of love." Prominent and humble people alike have worshipped here for nearly two centuries. In its churchyard lie buried not only the ancestors of many people in this community, but also of those now living in other sections of the state, and of some in other states.

Beautiful Monticello Methodist Church, when dedicated in 1861, had a flourishing congregation; many of the section's wealthy planters were among its members. Services have continued to be held here since the church's dedication; the old pewter communion service, which was donated by Dr. James Bolton Davis, is still used.

Located near the intersection of the old Monticello Road and the Newberry Highway, Rock Creak Baptist Church, organized in 1790, is open for worship every two weeks. The old Rock Creek School House occupied part of its churchyard for perhaps more than a hundred years. Recently demolished, it was one of the few ancient one-room schoolhouses left standing in South Carolina. "Big Meeting," a week-long summer event, with "preaching" every morning, afternoon and evening, was a colorful practice of this church in years gone by. At every mid-day of this meeting, spiritual exhortations would be set aside while the congregation flocked into the shady yard, carrying baskets bulging with enticing delicacies. Laid out on linen-covered tables, this entrancing food could not be resisted, nor easily forgotten.

The first Negro church in Fairfield, erected in 1867, was "White Hall," the African Methodist Episcopal Church. On Highway 215 in the St. Barnabas Community, this church had as its first pastors Rev. Moses Martin and his brother, Rev. Benjamin Martin. The land for the church was donated by these brothers.

The scourge of war has accompanied our progress in the new world. In such dread times this section has brought to the forefront the same dauntless spirit of our pioneering fathers. Many native sons have been sacrificed in these struggles; also many became heroes and outstanding officers. Two thousand men were furnished by Fairfield in the War Between the States. They have been described as brave, high-minded, daring soldiers. Monticello and Jenkinsville contributed their share of these men. The famous "Monticello Guards," composed of 112 men, made their dare-devil imprint in the record of battle; many of these names are still in this community. Captain Hayne McMeekin, Monticello planter and school master commanded "Company F" from Fairfield.

Among stories handed down about individual deeds of valor by our soldiers is one concerning John Rabb, Color-Bearer, from Monticello. At the Battle of Seven Pines, 1862, he distinguished himself, according to General John Bratton, from whom I quote in part: "When our regiment was half-way across the abettis, a grand volley was poured upon us from the thicket beyond — the entire regiment squatted involuntarily in the brush. As the crash died away I shoulted "Forward!"; none save our color-bearer seemed to hear. He advanced on and over the obstructions, not able to move, even under the highest, without lowering his colors. None who saw it can ever forget the splendid picture presented by our glorious and handsome boy, John Rabb. Never were colors borne with a loftier devotion to duty or quieter disdain of danger. He advanced, alone, halfway to the enemy, and it looked as if our colors would be handed over to them, when our entire regiment seemed simultaneously to take in the situation and made a desperate rush to overtake them. Our line poured like a wave over and under and through the obstructions, and coming up with the colors, continued the impetuous advance, until we swept over them." — John Rabb was subsequently killed while carrying colors of the regiment in the Battle of Gaines Mill.

An old cutglass decanter owned by Mr. and Mrs. Albert McMeekin of Monticello carries in its history an allusion to the War Between the States. Belonging to the Gibson family (ancestors of the McMeekins), it was among the valuables pilfered by the yankees. In their eager rush to pillage further, the depredators lost the decanter, which was later found by slaves and returned to the family. It has since been used for christenings in the McMeekin family.

Sherman's thrust through here, leaving wholesale destruction in its path, was met courageously by our people. The seemingly insurmountable problem of rehabilitation and the bleak days of reconstruction were faced with great fortitude. The wounds from this tragic conflict have been slow in healing; its scars have been difficult to hide.

In other wars — 1812, Mexican, World Wars — I and II, and the Korean conflict — a high percentage of eligible males from this vicinity have defended their country. Their families have felt the honor and the tragedy which war deals out inexorably to its fighters.

The development of cotton culture, based on the slave system, brought not only wealth and sumptuous living, but a need for regulations to govern its production. Monticello assumed a leading role in agricultural development. The "Monticello Planter's Society", composed of prominent planters, was very active in 1830, as was the "Anti-Tariff Agricultural Society" of Broad River. The Agricultural Convention of South Carolina met at Monticello in 1843, where planters discussed "curtailing of crops and increasing provision supply and stocks of all kinds." Earlier, cultivation of the silkworm was urged, as prospects had appeared to be favorable at the time. There are no reports to indicate that the silk industry was developed here, however several planters expanded the growth of the native mulberry tree to this end.

Heavy and continuous planting depleted the topsoil in Fairfield to such an extent that at the approach of the War Between the States the exhausted land was rapidly giving way to erosion. Such a condition was especially true in this section. This situation, along with the loss of slave labor and property, spelled the end of the plantation system. After the war agriculture was carried on by a share-cropping plan, in which the landowner furnished land and supplies, while the tenant performed the labors connected with crop production. Planting of cotton had been seriously stifled as a consequence of soil-impoverishment; landowners and their tenants were forced to diversify crops in order to make a living. The economic ruin of small cotton farmers left some farms abandoned in this community; others were left idle for the purpose of rebuilding the soil.

This situation continued until wholesale erosion damaged the entire county; through this section the red clay subsoil lay ruthlessly exposed, and gaping gullies formed a criss-cross pattern over the once fertile fields. The boll weevil brought the cotton industry further toward the brink of extinction when it swept the cotton belt in the 1920's.

The advent of the Roosevelt Administration saw the introduction of conservation measures which gave promise of higher economic gains in this area. The Jenkinsville Forest Protective Association was the first to be organized in Fairfield, and the second in the entire state of South Carolina. In 1933 this association established at Parr Shoals a reforestation camp for the purposes of combating soil erosion and the cutting of fire lanes. The State Forest Service has assisted farmers in the maximum production of trees through thinning, planting and other woodland improvements. Cooperative marketing, diversification of agriculture, experiments with pure seed, and good roads, have all contributed toward making farming a profitable business again. Much work has been done by the families in this area in farm and home improvement. The Monticello-Salem Community Improvement Project has worked most successfully toward this end.

Emphasis on pine tree culture has led to the virtual elimination of the row crop system. Fairfield County leads the state in the annual value of its forest products. The Monticello and Jenkinsville sections have contributed significantly to this produce. Pine culture, together with the raising of beef cattle and dairying, are the main economic pursuits of the present inhabitants.

Taken separately and statistically, the several railroad stations and hamlets which in their entirety were known originally as "Monticello," have varying facts of identity. Strother, at first called "Clapp's Ferry." was subsequently named Scherrer's Ferry, then Ashford's Ferry, and finally, Strother. Once a busy riverside station with six stores and a post office, its only distinguishing feature now is the bridge which crosses Broad River at this point. The lonely whistle of an occasional train is all that ever disturbs its inclosing silence.

The next railroad depot along the river was Dawkins, consisting of a post office and one store. It was named for the Dawkins family who were landowners of this area before and after the War Between the States. They moved to Texas many years ago. Bereft of its store, post office and operating depot, Dawkins exists now only as a name. Several miles down the railroad from here is Alston, which once had a park where travellers waited to catch or change trains. Here the railroad crosses the river to the Lexington County side.

In the Rock Creek Community is the pre-Revolutionary home of the James family, now occupied by Miss Susie James. John J. McMahan, State Supt. of Education in 1899, member of the Constitutional Convention of 1895, and a presidential elector in 1896, was born and reared in this community. A man of erudition and vision, Mr. McMahan lived ahead of his time; many ideas and meliorations advocated by him have since been realized. His constant plea was for the enlightment of public opinion. Also in this neighborhood is Rock Creek Church with its cemetery *and* the grave of the controversial ghost, Colonel David Provence. The latter is buried on a lonely mound just across the road from the church. Many are the twilights when his vaporous form has draped the barnyard gate of the late John D. Blair, whose residence "Rose Hill," was a short distance from the Colonel's aloof resting place.

Monticello, which at one time was considered as a location for the county seat of Fairfield, today is a village consisting of about two dozen residences, two stores, one church and a post office. The Monticello School, located five miles away at Salem Cross Roads, was built in 1929, consolidating six school districts. This school, having gone through several changes of name, is a continuance of the original James Rogers Academy, and has been kept in operation for more than a century and a half. Mrs. Nina McGill, a direct descendant of one of the signers of the Declaration of Independence, lives in Monticello. She is the great, great, great, great granddaughter of signer Charles Darrell Carroll, who lived in Carrollton, Maryland. Among other honors, this village claims the distinguished chemist, Dr. LeRoy McMeekin, as a native son. Head of the Protein Division, Eastern Regional Research Laboratory, U. S. Department of Agriculture, Dr. McMeekin won the 1951 Borden Award for his outstanding contributions to the knowledge of chemistry.

Parr Shoals, three miles to the west of Jenkinsville, contains the nuclear-powered electric generating station, which is a joint effort of the Virginia Power & Light Company, the Duke Power Company, the Carolina Power & Light Company, and the S. C. Electric & Gas Company. These companies cooperated in forming this pilot project to determine the feasibility and practicality of creating electrical power by processes of nuclear fission. Silas C. McMeekin, native of the Jenkinsville Community, and President of the South Carolina Electric & Gas Company, was instrumental in having this project located at Parr Shoals. His practical vision and comprehensive knowledge of the complexities of the electric power industry have made him a first-class administrator and pioneer in this field. Parr Shoals was named for the Parr family who owned large tracts of land near here before the War Between the States.

Long Run, between Monticello and Jenkinsville, and to the east of Highway 215, embraces part of the St. Barnabas Mission Community and the "Brick Church" section bordering on Little River. "Heyward Hall," the restored ancestral home of Captain James Kincaid, is near here. The two churches in this area, previously described, are Ebenezer Associate Reformed Presbyterian Church and Little River Baptist Church.

The hamlet of Jenkinsville, about the same size as Monticello, contains two stores, one church and a post office. A few lovely old homes are still standing in this neighborhood. The Jenkinsville High School and Community Center was built in 1927. In its schoolyard is a Ginkgo tree planted by the

Richard Winn Chapter of the D.A.R., in honor of George Washington. It is said that the village was named for a Mr. Jenkins, a blacksmith, who was the first settler on this spot.

The Wallaceville section, along Broad River, is several miles to the southwest of Jenkinsville. Dr. John Wallace, prominent physician to the Confederate forces, settled here in ante bellum times; his handsome plantation home was destroyed by the Yankees.

The lineage of most of the people living in this part of Fairfield County can be traced back to their Revolutionary ancestors, and even beyond that, for a few others. Very few names have been introduced since those early times. The history of our tenure is a testament of our love for this land, with its hills and rivers and forests; we hang on, planting and producing, keeping intact the peculiar spirit and character of our legacy of values.

THE OAKS

HELLEMS — LEMMON — WELLS

The home of the late John Montgomery Lemmon and his wife, Mary Ann Yongue Lemmon, is located five miles from Winnsboro on the Jenkinsville road. It was built by a Mr. Hellems who came to Fairfield from Texas. There were twelve hundred acres of land in the tract on which the house was built.

Mr. Hellems supervised the construction of the house and saw to it that not one inferior piece of lumber was used. This accounts for the excellent condition that it is in today after standing for more than one hundred years. In 1856 Mr. Hellems sold the house and plantation to John Montgomery Lemmon for the sum of ten thousand dollars, after residing in it for a short time.

The house is large and spacious, typical of the better plantation homes of the period. Two mammoth chimneys are at either end of the building which is fronted with a two story classic portico. A wide, one story piazza extends across most of the rear of the house, with a room at one end of it. A gabled roof covers the building. In the gable over the portico is a well designed fanlight window. The front doors leading to the porches are large and flanked with sidelights. The name given this place was THE OAKS, a very descriptive title for the old house was framed and surrounded by a magnificant oak grove avenue.

During the War Between the States Mr. Lemmon went into the Confederate service, leaving at home his wife and small children. A neighbor, Mrs. McCreight, stayed with them during the war years.

Very often passing Confederate soldiers stopped in for food and lodging. One day a wounded soldier came. Mrs. Lemmon dressed his wounds and burned the bloodstained shirt lest it be discovered by Federal soldiers who were reported to be in the vicinity. Surely enough they came on the heels of the Confederates, over-running the house and shouting demands for food and supplies.

Soon they were demanding silver and jewelry but Mrs. Lemmon was adamant. When they increased their demands, embellished by threats and profanity, Mrs. McCreight being more fearful of them and whose silver was buried in the box with the Lemmon valuables under the rail fence, said, "Oh, Mrs. Lemmon, please, give them mine!" Thus the secret was out.

Besides carrying off the silver, they looted the smokehouse, caught all of the chickens except one, took with them all of the mules, killing the one that refused to go.

One soldier was left for a final deed. He came running down the stairs, falling from the landing into the room where the family was sitting. He made this statement, "Lady, I have started a slow fire in the attic." We wonder if this could have been the Yankee soldier that wrote on the wall of the old Brick Church his apology for taking up the floor of the church to span the river?

With the warning of fire some of the slaves were called to carry water up to the third floor and a watch was set up until all danger had passed.

[218]

THE OAKS

After the war the education of the Lemmon children was taken care of by a paid governess.

Through the years the Lemmon family has been known for its hospitality to friends and relations. Visiting ministers were entertained with loving kindness. It is said that a stranger asking for a night's lodging was never turned away.

The Lemmon home is one in which God was reverenced. Bible verses were recited by each one at the breakfast table through the week as well as on Sundays, and each evening family prayers were held.

Never were grandchildren given more love and consideration than by this family. For years the two maiden aunts, Janie and Belle, planned the Christmas celebration for the entire family connections, having a large Christmas Tree, decorated and laden with gifts, in the parlor and a sumptuous dinner for the many guests.

This home is today owned and occupied by a granddaughter, Marie Lemmon Wells and her husband, Johnnie Wells. It is well cared for, having been completely renovated during the past few years. Many rare pieces of old family furniture still remain in their original places in the spacious old rooms and hospitality is still practiced as it was in the old days.

MACFIE PLACE

MILLING – MACFIE

Captain David Milling, born in 1797, came to this country from County Down, Ireland in the early 1820's. He landed in Charleston, South Carolina where he remainded for a short while and then moved to Columbia where he was a proserous merchant. Other members of his family had settled in Fairfield County at an earlier period. He purchased one thousand acres in Fairfield and later came here and settled permanently. He was twice married. His first wife was Jane Wright and they had several children. One son, James, was a prominent physician who graduated from the South Carolina Medical College in 1855 and immediately afterward settled in Louisana.

In 1850 Captain David Milling married Mrs. Sarah Yongue Milling who had several children by her first marriage. She was the widow of another David Milling, a kinsman of Captain David. She and Captain Milling had two daughters and three sons.

The house was built about the time that they were married and the family holdings had increased to two thousand two hundred acres and many slaves. The place prospered and the family was counted among the wealthy gentry of the county.

During the War Between the States the Milling plantation was in the path of Sherman. When the invaders arrived the meat supply in the smokehouses was so great that it could not all be carried off so the surplus was burned. The soldiers heard stories of the handsome silver that had been in the house before their unwelcome arrival. When it could not be found they questioned the old Captain who refused to reveal the hiding place. After

MACFIE PLACE

LXXIX

threatening to burn the house they took him to the big barn where preparations for his hanging were begun. His daughter, Margaret, then a young lady, learned of her father's sad plight and hastened to the barn to tell the men to release him and showed them where the treasure was buried.

In 1893, when Captain Milling's widow's estate was settled, their youngest daughter, Lorena, who had married James Macfie, bought the interests of her brothers and sister and retained the plantation and house which was famous for its corn and flour mills. The Macfies later moved to Winnsboro and James Macfie became sheriff of Fairfield County, an office that he held for many years. The place now belongs to Palmer Macfie of DeLand, Florida, a son of Lorena Milling and James Macfie.

This is a typically ante-bellum, Southern plantation house. It was a lovely old place but it has been unoccupied for a number of years and has fallen into a state of dilapidation and desolation.

LEMMON PLACE

OWENS — COPELAND — LEMMON

For three generations this has been called the BOB LEMMON PLACE. It is a stately, handsome old house, very similar in appearance to the LEMMON-WELLS place a few miles away, though this is a somewhat smaller building.

The property on which the house is located was formerly lands belonging to the Owens family, early settlers of Fairfield. It is assumed that the house was built by some of the Owens. Before the War Between the States the home was occupied by a widow, Mrs. Creecey. While living here she married a Mr. Copeland who was a native of Tennessee. He brought mules, hogs, and other livestock to South Carolina where he found a ready market for them with the affluent planters in Fairfield County. The Copelands lived here for a number of years and during that time it became known as the COPELAND PLACE.

In 1870 the father of R. Y. Lemmon, a well-to-do planter, bought the place from Doctor Owens and gave it to his son who married Miss Agnes Milling, a daughter of a prominent family in the neighborhood. R. Y. Lemmon was known to his friends as "Redhead Bob Lemmon." He was a popular man in his community and throughout the county. He was a member of the Legislature from Fairfield for a number of years.

This beautiful old home still belongs to "Redhead Bob's" descendants. Two of his sons live in the house and operate the large plantation and a country store. Stately pines, broad green pastures, and fish-filled ponds cover the spreading acres surrounding broad cotton and grain fields.

The house sits well back from the road, at the head of a wooded avenue, enclosed by an old fence. The place is neat and the remains of the old garden still give it a comfortable, home-like appearance.

LEMMON PLACE

LXXX

MARTIN PLACE

MARTIN

Before 1813 the plantation, of which this old house is the seat, belonged to Robert Martin of Charleston. During 1813 it was settled by his brother, William A. Martin, who brought with him slaves and who set up an orderly and prosperous plantation which he managed for his brother Robert. The house was built in 1816.

The building is in a beautiful setting on an elevation which affords a wonderful view of the surrounding country-side. It is encompassed with lush, green lawns, well-placed shrubs, and colorful flowerbeds. Two stone shafts partially covered with dwarf English ivy are on either side of the walk leading up to the front of the house. At one time these were gateposts for a fence which divided the yard from the cotton fields. Ancient outbuildings and the original old well are still in use. The kitchen, which was detached from the main dwelling, has been removed so as to give a more spacious aspect to the grounds at the rear of the house.

The house proper is a large rectangular building with a gable roof and fronted with a one story piazza supported by six large square columns on granite bases. Wide granite steps lead up to the porch. At either end of the house are enormous brick chimneys covered with a cement plaster. There are four large rooms on the first floor and a gracious entrance hall from which a beautiful stair ascends. The second floor consists of two very large rooms on the front and two smaller ones on the rear. Originally the back rooms were not connected with those in the front. They were used for the Negroes who were locked in each night to protect them from wandering off the plantation and being stolen by outlaws and smugglers. The men were locked in one room and the women in the other.

In the center of the upstairs hall, over the front entrance, is a small trap-door which was cut during the War Between the States. The family valuables were hidden here in the space between the floor and the hall ceiling. The upstairs hall was carefully carpeted so that the spot would not be noticed and when the invaders arrived the hiding place was not detected.

William Martin purchased the plantation from his brother Robert for the sum of $10,000.00 and at his death it passed to his son, R. L. Martin, who was born in the old house on April 30, 1843. Robert L. and his brother David enlisted in the Confederate Army. David was killed at Boonesboro, Maryland and Robert was wounded at the same place. He recovered and returned for service to be wounded for the second time at Chancellorsville. After this recovery he went back to the front, where during the Battle of Chicamauga, he was shot again. Later, at Travillion Station he was wounded for the fourth time. This time he was badly mangled and chances for his recovery seemed dim. When he became stronger he asked his attending physician, Doctor Butler, if he might go home. The good doctor replied, "Martin, I'm giving you a furlough home but I know you will be dead when you get there." Robert Pleaded, "Doc, you just give it to me; I'll try it!" It was given and he did try it and made it. After a stay at home he became well and rejoined

MARTIN PLACE

the army and was with Hampton's Cavalry at Smithfield, Virginia, at the time of the surrender.

When Sherman's troops came through the Monticello section some of his men took quarters in the Martin home. The handsome rosewood piano which is still in the drawing room of the old dwelling is said to have been responsible for the house being spared. Some of the officers were music lovers and songsters and a member of the family played for them by request during their stay. When they left they thanked the musician for entertaining them and stated that they would not burn the house.

The plantation passed from R. L. Martin to his son, Doctor D. H. Martin. Doctor Martin's sister, Mrs. Julia Martin Simms, who was on the staff of Winthrop College at Rock Hill, South Carolina for thirty years, restored and occupied the old place as her home and lived there until her death. The present owner, David H. Martin, bought the property from his uncle, Doctor D. H. Martin, and now resides here with his wife. They love the old homestead and care for it with pride and affection.

The building is in excellent condition, having been modernized and restored and completely redecorated. Large, handsome mantels adorn the main rooms. Though simple in design they are well proportioned and dignified. The rooms are wainscoted to chair-rail height and are either plastered or panelled above. The wide, naturally finished flooring boards and the simple but well designed stair add to the charm of the interior which is furnished with antiques and heirlooms acquired through the generations by the family. One unusual piece is an elegant English-made press that came with the Martins to America, as did the two graceful canopy beds. The dining room is furnished with a unique suite that dates back to the prosperous days "before the war." In one corner of this room is an enormous corner cupboard of unusual design and filled with cut glass, silver, and old china. Above the table in the center of the room is a beautiful brass and glass kerosene lamp chandelier. There is not a room in the old house that does not have some furnishings that were used by former occupants of the bygone days.

FURMAN INSTITUTION

The FURMAN INSTITUTION was chartered and established in 1825. This was an academical school and a theological seminary for the education of youth sponsored by the Baptist of South Carolina. Doctor James Furman, the spiritual father of the school, was the son of Richard Furman who came to South Carolina as a surveyor before the Revolutionary War from New England. The family was interested in education. Their school was first opened in Edgefield, South Carolina, in 1827 but due to financial difficulties and other reasons it was moved to the High Hills of the Santee at Statesburg. It operated there for a few years and was moved again, this time to Fairfield County.

After the Reverend Doctor Jonathan Davis of Fairfield County was made Chairman of the Board of Trustees a tract of land consisting of 557 acres was purchased in his county and the school was opened there. The location

FURMAN INSTITUTE

was a little more than three miles west of Winnsboro. At first a frame building of thirty by one hundred and twenty feet was built to house the students, classrooms, and library. This was in 1837. In May of the same year the building and its contents were destroyed by fire. One student, a Mr. Goddard of Georgetown, South Carolina, perished in the flames.

The school was operated on the manual labor plan. Each student worked a task in the field every day to help defray his expenses.

In 1838 two more buildings were erected. One was of three stories and was built of brick. This was used for an administration building, classrooms, and chapel. It still stands atop a high, barren hill, vacant and weather-beaten, like a gaunt ghost of the past. The second building was also of brick construction. It is a rather attractive, spacious, two story structure with a one story piazza across the front. It was used as a residence for the faculty. Now it is the home of the Timms family who have lived here for many years.

Besides the two brick buildings there were a dozen or more small barracks buildings eighteen by sixteen feet in which the students lived.

During the years that the school remained in Fairfield it had a struggle to remain in operation. In a short while the manual labor department proved to be a failure. This was closed in 1841. The classical school dragged on for some time longer but was finally forced to close for a while; then it was reopened. The department of Theology, however, continued to flourish and grew to be the best school of its kind in the entire South.

In spite of the progress made in the Seminary the Baptists raised more funds and decided to move the school again. In 1851 it was taken to Greenville, South Carolina. The new Furman planned to offer courses in law and medicine and was rechartered as Furman University. It has grown now to be one of the largest and most popular institutions of learning in the state. Several years ago the campus was moved again; this last time from the City of Greenville to a beautiful site at the foot of the mountains a few miles west of the city.

HEYWARD HALL
KINCAID — ANDERSON — HEYWARD

This imposing manor house is of pre-Revolutionary construction. It was built by Captain James Kincaid in 1774, shortly before the war.

The house itself is a large square building designed on Georgian lines with a hipped roof covering the building and with porticos at the entrance. The thick walls are constructed of old English bricks that were brought to this country as ballast for ships. The locks, grill-work, ornaments, and hardware all came from the mother country. A great solid mahogany stairway is one of the main features of the house. All of the mantels are elegantly carved and beautifully proportioned. The woodwork and trim was also done by hand.

Ever since its erection this old house has been a show place but in comparatively recent years it was renovated and completely restored. Great

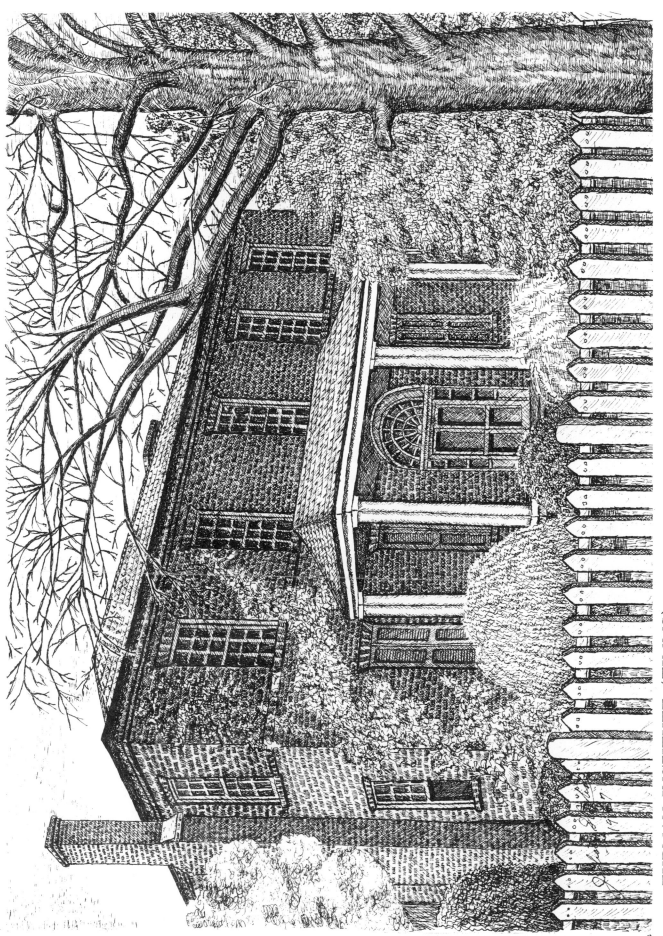

FURMAN INSTITUTE (TIMMS)

LXXXIII

attention, too, has been given to the gardens and parks surrounding the house. All in all, this place ranks among the "firsts" of the old homes of the Upcountry. The restoration of this estate was done by the late Mrs. Dan Heyward over a period of several years.

The original gardens and parks were laid out by Captain Kincaid and they were acclaimed to be one of the most beautiful and effectively executed in the Piedmont. They consist of a series of terraces, each from six to ten feet below the other. Boxwood is used to an advantage in the more formal areas and native trees vie with one another in the park for beauty and grandeur.

An old mounting block of solid stone is in front of the house, a relic of the olden days when it was in constant use by the grand ladies and gallant gentlemen of the past. Swinging in a curve from the front door to the road and on down through the woods is a walk of granite blocks.

Many of the old outbuildings are still on the place. One of the most interesting is a small house in the back yard. It has a rock floor and in the old days was called the "icehouse." Before commercial ice was introduced this precious commodity was furnished by nature. During the winter months ice was cut from the nearby river and stored in this building for use during the sweltering summer months. Just to the side of the icehouse is a round, stone-lined well that supplied water for the household. It is very deep and even in hot weather its water is chilled and refreshing.

Captain Kincaid's plantation was spoken of as a model place and his ideas and methods were studied and used by many other planters. Several sources credit him with the invention of the cotton gin. For some time he had a model on his plantation that he had been using and perfecting. During this period Eli Whitney visited in his home. Whitney was most enthusiastic over this new labor saving device. He studied it and made drawings of it and some time later he made a model and secured the patent. In Fitz-Hugh McMaster's HISTORY OF FAIRFIELD COUNTY this controversy over the cotton gin is discussed at length on page fifty-three.

Captain Kincaid will long be remembered and blessed by many as the man who first brought the tomato to this country and developed it as a food. Kincaid was a retired sea captain and during the Revolution he served under General Francis Marion and General Thomas Sumter with distinction.

Like the manor houses in England after which this old landmark is patterned the place also has its ghost. For many years and several generations some of the inhabitants of the countryside tell that on moonlight nights a lovely lady clothed in a flowing white nightgown which glistens in the moonglow may be seen walking from the house to the cemetery at Ebenezer Church which is but a short distance away. She is said to be the ghost of a lady who lived there many, many years ago. In real life her husband had died young. She was very much in love with him and often on moonlight nights when she could not sleep she would gather flowers from the garden and take them to his grave where she would sit and grieve for hours.

After the passing of the Kincaids the name of the house was changed from KINCAID MANOR to ANDERSON MANOR. A Kincaid daughter who married an Anderson came into possession of the estate. The Andersons were planters and operated a quarry which was later sold. The Heywards bought

HEYWARD HALL

LXXXIV

the house and headed the operations at the quarry. The name of the old manor house has been changed again. It is now called HEYWARD HALL.

The Heywards completely restored the property and had the house handsomely furnished and decorated and the gardens and grounds relandscaped. Since the death of Mr. and Mrs. Dan Heyward the house has been unoccupied.

EBENEZER

ASSOCIATE REFORMED PRESBYTERIAN CHURCH
(THE OLD BRICK CHURCH)

EBENEZER is often called or referred to as the birthplace of the Associate Reformed Presbyterian Church in South Carolina for it was in this historic little building that its first pastor, the Reverend James Rogers, acted as moderator and organized the Associate Reformed Synod of the Carolinas in 1803.

The building was erected in 1788 by the people of the Lower Little River section of the county. They were predominantly Scotch-Irish Presbyterians, highly religious, and staunch and fervent in their beliefs.

The sanctuary is small and rectangular in design, very plain, and covered with a gabled roof. It is well lighted and ventilated with long, unornamented windows. The bricks for the thick masonry walls were made by members of the congregation who also constructed the church and built the simple but well-appointed furniture. The pews are straight-backed and severe. The pulpit is merely a dias, three steps above the floor level, with a plain rail around two sides; the back is against the wall. It is entered by a pair of steps on the front, one set on either side of the center which contains the Bible stand. There is also a slaves' gallery where the house servants worshipped with their masters and were taught the fundamentals of Christianity.

The Reverend James Rogers, a native of County Monaghan, Ireland, and a graduate of the University of Glasgow, became pastor in 1791. He was thrice married. His first wife was Jane Wilson Murray; the second, Celia Davis, and the third, Jane Adger, all natives of Fairfield. Aside from the organization of the Associate Reformed Presbyterian Church in South Carolina, he founded the Jefferson-Monticello Academy in 1800 and was its president for more than a quarter of a century. He died at his plantation, WHITE HALL. During his pastorate the church and the academy prospered. This prosperity continued until the outbreak of the Confederate War when all of the young men in the congregation joined the Confederate Army. The casualty list from this section of the county was unusually high.

Among the pastors who served the church in later years are James Boyce, Thomas Ketchin, C. B. Betts, and A. J. Kirkpatrick.

During the war, in 1865, Fairfield County was invaded. Ebenezer was in the path of General Killpatrick's Union Cavalry. Near the church there were skirmishes with the Confederates who had the advantage of being located on the ridge. When the Union Cavalry reached Little River they found that the Confederates had burned the bridge. In order to avoid the bullets of

EBENEZER CHURCH   LXXXV

the sharpshooters in the hills above them, the Yankees took advantage of the little church and ripped out part of the flooring and woodwork to hastily construct a bridge over which they might cross the swollen stream and move on beyond the ridge.

After they left a note of apology was found inscribed on some of the woodwork that remained intact. It read thus:

"To the citizens of this county —
Please, excuse us for defacing your house of worship.
It was absolutely necessary to effect a crossing over the Creek.

(Signed) A Yankee."

In the peaceful little churchyard at Ebenezer, enclosed with its weathered, time-mellowed granite wall are many tombs bearing illustrious names of great South Carolinians. Some of them are: the Kincaids, McMorrises, Andersons, Sloans, Rabbs, Watts, Irbys, Macfies, Ruffs, Harpers, and Players.

LITTLE RIVER BAPTIST CHURCH

The Reverend Jacob Gibson was Fairfield's first Baptist minister. He was a highly educated man, a teacher and a preacher, who spent his useful life in preaching the gospel and instilling literary refinement into his neighbors and followers. He and his family came to Fairfield County from Virginia in 1762 and settled in the Little River section near what is now known as the BRICK CHURCH or EBENEZER Associate Reformed Presbyterian Church. In 1767 he gave the land, organized, and helped to build the LITTLE RIVER BAPTIST CHURCH.

The present building was erected in 1845. The same builder designed this and the MONTICELLO METHODIST CHURCH. He was an excellent carpenter and a gifted artist as can be seen in the beautiful, detailed work and the designs of these buildings. The wood-work, hand carving, rosette, gallery, and chandeliers bear witness to his good taste and talent. When this building was completed it was dedicated by the Reverend Doctor James C. Furman of Furman University in Greenville, South Carolina and a former resident of the Jenkinsville-Monticello community.

During the War Between the States this old house of worship was damaged by the Northern troops. The imported prisms of the chandelier were smashed, some of the furnishings abused, and the building left in a general mess.

Until 1867 the Negroes of the community used the gallery and came in a spirit of reverence to worship with their former masters. They were still welcome but the new teachers and politicians from the North taught them to be distrustful and to hate their old masters and white friends and to build their own churches where their own preachers and the Carpetbag missionaries could direct their thinking.

As the years passed by many families left the community and the little church had a struggle for existence. Finally it was closed and the former members worshipped at more assessable locations. This was the case for about forty-five years. During that period the Negro Episcopal Church in the com-

LITTLE RIVER BAPTIST CHURCH

LXXXVI

munity, Saint Barnabas, was burned. Its members did not have the means to rebuild. They were offered the use of LITTLE RIVER BAPTIST CHURCH building which they accepted for about a decade and until they were able to rebuild.

Due to improved roads, transportation, renewed community pride, this little church has been restored and reopened to serve the descendants of its former members and their new neighbors. It is elegantly furnished with much of its original equipment. The handsome marble topped communion table and chairs that adorned the little building in its beginning have been restored to their former places. A handsome new pulpit and matching accessories was given as a memorial to the late Claude Jeter, of Detroit, Michigan, a former member of the church and son of the community, by friends from his adopted home.

Services are now held regularly every Sunday and the old congregation has taken on a new growth and prosperity.

HOLLEY PLACE
HOLLEY

When this old house was built it must have been a beautiful, gay, and fashionable home. It is now nothing more than an empty shell, gloomy and eerie with the dark open windows staring hauntingly at the casual passers-by. The grounds are overgrown with brush and weeds but the two great granite gateposts still stand guard and mark the spot where carriages filled with the gentry of the countryside once stopped.

No records have been found on the place other than it was the home of the Holley family for generations. The late P. B. M. Holley as one of the last of the family to own it.

HOLLEY PLACE

LXXXVII

McMEEKIN PLACE
McMEEKIN — CURREY — EPISCOPAL CHURCH

One of the most mysterious and historic old homes in Fairfield County is what for many years was known as the CURREY PLACE and is now called SAINT BARNABAS. It is located in the JENKINSVILLE—MONTICELLO section between the two settlements, an area that was known for its fine homes and culture from 1800 until the Confederate War. This and several other old plantation homes still bear a haunting witness to their days of affluence and gracious hospitality. Many others, among them the famous Allston plantation, whose lowcountry live oaks and tall, tapering granite shafts mark what was once a long avenue and gate-posts for the thirty-six mansion which rivaled Nicholas Peay's MELROSE; WHITE HALL, Colonel Hugh Stevenson's elegant home, and several others were in this neighborhood where beautiful women, fast horses, and fabulous parties were "the order of the day."

Very little of the early history of this place can be found but it must have been a McMeekin home. Near the house, in a small plot enclosed with a heavy wrought-iron fence, are two old graves. One is in memory of General Thomas McMeekin who died in 1847 in his 74th year. The other is the grave of his wife, Margaret, who died in 1822 in her 49th year, and their son, John, who died in 1836 in his 20th year, the last two mentioned were formerly interred in the churchyard at EBENEZER a few miles away, some time called the old BRICK CHURCH. They were brought from there to this spot in 1849 according to the inscriptions on the tomb.

Little information can be found on the General although he is an ancestor of some of the McMeekins in the community. He was evidently a general in the War of 1812 or a general in the state militia.

The house is unusual in design. The ground floor is constructed of thick, plantation-made brick walls. Massive brick chimneys, two on one side and one on the other, with several inside chimneys provide fireplaces for the rooms. The design of the front is dominated by an unusually large triple window in the gable overhanging the front porch which extends across the front of the building. A rear wing with a gallery-like porch on one side juts back from the main body of the structure. The front porch is supported by massive square wooden columns. Smaller wooden posts support the gallery on the rear. An old hand-dug well, enclosed with brick is still prominent. It is quite near the house, just off from the back porch. The house though empty and deserted still stands proudly and defiantly.

The Episcopal Church of South Carolina purchased this property and established a mission for Negroes here. It is called SAINT BARNABAS and is the community center for the Negro Episcopalians.

McMEEKIN PLACE

HAPPY VALLEY

HARPER — McPETERS — FEASTER — PETTIGREW
GLADNEY — ROBERTS — HALL

This homey, very old country place was recently purchased by Mrs. John Bratton Hall (Cleora Clowney). She is now in the process of restoring and renovating the house and in improving and clearing the grounds. Since the death of the former owner the place had fallen into bad repair from neglect.

In 1920 Mrs. Genie Aiken Gladney Roberts and her brother bought HAPPY VALLEY. At that time or a little later the place was put into good repair and Mrs. Roberts made it her home and spent the last years of her life there. She was a highly educated lady who had spent most of her adult life in study and in teaching in colleges. She was considered an authority on South Carolina History and devoted a great deal of time in research on this subject.

Mrs. Roberts bought the tract from Florence G. Feaster who had inherited it from her father, Trezvant De graffenried Feaster. Mr. Feaster bought the place in 1890 from George Butler Pettigrew for an investment. Mr. Pettigrew had acquired it in 1885 from Annie C. McPeters and Maria Harper who had become the owners of HAPPY VALLEY in 1874.

HAPPY VALLEY is also known as the HARPER PLACE. Its name came from one of the first owners, a Judge Harper, who is spoken of in Fitz-Hugh McMaster's HISTORY OF FAIRFIELD COUNTY thus; "Before 1785 the citizens had no court nearer than Camden, that venerable town being the center of a very large judicial district. At the above mentioned date Judge Harper used to spend his vacations in the western part of Fairfield.

HAPPY VALLEY

LXXXIX

HIGH POINT
THOMPSON — GLENN — JETER

The HIGH POINT property goes to a land grant from the King of England, dated 1773. The grant was to William Thompson who was the builder of the present house in 1800.

HIGH POINT is the name that Thompson chose for his new home and plantation. It is very well named for the house stands on the highest point on the ridge between Columbia and Spartanburg, an elevation of some five hundred feet or more. The view from this site is majestic. High hills and valleys extend to the horizon on all sides, their vivid greens melting into various tints of purple against the clear blue sky and billowing white clouds.

The house is a typical plantation home of the period, a large, rectangular, two storied building. On one side is a mammoth chimney that is completely covered with English ivy, well-trimmed beds of which cover the ground on the front and sides. The house is unique in that it has large inside chimneys also. A wide porch extends across the front. It is supported by generous, square, panelled columns. There are two entrance doorways on the front. All of the windows are flanked with the original, hand-made louvred shutters. Giant magnolia trees provide a shady coolness for this friendly, homey old house, and when in bloom their fragrance permeates the air. A well-pruned crepe myrtle hedge screens the yard from the road.

Except for the handsomely carved oversized mantel the interior is simple but spacious. The drawing room is furnished with priceless family heirlooms, some of which were among the original furnishings of the house.

In 1845 Mrs. William Thompson deeded the place to her son-in-law, H. A. Glenn. The present owners are Miss Kitty Glenn and her sister, Mrs. E. Claude Jeter reside in the comfortable old home. They are descendants of the Thompson's and the Glenns who have lived here for more than one and one-half centuries.

During the War Between the States this old house was visited by the invaders but its treasurers were successfully hidden and saved. In the guest room ceiling is a trap-door, the only opening into the attic. The valuables were secreted here; and the tall, canopied, cedar-poster bed was placed under it and completely hid the opening. In their search for an entrance into the attic the plunderers smashed several of the closet doors and the walls in some of the rooms but to no success.

An interesting family cemetery, containing the grave of William Thompson, is near the house. It is well kept and is used by the descendants of this pioneer.

The old house is in excellent condition and is cherished and well cared for by its owners and members of their family, whose people have ranked among the first families of the county down through many generations.

HIGH POINT

FAIR VIEW

THOMPSON — GLENN — McEACHERN — MARTIN

This lovely old columned country manor house was built by the Thompson family who held extensive grants of land in this area before the Revolutionary War. The house was built some time after 1800. In 1830 Doctor John Milton Glenn bought the property from the Thompsons.

Doctor Glenn and his talented wife were very gay and hospitable social minded people as well as being large slave holders and successful planters. Their home was almost constantly filled with guests and the place was one of the social centers of the Jenkinsville-Monticello community.

The Glenns took great pride in their grounds and gardens which were immaculately kept. The formal boxwood plantings, in geometrical patterns, were on either side of the big front yard. Stately magnolias flanked the house and the semi-circular driveway leading up to the building which crowns a high rolling knoll.

Louise, the Glenn's only child, was twice married. Her second husband was Furman McEachern, a salesman who at one time (1909) served in the Legislature from Fairfield County. She deeded FAIR VIEW to him after they were married. After her death McEachern married Mary Chappell and gave her the plantation as a wedding gift. The widow McEachern did not live in the old house and it was rented for a number of years during which time the gardens were greatly abused. The boxwoods became overgrown and were cut down rather than being pruned and trimmed.

The present owner and occupant of the old home is the Reverend L. K. Martin, a retired Presbyterian minister from Georgia. He saw the old place, became attracted to it and purchased it from Mrs. McEachern during the 1930's.

During the Confederate War the house was set afire by the Northern troops and left to burn. After their departure the flames were extinguished and the grand old place was not destroyed. It still stands proudly on its high, green hill among the gaint magnolias.

FAIR VIEW

XCI

MAYFAIR

ALSTON — COOK — CHAPPELL — BRUCE — McMEEKIN

MAYFAIR was designed and built by Colonel William Alston in 1824. Colonel Alston was a member of the prominent and powerful Allston and Alston families who controlled and planted most of the famous rice plantations on the Waccamaw River in Georgetown County. These people were avid politicians, social and civic leaders, supplying South Carolina with two governors. Governor Joseph Alston, son-in-law of the Vice-President, Aaron Burr, was governor of the state during the War of 1812. His only child died in the summer of 1812 and his wife, Theodosia, was lost at sea in the same year. His early death some few years later in 1816 was attributed to grief and melancholia brought on by the loss of his loved ones. Governor Robert Francis Withers Allston was chief executive of the state in the stormy days just prior to the War Between the States. He was a scholarly, wise, and widely traveled man and did much to promote education, culture, and art in South Carolina. He died while still in his prime and before the war ended.

After MAYFAIR was completed Colonel William Alston presented the house and plantation to his daughter, Mrs. Burrel Cook, as a wedding gift. The Cooks entertained lavishly and were leaders in the social and political activities in Fairfield County, Mr. Cook having served several terms in the State Legislature. This family held the place from 1824 until 1883 when it was purchased at auction by Thomas Chappell.

The family of Thomas Chappell resided here until 1945. At that time it was purchased by his granddaughter (Mary Douglas Chappell), Mrs. R. C. Bruce. Mrs. Bruce repaired and partially restored the home occupying it at intervals for several years. Recently MAYFAIR was sold to Mr. Silas Mc-Meekin of Columbia, South Carolina, a relative of the Chappell family and a native of the Jenkinsville-Monticello community.

This is quite an elegant house and reflects the Lowcountry influence of the builder both in style and design. The stairs, mantels, woodwork, and the entrance are especially beautiful. The carvings and decorative designs are among the finest to be found in the county. The back stairway is enclosed. The reason for doing this was to protect the young ladies of the household from exposing their ankles and limbs as they descended the stairs.

CHAPPELL PLACE

RUFF — CHAPPELL

A short distance from the main crossroad at Jenkinsville is a delightful old country home. Surrounded by broad green fields with wooded hills in the background is the old Ruff or Chappell house. The building itself is deceiving; on first glance it appears to be rather small and of a fairly late vintage. The deception is due to a room that has been added at one end

MAYFAIR

of the porch on the front which was originally an open porch. The present porch is quite spacious and has been screened for summer comfort which gives it a modern appearance.

In reality this is one of the oldest homes in the county, having been built in 1795 by Daniel Ruff, a member of one of Fairfield's pioneering families. The drawing-room is the main feature of the building. It is a large broad room, lighted and ventilated by long windows and decorated with a most handsome mantle of excellent proportions and design. The room is wainscoted to the chair-rail which is of a more simple design. The furnishings, for the most part, are lovely old family pieces that are all in fine condition.

The big yards surrounding the house are accented with well-placed shrubs and flowerbeds. A semi-circular boxwood drive leads to the front door. A rare desert willow is out-standing among the shrubs adorning the grounds. It has a beautiful spiny foliage and a delicate pink blossom growing in large clusters at the ends of the branches. There is but one other plant like this in the state (so the owners of the house have been told.)

In early days the second floor of the building housed frames of "silk worms" and weaving equipment for making silk cloth. One ancient mulberry tree still remains on the grounds where once there was a grove. The tender leaves of these trees were gathered and fed to the silk-worms who spun themselves into their silken cocoons which were processed and woven into fine fabrics by the industrious people who lived here when this great country was in its infancy.

During the ante-bellum period this plantation also produced quantities of cotton and it was during this time that the property passed from the Daniel Ruff's son, Silas Ruff to the Chappell family.

When Sherman's troops came through in the declining days of the Confederacy the Chappells were living here. Their hams, other foodstuffs, and valuables were successfully hidden from the plundering hordes in the stairs. Several steps were carefully removed, the goods concealed under them, then, replaced in such a manner as to leave no traces or marks of having been disturbed. A fine saddle-horse also escaped the soldiers. It was taken into the woods near the house and hidden in a deep ditch. Miss Sallie Chappell, then a very small girl, hid her beautiful doll under a pile of leaves near the yard fence. When the intruders were leaving one of the soldiers discovered this little treasure. He picked it up, hung it on the clothes-line and called back, "Little girl, I found your doll!"

This little girl later became the mistress and owner of the plantation. She lived here and attended to the farming operations as long as she was able, living to a ripe old age. She never married and during her last years had to leave the old home that she had loved and cared for for so long and live with relatives.

After being vacant for a quarter of a century her nephew, the present owner, Mr. Douglas Chappell, and his family moved into the house and restored it. The house is now in excellent condition, well cared for, and a place of beauty and serenity. Mrs. Chappell is a great-great-granddaughter of the original owner and builder of the grand old house.

CHAPPELL PLACE

DAVIS PLANTATION
DAVIS — ROBINSON

After the Revolutionary War the Monticello community became one of the wealthiest sections of Fairfield County. Many handsome mansions were built during this period of affluence which lasted from the 1780's until the Confederate War in the 1860's. A few of these survived the Federal invasion by General Sherman's troops, among them the old Davis home which is now one of the proudest and most elegant mansions in the county.

The main body of this house is covered with a hipped roof through which two mammoth inside chimneys protrude. It is fronted with a classic gabled portico supported by four tremendous round columns resting on heavy masonry bases. A beautiful fanlight window adorns the center of the portico gable which overhangs the upstairs balcony and the first floor veranda. Wings extend on one side and to the rear of the building.

Doctor James B. Davis, who lived here, was one of the most colorful figures of his time. He was a son of the illustrious Doctor Jonathan Davis and his wife Rebecca Kincaid Davis, a daughter of Captain Kincaid of Revolutionary fame. Doctor Jonathan Davis was a highly educated man, a Baptist minister, and a successful planter and educator. It was due to his efforts that the Jefferson-Monticello Academy and the Furman Institute were established in Fairfield. Doctor Furman, founder of the Institute, married two of his daughters.

James B. Davis was born December 31, 1809, on his father's estate near Monticello. He was educated at the Jefferson-Monticello Academy, South Carolina College, South Carolina Medical College, and the Medical College of Pennsylvania. He has been described as one of the most handsome and talented men of his era. His wife, whom he married in 1830, was Mary Elizabeth Scott of Richland County, a most charming and gracious young woman who was noted for her beauty and grace both in this country and abroad.

After practicing medicine for two years in Winnsboro, Doctor Davis gave up his public pratice and retired to the family plantation where he devoted his time to his agricultural interests and to the breeding of thoroughbred horses and livestock. In these fields he became a leader. He was an active figure in the Fairfield Agricultural Society and in the State Agricultural Society. His fame in these pursuits were proclaimed abroad and in 1845 he was appointed Minister of Agriculture to Turkey where he and his family lived until 1849.

While in Turkey he became a close friend of the Sultan Abdul Mojid, who was interested in the promotion of the cultivation of cotton in his empire. In gratitude for the excellent work by Doctor Davis the Sultan bestowed rich and handsome gifts upon the family. Upon their preparation for returning home he presented Mrs. Davis with a purse of $20,000.00 for herself and her heirs. To the doctor he gave rare and valuable animals, some of whose breeds had been carefully guarded and never before been allowed to leave the country.

Failing health and the loss of the sight in one eye prompted Doctor Davis to return to America for the Turkish climate was against him. His animals

DAVIS PLANTATION

were left on the Sultan's farm in the care of an agent. Their shipment was delayed due to the fact that the Cashmere goats had to be brought across the desert in baskets on the backs of camels. When they arrived in England they attracted the attention of the Earl of Derby who tried to purchase a pair of the goats. Doctor Davis stated that they were not for sale but that he would trade a pair of them for some Brahman cattle that had been in the Zoological Garden of London. These animals were known as the Sacred Cows of India and had been brought to the Gardens for exhibition by the British East India Company.

Several days later the Earl arranged for the trade, "a magnificent white bull, and a beautiful fawn-colored heifer, and for this pair he received in exchange one pair of Persian Goats, leaving the nine that were brought to the United States with the Brahman Cattle, and a pair of black water buffalo, which Doctor Davis had purchased in Turkey . . ." These were the first Brahman Cattle to be brought into this country.

In August 1849, Doctor Davis and some of his animals arrived in Charleston. The Steamship HUNTINGTON had arrived earlier, in June of the same year, with the first of the stock. For a short while the Davises lived in Charleston in a house on the corner of East Bay Street and Longitude Lane. They later moved to a home that he purchased near Columbia on the Garner's Ferry Road. After his father's death he returned to the family estate at Monticello where he died in 1861 at the age of fifty-one.

Upon his return to Fairfield Doctor Davis was given the nickname of "Turkey Jim" by his neighbors. He is buried with other members of his family on his plantation in the old Davis Cemetery not a far distance from the house.

His treasured herd was not destroyed during the War Between the States. After those perilous days members of the family sold some of the stock in Kentucky, Texas, Florida, and Georgia.

The Davis family continued to own this grand old house until it was purchased by the father of the present owner, Mr. Ross Robinson. The Robinsons keep the place in the true Southern tradition. The spacious halls and elegant rooms are furnished with family heirlooms and the grounds are well-kept surrounded by green pastures whose white fences enclose herds of fine cattle and beautiful saddle-horses.

MONTICELLO METHODIST CHURCH

The MONTICELLO METHODIST CHURCH was one of the first Methodist

congregations in Fairfield County. The original building was erected some time before 1820. As the membership grew this little house of worship was enlarged on several occasions. The present building was erected in 1861.

This building, although it has but recently passed its century mark, is a fine example of the rural churches of the ante-bellum period. On the exterior it is plain but classic, a rectangular structure covered with a gabled roof supported by four large columns on the front, a spacious tall porch is fronted and flanked by five easy-rising steps.

MONTICELLO METHODIST CHURCH

The interior is handsome. The pews and furnishings are plain but the woodwork and decorations show good taste combined with an air of elegance and refinement. The doors are topped with glass Gothic arches and the windows are long, slender, and airy, shaded with movable slatted shutters. Around the back and side walls is the slave gallery resting on graceful columns. The carvings and the bannisters used in the gallery are truly works of art.

The chandelier and the "chandelier ring or rosette" are most unusual and rare. The framework is brass, circular in shape, with eight brackets extending from the center to support eight large kerosene lamps.

During the War Between the States a division of Sherman's destructive army under the reckless General Kilpatrick came through the Monticello section burning and looting many of the plantations and homes as they came but for some unknown reason they did not molest this little architectural gem.

This church is still in use and is the pride of the community. It is well kept and landscaped, sitting back from the road in easy view for the passersby to see.

MONTICELLO STORE
and
POST OFFICE

DAVIS — McMEEKIN

The MONTICELLO STORE and POST OFFICE is one of the few reminders of the once famous Jefferson-Monticello Academy that served as a flourishing educational institution for so many years in Fairfield County. Most of the other buildings have either been destroyed by fire or razed.

It is a typical early American country store building covered with a gabled roof, the front of which covers an open porch supported by four large hexagonal columns which give it an air of distinction.

William Edrington states in his HISTORY OF FAIRFIELD COUNTY that when he attended the Academy in 1822, "I had as classmates William B. Means, Robert Means, James B. Davis, William K. Davis, and C. DeGraffenried . . . These, together with William M. Nyers, Thomas B. Woodward, James A. Woodward, Cullen Powell, John H. Means, and myself were boarding with Colonel Jonathan Davis, and our sleeping department was in his old storehouse recently fitted up for that purpose." This must have been when the wing and ell to the rear of the building was added.

The store continued to be a part of the Academy as long as the school lasted. Since that time it has been used as a community store and post office. It is now the property of Mr. Albert McMeekin, a life-long resident of Monticello, who operates the store. Mrs. McMeekin is the Monticello Postmistress and is known and respected throughout the community for the many gentle courtesies that she dispenses daily, beyond the call of duty, for her neighbors and the people of the community.

[254]

MONTICELLO STORE & POST OFFICE

XCVI

TRAPP PLACE

TRAPP — GOODLETT — SMITH

This unique old house is called the TRAPP PLACE, taking its name from early owners who lived here for several generations. The builder of the house is unknown but it must be of an extremely early vintage judging by its construction. The property was given to a Mrs. Trapp by her father (name unknown) when she married William Trapp.

The present owner, Mrs. Carrie Goodlett Smith (Mrs. Caldwell Smith) bought the place from descendants of the Trapps after the death of her first husband, Mr. Goodlett. She repaired the house which although run-down was still solid, built of large hand-hewn logs. At that time only two of the windows had panes in them, the others were only gaping openings in the walls.

The walls of the house have been covered with weatherboarding and ceiled on the interior which is quite simple and plain with no ornamentations or decorations but it has a definite early-American character.

The yard is fenced in and is filled with shrubbery and a profusion of colorful flowers which gives the old place an air of cheerfulness.

FONTI FLORA

PEARSON

The Pearsons were among the first settlers to come to Fairfield. They have been cultured social and political leaders for generations and about two centuries. The PEARSON MANUSCRIPTS kept and recorded by members of this family has done much to retain the history of the county. One of the first of the name was a leader of the two Seventh Day Adventists congregations who settled here before the American Revolution.

Through the years this family acquired much land and amassed a fortune. It was during this period of prosperity before the Confederate War that Doctor George Butler Pearson built the handsome mansion at FONTI FLORA and made it the seat of his estate.

The site was chosen with care and the name is most descriptive. Fonti Flora means fountains and flowers and fountain is a very literal name for on the place are numerous strong springs around which wild flowers grow in profusion.

The home that the doctor built is large and comfortable, majestic, and bordering on elegance. It is fronted with a two story gabled portico supported by six massive wooden columns. In the center of the front gable is a beautifully designed window with a fan-light of glass panes. The rooms are large and airy with high ceilings, handsome mantels, cornices and wainscotings, all made by hand and carved by artists of the trade. An imposing stairway rises from the long, wide hall and leads up to the second and third floors. Some of the original furnishings and paintings still grace the rooms and adorn the walls of the old mansion. In the drawing room are portraits of the Pearson family painted by the famous artist, Scarborough.

TRAPP PLACE

XCVII

The grounds have returned to their pristine loveliness. Except for the boxwood garden to the right of the manor house the setting is one of pure natural beauty. When the house was first built the grounds or park was exquisitely landscaped in the formal English tradition. This park surrounding the house included twenty-five acres of rare shrubs, flowers for each season, an orchard of fruit trees and one of nut trees; a vineyard, a rose garden, and a boxwood garden. The walks and drives were laid out in geometrical patterns and were lined with boxwood.

The usual outbuildings were well grouped to the sides and to the rear of the main dwelling. The remains of the old kitchen are still evident although now it is just a mass of huge stones. Among the auxiliary buildings was the "Doctor's Shop." Doctor Pearson was a naturalist as well as a physician and he grew and collected rare herbs from all over the world. From these he compounded his medicines which were used extensively throughout the countryside.

When the invading armies from the North came through in the Sixties FONTI FLORA was looted. Valuables were stolen and destroyed and rare books were taken from their shelves never to return again. The house itself was set fire to and still bears the black scars of those dreadful times on the charred wainscotings in the room where the fire was started and later put out by faithful servants who were responsible for saving the old mansion.

One member of the family to witness these horrible scenes was an old man in his "second childhood." His violent protests and high-sounding oratory amused the soldiers who taunted him just to hear him talk and rave. Before leaving they brought a horse into the grand hallway, bound the patriarch's hands behind him and mounted him backwards on the frighened animal, driving it with whoops and cheers up and down the hall until the old man was finally thrown off onto the hard floor. With jokes and jeers they left him there on the floor of the smoking house. After their departure the servants carried him out and extinguished the flames.

Another hair-raising event took place in this old house. A young mistress of the plantation was alone in the building with her small children one night. Living on the place was a demented but thought to be harmless old Negress. She did small tasks and was cared for by the family in appreciation for services that she had rendered in days gone by when she was well and in her right mind. On this particular night the mistress of the house was awakened by the old woman who was standing over her with a raised hatchet in her hand. She told the bewildered and frightened woman that she had seen a vision that night and that an angel had told her to go to the "Big House" and kill her mistress.

The horrified young woman was terror-stricken! She pleaded and argued that her life should be spared for the sake of her small children. In spite of the entreaties the old crone would only shake her head and say that the ugly job had to be done just as the angel had instructed her although she was "awful sorry" that her "young missus" had to be the victim. Finally, almost at her wit's end, she remembered that the old woman loved whiskey. When this fact came into her mind she reasoned in another way and told her that some liquor was in the house but that it was so well concealed that no one could

FONTI FLORA

XCVIII

find it if she did not take them to it. The old woman showed immediate interest and let her thirst overcome her angel's command. She permitted her victim to get the spirits for her. The cunning housewife insisted that she drink some before using the hatchet for it would give her more courage. The old woman heeded and took one drink and then another until she became so drunk that she could no longer hold the death weapon. The next day the unfortunate old creature was bound and loaded into a wagon and was taken to town by some of the plantation hands where she was placed in the county jail from whence she was committed to the State Asylum.

FONTI FLORA still remains in the Pearson family. Its present owner is Mrs. George W. Tomlin of Columbia, South Carolina, who was born Katherine Pearson. Mrs. Tomlin and her family dearly love the old place and are now in the process of a restoration which is being supervised by Mr. Tomlin.

ROSE HILL

HALL — PROVENCE — LONG — BLAIR — PARKER

This property was given to Elizabeth (Lizzie) Hall by her father as a dower when she and Colonel David Provence were married. Colonel Provence came to South Carolina from Kentucky in 1836. After he and Miss Hall were married he enlarged and remodeled the house adding a wing to the rear and the bay windows on the front. A Mr. Jennings who worked for him did the work.

The house is an odd little building. Entering it from the front is a reception hall with a room on either side and from which the stairway extends to the second floor. To the rear of the hall is a large, long dining room and another smaller room. The kitchen is behind the main building but connected to it by a covered back porch. The bedrooms are on the second story and a porch extends across the front.

Colonel Provence was an eccentric gentleman, very proud and proper. He loved horses and racing and enjoyed entertaining and being entertained. His grave is a short distance from the house and across the road from the Rock Creek Baptist Church and cemetery. One story is that he requested to be buried here and not in the cemetery with "the common herd." Another is that he was a Catholic and requested not to be buried with "the heretics." The third story is that due to his faith the members of the church objected to his interment among them. Be all of this as it may the fact remains that the solitary grave with a handsome marker stands alone on a hill opposite the church.

After the Colonel's death quarrying operations were begun at Blair's and the first of the operators and stonecutters were Italians. They heard local stories about the late Colonel and that he was a rich man who had requested that a fortune be buried with him. Believing this story a group of these men exhumed the old man's body during the hours of darkness and on finding no treasure except his watch and ring, left the casket and the almost mummified body beside the open grave.

ROSE HILL

XCIX

Occupants of the house and people of the community say that Colonel Provence still haunts the house and the road leading to his lonely grave. Strange noises are heard in the house and locked doors mysteriously open and slam.

Mrs. Hannah Long Blair, now in her nineties, moved into this old home when she was five. Her father was Captain James I. Long who bought the property from the Provence estate and later gave it to her after she was married. In recent years Mrs. Blair has passed title to her daughter, Mrs. George Blair Parker. She still resides here with Mrs. Parker and her family.

McCANTS PLACE

Of early American log construction this old remnant of the past on the outskirts of Winnsboro is said to be a haunted house. It has belonged to the McCants family for several generations.

McCANTS PLACE

C

PART V

FEASTERVILLE,
BLAIR
and
WOODWARD

THE FEASTERS (PFISTER)
and
FEASTERVILLE

by

ETTA A. ROSSON

Some time subsequent to 1735, a certain Peter Pfister, with his son, Andrew, and others, decided to leave their native Canton of Berne, Switzerland, and seek their fortunes in one of the colonies of youthful America. It required many days and not a few hardships for them to cross the Atlantic, but they probably knew much of the hard life while living among the mountains of their native land. There may have been other sons.

On reaching America, they established themselves in Lancaster County, Pennsylvania. About 1767, Andrew Feaster married in Philadelphia, Pennsylvania, a widow, Mrs. Margaret Fry Cooper. Her first husband's name was Peter Cooper. She had by him two or three children, Adam, Eve (or Elizabeth), and Peter. Andrew Feaster had also been married before. We do not know the name of his first wife, but by his first marriage he had a daughter, Martha, who married William Colvin.

Peter Pfister (Feaster) was now very old, and in discussing the problems if moving further South, over rough roads and through a region sparsely settled, someone asked; "But what shall we do with Uncle Peter?" He had grown old and infirm, and seemed hardly able to endure the laborious journey. But he had been listening, and promptly replied: "Take me along, and if I die, bury me by the road-side. God is just as near one place as another." On the hard journey, Uncle Peter did die, and his body was buried as he had directed. Somewhere in Virginia, in a churchyard, lies the dust of this brave old pioneer, the grave unmarked, but those in who followed after, he has continued to live as an inspiration. The family was six months on the journey South.

It appears that the Feasters had been connected with the Dunkard faith in the land of their fathers, and it is possible that they were drawn to Southern Pennsylvania in order to be associated with others of like religious convictions. After moving South, we find the next record of them in Wilkes County, Georgia, in 1774, petition "Andrew Feaster, 150 acres of land on Funderburg Branch. Wife, four sons, four daughters, aged 18 to 2 years, from Pennsylvania."

There is also in the Georgia records, petition of John Feaster, "asking 100 acres of land between Francis Pavy and Thos. Marthaison, on Great Ogeechee" (Granted conditionally), and other Georgia records.

Two or three years after the above record of Andrew Feaster, in Georgia, the British were agitating the Georgia Indians to attack the Carolinas and all the white settlers. Andrew moved back into a more thickly populated section with the large family he had to protect, and, unlike some others, failed to move back to Georgia. This is borne out by the fact that there is no record in Georgia of Andrew selling his land. He simply walked off and left it.

Andrew Feaster and wife, with his son, John, and others, finally arrived in Fairfield County, South Carolina. Martha, daughter of Andrew Feaster by his first wife, also came with them. We are told that with Andrew there also came his nephew, John Feaster (probably the one referred to in the Georgia records) from whom there descended in Edgefield County, South Carolina, Andrew, Lawrence (Laurens), Elizabeth, and Irene Feaster, who were brought back to Fairfield County by Andrew and Mary Norris Feaster, after a visit they made with Mary Norris' family.

Andrew Feaster and family settled in Fairfield County on what was later known as the Wyatt Coleman place, later owned by the family of Hugh Stevenson. Here the family decided to cease their wanderings, establish their homes, and engage in agriculture. Among these hills, which doubtless reminded them if their beloved Switzerland, descendants of the Feasters have resided for more than 170 years.

Andrew Feaster was born in 1735, and died July 15, 1821, aged 86 years. Six children were born to him and Margaret Fry Cooper, as follows:

(1) Martha (daughter by his first wife, name unknown), married William Colvin when she was 16 years old. On the day she married, she knew for the first time that Margaret was only her step-mother, and she wept bitterly.

(2) Susan married Moses Cockrell.

(3) John, born 1768, died in 1848, married Drucilla Moberly, daughter of Samuel Moberly, Private Quartermaster and Riding Express, in the Revolutionary War; and his first wife, Mary (Polly) Waggoner, daughter of Hans or Jans Waggoner, who built Fort Waggoner, in the Cherokee Indian War, 1760.

(4) Margaret, married Ezekiel Wooley.

(5) Alice, married Hudley McShane.

(6) Andrew, born 1776, died January 25, 1808, unmarried.

(7) Jacob, married Margaret Cannamore. No children.

Andrew Feaster served in assisting in the establishment of American Independence during the War of the Revolution as follows: "Furnished a mare and a field of growing grain to Colonel Henry Hampton's Dragoons." (See South Carolina Stubs to indents, Book O, page 321.)

The name Pfister is of Swiss origin, and was changed to Feaster by Andrew Feaster, Sr.

The locality in which Andrew Feaster settled took its name, FEASTER-VILLE, from Andrew Feaster, and is so called today. He was a public advocate of the Dunkard faith, and preached frequently, as tradition testifies, in advocacy of that faith among his neighbors. His son, John, born 1768, also advocated the same doctrine in public, and it was he who built and gave the land and buildings for Liberty Universalist Church, at Feasterville, the Feasterville Male and Female Academy, and Feasterville Boarding House. The church was built in 1832, and organized in 1877, but the group' of Universalists, as they called themselves, instead of Dunkers, was there before 1777.

[267]

Mrs. Jennie I. Coleman's record of the building of the "Boarding House," and the Feasterville Male and Female Academy just across highway 215 from Liberty Universalist Church, is as follows:

"Mr. and Mrs. J. W. Ladd came from Virginia to Winnsboro, South Carolina seeking work. He was a painter of portraits, and came to Feasterville to make a portrait of my great-grandfather, John Feaster, about 1840. The portrait is still in the family. Mrs. Ladd came with her husband, and spent the time at the Feaster home. She was pleased with the neighborhood. Especially, she noticed the number of fine, beautiful girls and remarked to Mr. Feaster that there should be a school for them. He at once said, 'If you will teach it, I will build the house.' It was finished about 1845, and always has been known as the 'Boarding House'." His son, Andrew Feaster, supervised the building, two stories, four rooms upstairs for the young ladies, and four downstairs with a double kitchen in the back yard, and everything desirable, on a five and one half acre plot of land.

"When all was finished in 1845, the Ladd family moved from Winnsboro. Her mother, Mrs. Stratton, from Virginia, came with them, to keep house. Many ladies came to the school from Laurens county, Chester, Newberry, Blackstock, and all around the neighborhood.

"Mrs. Ladd, a fine musician, gave lessons to a number of girls, taught music, various kinds of fancywork, beautiful quilting, painting, and needlework of many kinds. There were families of Feasters, Colemans, and neighbors, to keep the surrounding alive and interesting."

Mrs. Ladd, on leaving the community, went back to Winnsboro to live, and was there when Sherman came through from Columbia. She was a very remarkable woman, and most of us have heard the story of her saving the Masonic jewels from the Northern troops.

The Reverend B. D. Clayton, in his book, "FORTY-SEVEN YEARS IN THE UNIVERSALIST MINISTRY," states that he taught in the Academy from 1864 until the end of 1865. We know Mrs. Ladd was teaching there in 1848. Mrs. Julianna Stevenson Coleman stated that she went to school there in 1848, and boarded with Mrs. Ladd in the "Boarding House." Other girls rode horseback from their homes. Miss Margaret Narcissa Feaster, daughter of Andrew Feaster and Mary Norris, was teaching in the Academy in 1860-61, according to her diary. Mr. Feaster Lyles and his sister, Isabelle, taught there after the war.

In his will, dated November 25, 1847, John Feaster states:

"My will is that the lot of land on which the Female Academy and Boarding House stands at Feasterville, containing five and one-half acres, I give and bequeath to my three sons, Jacob Feaster, Andrew Feaster, and John M. Feaster, in trust and for the benefit of the Feasterville Male and Female Academy, and I hereby appoint and constitute them trustees of the same." From that time, when a trustee died, or removed from the community, another trustee was selected by the two other trustees. The trustees control the "Boarding House" property, but may not sell it. When the building ceased to be used as a residence, it came to be used as a community building. The grounds were landscaped in 1937 by Mother Walker of Winthrop College.

Coleman Masonic Lodge No. 97, organized by the Colemans and Feasters in 1860, occupies the front upstairs rooms for their meetings.

In the Feaster Family Cemetery at Feasterville, Andrew Feaster's monument bears the following inscription:

ANDREW FEASTER, SR.
Departed this life
15th July 1821
in the 86th year of his age
a native of the
Canton Berne
Switzlerland
Margaret, his wife,
departed this life
10th Octr 1823
aged 95 Years
A native of Philadelphia.

John Feaster built a two story frame building near the Cemetery, about 1806. This house had the first glass window panes north of Beaver Creek, and people came for many miles around to see them.

Also, an American eagle, in colors, was painted on the ceiling of the front porch, and when the Northern troops came through during the War Between the States, they did not burn the house for this reason.

In the time of John Feaster, indigo was the money crop. Because of competition with India, it ceased to be profitable, and many of the planters of this section thought that they were unable to change to anything else so sold their farms and went West. John Feaster said, "Don't leave your land to go where they are crowding in." He stayed in Feasterville, changed over to cotton and became very prosperous.

Some of the early pastors of Liberty Church were: Reverend Giles Chapman, Mr. McMorries, the Reverend Doctor Shinn, Doctor D. B. Clayton, Mr. Andrews, and others. The last was Doctor Thomas Chapman of Atlanta, Georgia and Saluda, South Carolina.

CLOWNEY HOUSE

ASHFORD — CLOWNEY — METTS — BROWN

his old house sits high on a hill overlooking the broad Broad River and on across many miles of Newberry County. The early history of the place is somewhat cloudy. It is situated on lands that belonged to one time to the Strothers and later to the Ashfords.

To the rear of the building and quite near the highway from Newberry to Winnsboro is an intriguing old cemetery enclosed with a heavy granite wall. The ancient graves that are marked tell of the people who lived here before 1800. Some of those interred in the plot are Ashfords. The map of Fairfield County in Mills Atlas was made in about 1820 and shows this as Ashford property with the ferry below called Ashford's Ferry and the road to Winnsboro called the Ashford's Ferry Road. Through Colonial, Revolutionary, and Confederate eras on up until the present, this has been one of the most travelled and historic arteries of traffic to and from the county.

The old house on the hill, though now neglected and over-grown with brush and grasses, still stands. Upon close observation it is a quaint building and the Victorian "gingerbread" woodwork in the gables is deceiving as to its age. Upon closer inspection the bricks and fundemental construction shows that it is of a much earlier period. Inside chimneys allow each of the rooms a fireplace. It is a simple rectangle of one and one-half stories covered with a gabled roof. On one side is a very plain shed porch covering the main entrance. An oversized, elongated window capped with a gabled cornice, lights and ventilates the second floor. Another interesting feature is the design of the first floor windows. They, too, are elongated, nine panes over nine, with frames including louvred openings above the windows proper.

Tradition says that this building was constructed to serve as a ferry house, a place in which the ferryman lived and with accomodations for guests in case of bad weather or hindered crossings of the river. It is said to have been built by the Ashfords whose home was nearby.

About the time of the War Between the States, and for many years afterward, this old house was occupied by William Clowney and his family. Since that time various tenants have lived here. It is now the property of Mrs. Hunter Brown of Newberry who has extensive tree farms in the area.

One interesting and rather romantic story is told about the place. A beautiful daughter of the house was in love with a young man but her father discouraged their marriage. The young man left Fairfield and went to Texas, where he made a fortune, and returned years later to claim her for his bride. Again he was discouraged but before returning to his adopted state he persuaded his sweetheart to elope with him. The attempt was unsuccessful for the father discovered the ladder at one of the gable windows and knew what was about to take place. He went to his daughter's room, found her bags, and hid them, forbidding her to carry out the proposed elopement. The lover returned at the appointed time, waited for several hours and when she did not make an appearance he returned to the west. Many years later, when they

CLOWNEY HOUSE

were both well along in middle-age he heard of her father's death and came home again for his love. This time they were married and returned to Texas and their descendants are now counted among the well-to-do first families of that state.

ROCK CREEK BAPTIST CHURCH

The ROCK CREEK BAPTIST CHURCH appears to be a new building but such is not the case. It has merely been repaired and brick veneered in recent years which gives it this "new look." The congregation dates back to the very early 1800's and the little building probably to the 1830's. No history of this church has been made available but it is known that at one time a school was also located on the site and was sponsored by this congregation.

FAIR VIEW
MEANS — BLAIR — FRAZIER

FAIR VIEW is situated on one of the highest hills along the Broad River in the Blair section of Fairfield County. For many miles from the Newberry County side of the river it can be seen boldly looking down from the pinnicle that it has crowned since its erection a few years after the Revolutionary War. This house was built to stand; it still does, and proudly, too, in spite of having been neglected and deserted for about a quarter of a century. To reach the site one has to walk over rough, rocky terrain through a fast growing forest that is veritably making its way to the front door of the old mansion. This place is so remote and overgrown that it reminds one of the castle of the "Sleeping Beauty" in the fairy tale by that name.

The builder of the house was General Thomas Means of Colonial and Revolutionary fame who died in 1807 and is buried in the yard. His grave and the weathered old tombstone may still be found hidden among the vines, overgrown shrubs, and briar roses that cover the place. General Means also represented Fairfield County in the Legislature in 1798 and 1799. His son, John H. Means, was Governor of South Carolina.

The house is built of hand-made bricks that were made on the plantation by the slaves. The main body of the structure is a rectangular two story building covered with a hipped roof. From the rear extends a two story ell with a gabled roof. This ell has long porches or galleries extending the full length of both stories on one side. The solid brick walls are twenty inches thick and are plastered on the interior. This plaster is still in remarkably good condition considering that the house has been open to the elements. The drawing-room ceiling has a handsome molded chandelier ring in the center of a beautifully molded circular floral design. The bricks on the outer walls are plastered with cement. In a semi-circle over the front door and molded into the cement

ROCK CREEK BAPTIST CHURCH

is an American Eagle with outstretched wings bearing the shield of the United States. This patriotic decoration placed there by the Revolutionary soldier is disintergrating with time and exposure but during the Confederate War it saved the house from being burned. When the Yankees saw the United States crest and the American Eagle they would not set their torches to the building.

After General Means' death FAIR VIEW was sold to William Blair. During the long occupancy of the Blair family this old home was one of the social centers of the community. Stories may still be heard of the grand balls that were held here. William Blair was married three times and had a large family and connections as well as a host of friends who all took advantage of and enjoyed his unstinted hospitality. The place has remained among his descendants up to the present time, a period of about one hundred and fifty years. The current owner of FAIR VIEW is J. B. Frazier, Jr., a great-grand-son of William Blair.

An amusing incident is told by members of the family about the harrowing days when FAIR VIEW was visited by the Yankee soldiers. Captain William Blair was and old man and was at home during the occupation. The company which visited his plantation to loot and burn was under a Captain William Blair, a young man from New Jersey. When he was told by the servants that the owner of the place was also a Captain William Blair he was anxious to meet him and had the old man called out. The young captain was very affable and on seeing the patriach said, "My name is also William Blair. I am from New Jersey. I wonder if we are kin?" To this the old man retorted, "No! If I had one drop of damned Yankee blood in my veins I'd slit both of my wrists to let it out!" So saying he brandished a long knife to further dramatize his statement. This amused the young man and the house was spared and before he left he and the old captain were on more congenial terms although the old gentleman remained restrained and somewhat distant. The above story was told by a descendant of Captain William Blair who now resides in Newberry, South Carolina.

LYLES-CROWDER HOME
LYLES — FEASTER — CROWDER

In the western part of Fairfield County along the Broad River the land is extremely hilly, bordering upon being mountainous. The steep wooded hills and deep narrow valleys make it a rugged country. Hidden among the hills, usually on their crests, like gems in a tiara, are some of the oldest and most historic homesteads in the county.

One of these is a time-worn, weatherbeaten house that was built in 1812 by Major Thomas Lyles.

Major Thomas Lyles was a son of Arromanus Lyles whose father was Ephriam Lyles, one of Fairfield's first settlers. Ephriam and his brother, Colonel John, took lands at the mouth of Beaver Creek on Broad River. The family was from Brunswick County, Virginia originally but they came to Fairfield from Butte County, North Carolina, about 1745.

FAIR VIEW

Ephriam was killed by Indians in his new home and a Negro servant was murdered by them in the yard, but his widow, Ann, and her seven or eight children escaped.

Arromanus became one of the first citizens of the district. From 1790 to 1794 he represented the county in the state legislature. In 1796 he was one of the citizens who paid tribute to the memory of the Reverend Jacob Gibson, a pioneer Baptist minister, who died in that year.

Major Thomas Lyles married a Miss Peay, a daughter of another of Fairfield's first families. He was a representative to the legislature from 1832 until 1836. In 1839 his family consisted of three persons. When the census of 1860 was taken his plantation was valued at $32,000.00.

The house that Major Lyles built in 1812 is a sturdy and an attractive one. It was constructed to last and to be an heirloom for posterity. The bricks were all made by the plantation Negroes who mixed and packed the red mud with their bare feet, jigging, singing, chanting, and having a gay time in general while the work was being done. When the bricks were dried and cured they were laid in wet mud mortar and pointed up on the surface with lime. The walls of the building are entirely of brick and are sixteen inches thick.

The design of the house is typical of the period. It is a compact rectangular structure with a well-braced hipped roof. The roof is covered with thick hand-hewn shingles. For decoration the bricks in the cornice are laid in an angular pattern and a one story porch or piazza extends across the front just below the second-story windows. This is supported by graceful, slightly tapering, round columns. Over the front door is a semi-circular fan-light of very small glass panes. The broad entrance steps are of everlasting blue granite.

Originally the front yard was fenced in to protect an elaborately designed boxwood garden through the center of which is a wide brick walk. The fence and trellis over the gate was covered with a profusely blooming rose vine. Brick columns on either side of the entrance were topped with graceful wrought-iron urns.

Old houses such as this are filled with stories of romance, history, gaiety, love, sorrow, mystery, and well-guarded secrets. One of these stories will be told.

In late February, 1865, after the fall and destruction of Columbia, Sherman's devastating army moved into Fairfield. At that time Major Lyles was an old man, ill and bed-ridden. As the dreaded invaders came near his little domain he sent his family away for their safety. The household treasures were taken with them. His finest stock and the highly bred horses for which his plantation was famous were sent deep into the swamps of the Broad River and carefully hidden. The old man, alone with a few servants, remained on the place to receive the enemy. Before their arrival the bummers had been told that he was a rich old planter and that in all probability he had much treasure hidden away.

They came like angry hornets swarming all over the place. When they inquired about the owner the servants told them that their master was in the house and ill, too sick to be disturbed. The usual search for loot ensued; the barns were raided and then burned. Stock and poultry that was superflous for them to carry away was killed and thrown into the flaming out-buildings. The cotton house containing fifty bales of fine staple went up in smoke. The

LYLES-CROWDER PLACE

old house was ransacked and when no treasure was found the old man's bed-chamber was invaded.

He told them positively and emphatically that there was nothing of any value in the house or on the plantation. They did not believe him and swore at him telling him that if he did not reveal the hiding place of his loot that they would burn the house over him. To these threats he shouted, "Burn and be damned! I only have a few miserable years ahead of me."

With that some of the men placed a pile of litter under his bed and set fire to it. He did not flinch but remained in the great canopied bed until the smoke began to fill the room. He was too sick and too proud to move. When the soldiers realized this one of the officers said, "That is the bravest old man I have ever seen," and ordered the awe-stricken servants to remove the fire. This was done with all haste but even today, almost a century later, the owners of the old house point with pride to the charred spots on the floor in the front bed-room.

A boy taking the last of the horses to safety in the swamps was overtaken by the plunderers and the beautiful animal was taken from him. This steed was "Zuleika," the pride of the country-side. It belonged to one of the Lyles daughters and was acclaimed to be the best "ladys' horse" ever bred in the county. The day after the Yankees left, this beautiful creature was found by the road-side with its throat slit from one side to the other. The vile act was committed by the officer who had appropriated the animal for his own use. He did it because the horse had bitten him and refused to let him mount. This horse was as gentle and easy to manage as a pet kitten when handled by a lady but it had been trained to bite and refuse to carry any man, except its groom, who tried to handle it.

The proud old house still belongs to the family of Major Lyles. It passed from him to his grand-daughter, Sallie Lyles (Mrs. John C. Feaster), and is now owned and lived in by her daughter, Mrs. B. D. Crowder, now an octogenarian.

IVY HALL

LYLES — BLAIR

IVY HALL is one of the oldest houses in the Blair section. It was built by Arromanus Lyles, the first white child born in Fairfield County, before the American Revolution. The house with its surrounding five hundred and eighty acres continued to remain with the Lyles family until it was purchased from the estate of Captain Thomas M. Lyles by L. M. Blair in 1902. Mr. Blair extensively remodeled and restored the grand old landmark and since that time it has been the home of his family.

During the restoration the new owner was careful to retain all of the charm and personality of the ancient building. The large fireplace with their simple attractive mantels still add warmth and character to the spacious plastered and panelled rooms that are floored with wide hardwood planks. A broad one story porch supported by hand-turned wooden columns extends across the front of the building. This is covered with vines of carefully trimmed English

IVY HALL

Ivy that has shaded the house with a restful coolness for more than one hundred years. It is from these vines that the home took its name.

On the interior the house is unpretentious but it is large and comfortable and about it is an air of stately dignity. There are twelve large rooms on the first two floors with two wide halls running the entire length of the house. At each end of the hall and on the first floor are winding stairs with very plain pickets and rails which add to the refined simplicity of the panelled hall-way.

The structure is put together with wooden pegs and still is as sturdy as it was when it was first built. The finished lumber that was used in its construction was dressed in Charleston. In those early days it took a week for the wagons to make the round trip. The horses that pulled the wagons wore sleigh bells on their harness so that the family would be pre-warned of their return.

IVY HALL has long been known for its hospitality. If it could speak it could tell of many historic and interesting events. When General Sherman came through this part of the country this was one of the houses marked to be destroyed. A detachment of his men after looting the place filled a trunk in one of the upstairs rooms with litter and paper and set fire to it. After they left, Uncle Billy Mosely, one of the faithful servants, found the fire and extinguished it before much damage was done. Before he could conqueor the flames they had burned a large ugly place in the floor. As a reminder of that hazardous day the owners did not repair the charred planks but nailed a piece of thick leather over it where it can still be viewed.

LONG HOUSE
EDRINGTON — FANT — LONG

This picturesque little farm house painted white and neatly fenced in has stood since about the 1850's. This, however, was not the first house to occupy the site. Many years ago there was a much larger home here. It was built by the Edrington family who came from Virginia and settled in South Carolina shortly after the Revolutionary War.

The Edringtons accquired large tracts of land in the Blair section and built three large houses which have all been destroyed by fire. One of these was the home of William Edrington, the historian. It was looted and burned by Sherman's men along with its handsome furnishings of early Virginia antiques, valuable library, manuscripts and historical records. The other was a brick house that burned in the early 1900's.

The family who lived here owned a number of slaves and employed an overseer. Shortly after the present building was erected one member of the family learned that his overseer made a practice of flogging the Negroes. The master did not approve of this method of punishment and told the overseer that he must discontinue it.

Some time later he caught the overseer in the act of beating a man that he had tied to a tree across the road from this little house. The master became so angry that he shot and killed the overseer. This hasty act cost him most

LONG PLACE

of his fortune and he was forced to dispose of some of his property to pay his legal fees and costs.

Doctor Fant bought the house and plantation. He lived here during the War Between the States and for some time afterwards. Will Long, the present owner, bought the place from Doctor Fant's estate and has made it his home for many years. This past year he and his wife celebrated their golden wedding anniversary in the old house with hosts of their friends and relatives.

AIKEN PLACE
BELL — AIKEN

This once attractive little house has fallen into bad repair due to absence of owners.

For many years this was known as the BELL PLACE. The first owner recorded is Mr. William Bell. He and his wife lived their married lives here. Mrs. Bell was born and raised here and inherited the place from her parents but we have no record of their names.

Robert M. Aiken married Margaret (Maggie) Bell, a daughter of the house, and lived here and raised their family. They had four daughters. One daughter, Robbie, married C. B. Starnell. Their daughter, Margaret Rose, married James Kilgore. She is the mother of Starnell Kilgore who wrote a complete novel, AGAINST TOMORROW, while still in her early teens.

The Robert Aiken family moved to Columbia and a sister-in-law of Mr. Aiken lived here for a number of years. Her name was Victoria Yongue Aiken but was called Vic by her family and friends and now the old house is called the VIC AIKEN PLACE. After this family occupied the place it has remained vacant.

COLEMAN HOUSE
COLEMAN

Doctor Robert Coleman was the third child of Henry Johnathon and Mary (Polly) Feaster Coleman. Henry Johnathon was next to the youngest child of the fourteen children of Robert and Elizabeth Roé Coleman, the first Coleman family to settle in Fairfield County. Polly was the daughter of John and Drucilla Mobley Feaster, also early settlers.

Henry Johnathon and Mary had sixteen children. Three of the sons, Robert Williams, William Preston, and Benjamin Franklin, were all doctors. All of them graduated from Bellevue Medical School in New York. Robert and Preston practiced in the Feasterville area and Frank in Louisana.

When the Civil War started six of the nine sons enlisted with the Confederacy, Jacob, Preston, Allen, Franklin, Henry, and George.

Doctor Robert sent George, the youngest of his brothers, to King's Mountain Military School to prepare him for service in the Confederate Army, though he was only seventeen years of age. All of the brothers were enlisted in the

AIKEN PLACE

Buckhead Guards before going into active duty. They were in Company B, 17th Regiment. Preston served as Captain and Frank as a Lieutenant. Robert was also a member of the Buckhead Guards but did not go to the war because he was unanimously selected by the people of the community to remain at home. They felt that he could not be spared. Henry and George were the only two of the six brothers to return. George was the only one of the family to live a long life and it is from him that many interesting stories and facts have been recorded. Robert was a counselor in his neighborhood during the Ku Klux Klan days. It is said that his counsel was never unheeded during those trying times.

The father, Henry Johnathon, was a soldier in the War of 1812. He was given several grants of land for his services. Henry was a farmer and a hatter. His father, Robert, stated in his will that he would like for his thirteenth child, Henry Johnathon, to follow his trade of making hats. His shop was located on what is now Highway 215. Henry carried out his wish and supplied all of the surrounding country with beaver and other varieties of hats. The shop was a short distance from his old home which sat on top of the hill west of the shop site. The water for the family's use and for the making of the hats came from a spring which was just across the road from the shop. It was, and still is, known as Hatter's Spring. It is a powerful spring and furnishes water for many families as well as for the passers-by.

While Robert was a medical student in New York he saw a house that he admired very much. When he returned home later he had one like it built for himself. This was little more than a hundred years ago. It was built in 1858 by a Negro named Peter. The lumber from which the house was built was sawed from trees growing on the Coleman plantation. They were hauled by ox carts to Charleston to be dressed. There the boards were hand planed and most of them were long enough to extend the full length of the rooms. The two front rooms were about twenty-five feet square and had very high ceilings. The house proper contained seven rooms, beside the medical office, and large front and back porches with bannisters around them. It was built high above the ground on large brick pillars. It took a full year to erect the building which was put together with pegs and hand-made nails. During the construction the lumber was kept in a log house built for that purpose. It was called the "lumber house." Under the "big house" was a small cellar used for the storage of fruits and vegetables.

The outbuildings included a kitchen, dairy, carriage house, harness house, cotton house, and a small residence for the cook and carriage driver. The slave quarters were a little more than a mile to the north of the home. After the slaves were freed the more faithful ones were given a few acres of land. One of these was Wyatt Coleman, but the other names have been forgotten.

During the Civil War when Sherman was making his way through South Carolina, some of his men raided this home. They put live coals in the medical office which burned a spot in the floor. These coals were removed by one of the house servants. A locked drawer and a bureau were torn open in the search for valuables. The old dresser still bears the scar, which is ever a reminder of those horrible days. The ladies were demanded to hand over their jewelry; the silver-ware was stolen, as well as the meat and all other food supplies. All of the live stock was herded away. During the raid the

CVIII

COLEMAN PLACE

master of the house was concealed in the little outhouse in the garden. He stayed here several nights previously not knowing when the Yankees might arrive.

Robert's ancestors before him had also experienced the horrors of war. Hans Wagner was in the war against the Indians. Andrew Feaster was among those helping in the Revolutionary War and his father, Henry Johnathon, was in the War of 1812.

On November 9, 1847, Doctor Robert Williams Coleman and Nancy Amanda McConnell were married. Both of them are buried in the Feaster Cemetery along with all of the Henry Johnathon and Mary Feaster family, excepting two sisters who lived in Georgia. "Doctor Bob" was a planter and a physician. He raised fine horses and had a splendid orchard. At times he enjoyed piecing quilts, knitting, and crochetting. He served as administrator in settling many of the estates of his connections. Papers showing this are still in the possession of his descendants. The Coleman Masonic Lodge No. 97 was organized in 1860. The warrant for this lodge was granted to John Christopher Columbus Feaster, W.M., Robert Williams Coleman, S. W., J. W., and John Feaster Coleman. Robert was serving as Worshipful Master at the time of his death.

Robert Williams Coleman reared a large family of children. His home is still owned by his descendants. His daughter, Lizzie, and her husband, Yongue Coleman, lived and celebrated their golden anniversary here. Their daughters, Kathleen and Mary Bess Coleman, now live on the place. When the Coleman, Feaster, Mobley Reunion is held each year the brothers and sisters, grandchildren, great-grandchildren, and great-great-grandchildren attend it and they come to the old home where a second reunion is held of the Lizzie and Yongue Coleman descendants. A happy time is had when they all get together in the "House That Robert Built."

THE BOARDING HOUSE

In the ante-bellum days this old house was alive with lovely young ladies who were attending the Feasterville Academy. This building was, and still is, called the BOARDING HOUSE. It was designed and operated under the direction of Mrs. Catherine Ladd who directed and operated the Academy founded and supported by the Feaster family. Mrs. Ladd's mother supervised the running of the house and the preparations of the meals.

A more detailed account of this building will be found in the INTRODUCTION TO FEASTERVILLE.

THE BOARDING HOUSE

CIX

LIBERTY UNIVERSALIST CHURCH

This congregation dates back to the late 1700's. The present building was erected before the War Between the States. For more information on this old church see the INTRODUCTION TO FEASTERVILLE.

CX

LIBERTY UNIVERSALIST CHURCH

CLANMORE

FEASTER — FAUCETTE

CLANMORE, the home of the Faucette family in Fairfield County, is a beautiful, historic, ante-bellum house. It is built along Georgian lines, a stately and well designed mansion that is most imposing in its majestic setting among towering oaks and crepe myrtles. This well kept landmark seems almost to be an echo or a sentinel out of the past.

Facing east is the neighborhood of Feasterville, a section rich in history and tradition, it is located on the old main road between Columbia, Union, and Spartanburg. This is now State Highway 215 and is often referred to as the Monticello Road. The house was built about 1845 by John C. Feaster, a member of the prominent Feaster family from which the community takes its name. He and his wife lived there until 1868 at which time the place was sold.

Major Charles Washington Faucette became the new owner. Upon his return from the Confederate War he found his home in Winnsboro in ruins so he bought this house and plantation for his family residence. Soon after they moved into the community they gave the name of CLANMORE to their home. Since that time it has remained the seat of the Faucette family.

Although the house has passed its century mark it has been well kept and is in excellent condition. It is a two story brick structure having four rooms on each floor with halls extending the entire length of the house through the center, actually making two additional rooms. In the back yard, a short distance to the rear of the house, was a brick kitchen connected to the main body by a narrow covered passageway, through which the meals were brought into the dining room. In the kitchen was a great fireplace containing the necessary cooking utensils of the day, such as, pot-hooks, skillets, ovens, and even a turn-spit. On this spit many a pig was done to a delicious, dripping brown. Across the narrow hall and behind a small stairway leading to a room above was the storage pantry and smoke-house.

The kitchen no longer stands having given away to the ravages of time. Its walls crumbled and fell into decay. A new kitchen of well seasoned pine has taken its place, but the square old brick house remains in its completeness.

The very best materials were used in its construction, most of which came from the plantation. The bricks were baked in the owner's kilns and the heart-pine lumber came from the estate's forests. All of the doors, facings, and trim was done by hand. The framework of the roof is fastened with wooden pegs and the walls and partitions are of solid, double sized brick. The interior is finished with smooth plaster and the exterior walls are covered with white stucco. The house proper is large and square with a hipped roof and four double chimneys, two at each end, affording a fireplace for each room. Partially across the front is a porch supported by four massive stuccoed brick columns. The upstairs balcony is open on top and is enclosed with wrought-iron bannisters. Originally a set of matching columns covered with lattice and on which rose vines and ivy were entwined extended down the front walk. This made an impressive entrance from the driveway to the friendly, old-fashioned, double doors. The colonade and arbor was destroyed by the cyclone of 1886 and was never rebuilt.

[290]

CLANMORE

The rooms are about fourteen feet square, with wide, thick pine floors, big, sunny windows and hand carved doors. They are furnished with antique furniture that has been in the family for many generations. These rooms are well-appointed, friendly, and refined. The old parlor still has its portrait by Ladd, a delicately carved love-seat, a marble top table that came from Paris, and old square Nuns and Clark piano, a big armed chair with clusters of grapes carved in it, and a handsome brass fire-side set. In the living room is a Governor Winthrop desk and small library tables. There are two side-boards in the dining room. One is a delicate, serpentine front, Hepplewhite piece, over one hundred and fifty years old, that belonged to some of the Coleman kin. The other is a massive cherry piece of a somewhat later period but well past its century mark that belonged to another kinsman, Colonel Hugh Stevenson of WHITE HALL. One corner is filled with a huge corner cupboard and in the center of the room is a beautiful drop-leaf table. Old pieces of china, silver, and a painting or two finish the room off. In the halls are fragile little chairs, spinning-wheels, and a grand-father's clock; all dearly treasured heirlooms.

Probably one of the most interesting features of the old house is its quaint stairway with the balcony and "burned spot." The "burned spot" is a dark reminder of the day that the Northern soldiers attempted to set fire to the building.

They came one afternoon, took possession, and searched the house and surroundings for valuables and food. They frightened the slaves and gave the cooks orders to prepare supper. The officer conducting the search on the lower floor found two new home-spun dresses hanging behind the door in the small guest room. He took them down and slit them into strips with his sword, then threw them on the floor and walked over them. He then went into the hall and kindled a fire on the second triangular step of the stair. He left the fire to burn and began to shout orders to hurry on with the supper. He even made a trip to the smokehouse to secure more hams.

During this time Lula Feaster, a young niece of John Feaster, who was a refugee with her uncle's family, was so indignant over the destruction of her new dresses, awaited an opportunity to extinguish the fire with a cup of cold water.

When the officer returned he thought that the fire had smothered itself so he went to the upstairs porch and started another, which was also extinguished by this brave Southern girl.

After supper the soldiers decided to spend the night in the community and gave no further trouble and seemed to forget that the house did not burn. Had they really meant to burn it? This will never be known.

In 1867 Charles W. Faucette and his family moved into the home, where he reared his family and spent the remainder of his life, passing away in 1904, at the ripe old age of eighty-four. After his wife's death two years later the property was inherited by their only son, Charles W. Faucette, Jr. To him it was a heritage to be loved and cherished. Before his death he expressed a wish that the house would always be in the possession of some member of the family. The present owners are Miss Julia Faucette, Miss Mary Faucette, Andrew M. Faucette, and Marion D. Ogburn.

CLANMORE has always played an important part in the social life of Feasterville. This hospitable home with its upstairs ball room and downstairs parlors has been the scene of many balls, teas, dinners, and infairs before and after the Confederate War. The old stairway has often felt the slow, quiet tread of footsteps as lovely brides made their way down to the old-fashioned parlor, where before an improvised alter, marriage vows were said. -

CLANMORE
Home of the Faucettes
in
Fairfield County

by
Julia Faucette

Old house to live in,
Old wood to burn,
Old books to dream over
Old Poems to learn.

Old friends to talk to,
Old folks to love,
Old memories that linger
Like blessings from above.

Old china to use carefully,
Old silver to shine,
Old letters to sort out
Old records to find.

Old flowers to give fragrance,
Old gifts to share,
Old mirrors to glance into,
Old jewels to wear.

Old woodwork to polish,
Old floors to sweep,
Old sounds to listen to,
Old secrets to keep.

Old diaries to treasure,
Old Bibles to read,
Old cookbooks to fill out,
With recipes we need.

Old "burned spot" to look for,
Old Confederate Uniform to show,
Old canteen to drink from,
Old history dates to know.

Old staircase to walk up,
Old clocks to strike,
Old lamps to refill,
Old beds to sleep in at night.

Old windows to rattle,
Old boards to creak,
Old bricks to crumble,
Old roofs to leak.

Old doors to open wide,
Old greetings to send,
Old hearths to warm by,
Old clothes to mend.

Old portrait to be proud of,
Old albums to display,
Old family trees to rewrite,
Old scrapbooks to put away.

Old spinning-wheels to turn softly,
Old cradles to rock,
Old candlemolds to wonder at,
Old closets to lock.

Old wedding gowns to try on,
Old shawl and yards of lace,
Make oldest dreams of yesterday
Peep from their hiding place.

Old paintings to cherish,
Old castors to set out,
Old candle-sticks to admire,
Old quilts to count.

Old pianos to play upon,
Old songs to sing,
Old, old times to remember
and to long for again.

STEVENSON PLACE

STEVENSON — WEIR — BOLIN — BRICE — BLAIR

This old house is truly a ghost from the past. It is now impossible to reach except on foot or by horse-back, yet, once that it is discovered it stands boldly and proudly, almost defiantly, on a high, bleak and gullied hill, commanding a glorious view of the countryside for miles and miles. It has been said that from the third story window the lights of Winnsboro can be seen.

The site is so utterly deserted and desolate that there is little evidence that mortals ever knew the place except for the old house itself and an indestructible rose-vine at one of the porch corners.

The house is long, tall, and sturdy, still square and erect although uninhabited for almost two decades. It is built high above the ground with two full stories and an ample attic that in the old days served as a ballroom. The building is long and rectangular in shape, covered with a gabled roof with colossal chimneys on the ends. A one story porch supported by six square columns covers the front. A smaller porch of similar design extends over part of the rear. Fanlighted double doors open into the wide hall extending through the center of the house with two large rooms on either side and a graceful and impressive walnut stairway that continues to the third floor. The long, panelled windows on the front add to the decor. Two "shed-rooms" are on either side of the back porch. On the second floor are also four rooms and a broad hall. The third floor, an attic, is not divided and was used originally for balls and parties.

All of the mantles and interior woodwork are beautifully executed. The walls are plastered above the wainscoting. The house was built for a large family and for gracious living. In the old days a kitchen reached by a covered passageway was to the rear, behind which were barns, stables, outbuildings and Negro quarters.

In the front yard stood a store-house on one side of the avenue and a blacksmith shop on the other. Only one of the great trees that formerly lined the approach to the house remains.

The old house was built by Samuel Hemphill Stevenson, a son of John and Jannette (Murdock) Stevenson, for his bride, Cynthia (Yongue) Stevenson, a daughter of Martin and Jualianna (Cameron) Yongue. A dim date written into the plaster on one of the chimneys appears to be 184 — (the last numeral is not legible).

The Stevensons had a large family of which there were several beautiful daughters who married into the gentry of the community. Mr. and Mrs. Stevenson were gentle and industrious people noted for their hospitality and charity.

During the Confederate War this old home was a haven of refuge for the women, children, and old men of the neighborhood. Several times when there were rumors of slave uprisings they gathered here at nights and slept on pallets in the broad halls and attic ballroom. During the Union invasion some of these same people returned to find shelter after their own homes had been destroyed. Still later, during the black, disgraceful days of the so-called

CXII

STEVENSON PLACE

Reconstruction the helpless and frightened came again for protection and companionship.

After the death of Samuel and Cynthia the plantation passed to their daughter, Sarah Stevenson, who had married her cousin, James Stevenson. She left it to her daughter, Elizabeth (Lizzie Stevenson) Weir. She and her family lived here for a few years and then moved to Columbia. Later she sold the place to T. Randolph Bolin. Manuel Brice, a Negro farmer, purchased the house and plantation from Bolin. A few years later it was sold for taxes and was bought in by Ray Blair of Blair, the present owner, who has held the property for about a quarter of a century.

WOODWARD

MOORE PLACE

GALLOWAY — MOORE

This is one of the pioneer or pre-Revolutionary houses remaining in Fairfield County. In this particular section of the county many of the older homes were destroyed by the British and Tories, later by the Yankees and accidental fires. This old house has withstood all of these hazards and, if for no other reason, is unique for having survived the wars, elements, and time.

Originally it was a rectangular, hand-hewn log building of two stories, constructed of squared logs carefully mortised and pegged together. Not only the exterior walls but also those of the interior are of this sturdy construction. It is covered with a gabled roof with large chimneys on either end. The entire front is protected with a one story shed porch supported by square panelled columns. The windows of the second floor are small but those of the first have been elongated and a broad entrance-way of double doors is surrounded with a paned, glass frame. The logs on the exterior of the building have been covered with weather-boarding and the interior partitions and walls have been ceiled or panelled.

The history of the old building is rather obscure. For generations it was owned by the Galloway family. About the turn of the present century it was sold to Thomas Moore whose widow and descendants still inhabit, love, and care for the old homestead.

The woodwork and decorations of the interior are simple and plain but in true early-American taste. The center hall extending through the house with rooms on either side and the easy-rising stair make it both spacious and comfortable.

An avenue leads to the house from the road. It is shaded by giant, ancient oaks. The grounds are neatly kept but are not pretentious. They give one the feeling of being in a pure, early-American setting.

MOORE PLACE

CXIII

CONCORD CHURCH

The CONCORD PRESBYTERIAN CHURCH at Woodward is a simple, rectangular, red-brick building. It is covered with a gabled roof and rests on solid granite foundations. The building is dignified but severely plain, no decorations.

The congregation is older than its house of worship, dating back to 1785 when the Reverend Robert McClintock, of Ireland, held services in the vicinity. In 1793 several supplies from South Carolina Presbytery preached here; among them the Reverends Roseboro, McCollough, Dunlap, Cousar, Gilland, and Davies.

The first "stand" or place of worship was located about five miles southeast of this building but was moved to the site about 1796. Here a log building was erected, each man of the congregation furnishing a log. The first one laid was by John Cork. During a hurricane this building was destroyed but it was replaced by another of the same construction. In 1818 the brick building was erected.

The Reverend Robert B. Walker enrolled and organized the church in 1796. The elders at this time were James Arter, James Caldwell, James Hindman, and Abraham Miller, John Sterling, James Robinson, and James McKeown.

The Reverend William G. Roseboro came to CONCORD in 1800 and served until 1810. He was followed by the Reverend Francis W. Porter who supplied until 1813. The Reverend Robert McCollough came next and remained until 1824. During this period the following elders were installed, Samuel Penny, Samuel Banks, Samuel McCollough, James Douglas, and Hugh Thompson. The Reverend William B. Stafford was installed in 1825 and served until 1834.

In 1836 the Reverend John Douglas became pastor but before he came Robert Caldwell, John Banks, and William Wilson were installed as elders and in 1836 John McCollough, Alex Hindman and Henry Moore were also installed. At this time the church had sixty-four members. James Wallace was pastor in 1848 until 1853 and from 1853 until 1858 the church was served by the Reverend W. J. McCormick. During his pastorate John Neil and Thomas Carlisle became elders. The Reverend G. W. Boggs supplied for a short while until the Reverend T. W. Ervin became the next pastor in 1859 and served until 1876. During his pastorate the following were installed as elders; A. B. and John C. Douglas, J. M. Blain, W. W. Brice, and A. H. Dunbar. The Reverend James Douglas served in 1878 until the Reverend John C. McMullen became pastor in 1879 and remained until 1884. During his pastorate William Douglas, J. E. Craig and W. Banks Thompson became elders.

Since this time the old church has had many faithful ministers and laymen. It is still an active, thriving church and its communicants are all well acquainted with and are proud of its service to the community for more than a century and a half.

CONCORD CHURCH

CXIV

LEWIS PLACE

WOODWARD — MILLER — WOODWARD — LEWIS

This attractive country home is one of a very early vintage. Its exact age cannot be determined but from the construction and the materials used the building could well be placed in the pre-Revolutionary era.

The house is situated on a high, rolling hill not far from historic old CONCORD CHURCH. The main body of this one and one-half story structure is built entirely of massive hand-hewn logs, mortised and pegged together. The interior walls are of the same construction. The building is a simple rectangle with a wing to the rear and is covered with gently sloping gables. On the front the roof extends over the long, wide porch and is supported by square columns that rest on solid granite bases. The porch is enclosed with plain picketed bannisters.

The outside walls have been covered with weatherboarding and those of the interior have been panelled. The interior has been renovated and modernized. The old flooring planks had become worn so thin that they had to be recovered. In recent years when a door was being widened some relics of the past were found between the logs under the panelling. An old saw belt and a newspaper announcing Abraham Lincoln's election to the presidency of the United States, listing the way in which the individual states voted, were found.

The Woodward family built the house and lived here until about 1845. During that year the house and a large acreage was purchased by Doctor George Miller. At this time the settlement and railroad station at Woodward was called Midway due to the fact that it was located midway between Columbia and Charlotte. The Miller family lived here until after the Confederate War. It was purchased from the Miller estate by Ed Woodward, a descendant of the former owners. This family occupied the house for several years and then leased the place to a Christie family who lived here until it was bought by Walter Lewis in 1911.

Walter Lewis' son, Robert A. Lewis, now owns the plantation and lives in the old house. He takes great pride in the place and keeps it in excellent repair. The grounds are neat and pleasingly landscaped and the old home has the atmosphere of early American antiquity and hominess about it.

LEWIS PLACE

ALBERT BRICE PLACE
BRICE

Located at the head of a densely wooded avenue, this old house is an attractive "cottage-type" plantation home that was built just before the War Between the States. Calvin Brice was the owner and builder. He was an ambitious young man and planned for this house to be the seat of a flourishing cotton plantation. The war, however, altered his plans and before his home was actually completed he had to leave it and go into the service of his state.

During the war years the house was left in the care of a faithful Negro servant, Aunt Sallie. She cared for and protected it well and when the conflict was over and the family returned her services were never forgotten. She lived to be quite an old woman and was always respected and cared for by her "people."

This place is now owned and occupied by Albert W. Brice, the youngest son of the builder, who has occupied the place since birth. Mr. Brice is now in his eightieth year, a dignified old Southern gentleman; the type that one likes to imagine inhabited all of the ante-bellum plantations of the Southland.

OAKLAND
MOBLEY — PATRICK — REES

John Mobley, who lived from 1794 until 1879 was the builder of this once proud old mansion. He was the youngest son of Samuel and Mary Wagner Mobley. John Mobley's wife was Catherine "Katsie" McLean who was two years younger than he and who died two years earlier, in 1877. The house was built during the 1820's.

The following is quoted from Mobley family records, "From his youth he was a most interesting personality. Shrewd and money making until fifty, like a sage he tired of it from that time forward. Before the War he was one of the richest men in Fairfield. He was the first man of that county to present himself for the Civil War. The officers refused him on account of his age, and his son, Andrew Jackson Mobley, then stepped forward, and has the honor of being the first Confederate soldier to enlist from Fairfield."

John Mobley was a wonderful man, "deferred to, and fawned over by his hypocritical friends, and feared by his foes. The Great Reaper gathered him after the close of his four score years and five. His body reposes in the cemetery of his gift. The rows of earth about him, mark the last resting place of his people. The ministering angel and companion, 'Katsie,' is there, too, beneath the sod, by his side."

The cemetery referred to is a short distance from the house across the main road from the avenue. It is called FELLOWSHIP CEMETERY. Andrew Jackson Mobley and his wife, Alice Eugenia Bynum Mobley are also buried here. After John's death the old home became the property of Andrew Jackson Mobley and his family who lived here until he had financial reverses and lost it. The place was purchased by T. G. Patrick of White Oak. It now

ALBERT BRICE PLACE

belongs to his grand-daughter, Jane Matthews Rees, of Fayetteville, Tennessee who inherited it from her mother.

During the life of John Mobley the old house was one of the grandest mansions in the county. One unique feature in its design is the way in which the columns of the first floor front porch are built. They are wide, square, and panelled. The panels facing the avenue leading to the house and those facing the building are glass. There are doors in them so that lamps could be placed inside that would light the porch and driveway. The reception hall is unusually large as are the rooms flanking it. Handsome mantels and woodwork once adorned the interior. The third floor was used as a ballroom and the kitchen and big dining room was detached from the home proper but connected with it by a covered passageway.

The grounds were formally landscaped by a professional and were the pride and envy of the countryside. The plantation was called OAKLAND. John Mobley's father's home was but a short distance away. It was also a grand mansion that was approached by an avenue of giant cedars. This place was called CEDAR SHADES.

The Mobleys are listed as being among the largest slaveholders in the state. Tradition tells us that when formal entertainments were held at either of these mansions Negro boys with torches were stationed in the trees along the avenues to light the way for approaching guests.

Now all that remains of CEDAR SHADES are a few scattered bricks and several giant trees. FELLOWSHIP CEMETERY, although overgrown and suffering from damages from falling limbs and deliberate desecrations is still filled with dignified old tombs, some of them enclosed with handsome wrought-iron fences. The OAKLAND HOUSE still stands four square and like a gallant old warrior, erect and proud, refuses to give way although it has been stripped of its mantels and elegant adornments. Even the beautiful old stair rails have been removed and now the steps and the long flooring planks are being carefully taken up, piece by piece.

Overgrown crepe myrtle and boxwood trees are the only traces and re-minders of the once famous formal gardens that are now a rank, growing wilderness, almost choking the old mansion itself.

[304]

OAKLAND

INDEX

INDEX – Continued

INDEX – Continued

INDEX – Continued

INDEX – Continued

INDEX – Continued

INDEX – Continued

INDEX – Continued

INDEX – Continued

INDEX – Continued

INDEX – Continued

INDEX – Continued

INDEX – Continued

INDEX – Continued

INDEX – Continued

INDEX – Continued

INDEX – Continued

INDEX – Continued

INDEX – Continued

INDEX – Continued

INDEX – Continued

INDEX – Continued

INDEX – Continued

INDEX – Continued

INDEX – Continued